Traces of a Stream

Pittsburgh Series in Composition, Literacy, and Culture

David Bartholomae and Jean Ferguson Carr, Editors

Traces of a Stream

Literacy and Social Change Among African American Women

Jacqueline Jones Royster

University of Pittsburgh Press

Pittsburgh Series in Composition, Literacy, and Culture

David Bartholomae and Jean Ferguson Carr, Editors

Published by the University of Pittsburgh Press, Pittsburgh, Pa. 15261

LIBRARY OF CONGRESS CATALOGUING-IN-PUBLICATION DATA

Royster, Jacqueline Jones.
   Traces of a stream : literacy and social change among African American women /
   Jacqueline Jones Royster.
      p.   cm. — (Pittsburgh series in composition, literacy, and culture)
   Includes bibliographical references and index.
   ISBN 0-8229-4122-8 (acid-free paper) — ISBN 0-8229-5725-6 (pbk. : acid-free paper)
      1. English language—Rhetoric—Study and teaching—Social aspects—United States.
2. Afro-American Women—Education—Social aspects.   3. Afro-Americans—
Education—Language arts.   4. Literacy—Social aspects—United States.   5. Afro-
American women—Social conditions.   6. Language and culture—United States.
7. Literacy—United States.   I. Title   II. Series
PE1405.U6   R68 2000
302.2'244'08996073—dc21
                                                          99–050942

To our women ancestors of the zamani,
who were then courageous and bold, who are now our everlasting strength;

To the noble and undaunted spirits of African American women,
including Lilla Ashe Mitchell, who remain steadfast in the face of trying times;

To my students at Spelman College, The Ohio State University,
and the Bread Loaf School of English,
who helped me to know that the kind of research I do needs to be done
and acted upon.

Contents

Preface and Acknowledgments

Over the course of my work on this project, I have come to a deeper understanding of what it has really been about—acknowledging that it has been about many things. Often it has appeared to be about everything. Most consistently, however, it has been about teaching me how to conduct research, that is, qualitative research, on a particular group of people—African American women. My apprenticeship has been long and enlightening. I have learned to engage in a painstaking process of recovery and reconstruction; to use multidisciplinary sources; to count experience variously, especially when the people whose experience it was are no longer alive and when they did not always leave clear records of themselves. I have learned to cross-reference tidbits of information in making sense of evidence; to recognize an important story when I see it; to develop strategies for retelling it respectfully despite the inevitable missing pieces. What I have learned best, however, is the value of two virtues: the importance of caring about "the subject" and the importance of patience.

In caring about the subject, I emphasize that there are really two subjects in this book: literacy and African American women. Concerned with both points of focus, this book is keyed by the question: What happens when we bring together what we know now about literacy with what we know now about African American women? On one hand the theoretical, empirical, and methodological bases for literacy studies have changed, operating now on the assumption that the territory of literacy is both text and context, not one or the other; and that, in being so, literacy also connects more generally to other symbolic systems of representation, for example oral practices, signs, or other visual systems, all of which collectively constitute a communicative matrix. Paying attention to the ways and means of literacy as a communicative practice, therefore, underscores the notion that literacy functions rhetorically as part of the sociocultural fabric of our lives. Clarifying such layers of complexity has been central in helping researchers and scholars to see in more full-bodied ways what is happening with literacy across communities, in this case among African American women.

Further, as the bases of literacy studies have shifted, so too has the knowledge base of the material conditions and the activities of African American women. We know more than ever before about both their lives and their times, and we have benefited from an array of interpretive tools from several academic disciplines in assigning meaning to their experiences. Between the two subjects of literacy and African American women, there is much room for discovery. The discovery begins when we bring African American women into bold relief as users of language, and it continues with analyses of how their literate practices enrich the knowledge base of the ways and means of literacy more generally. The intersection between these two richly endowed subject bases is a site for the production of scholarship that has the potential to be generative.

At this intersection, it has been most instructive for me to discover the sustaining effects of acknowledging consciously my vested interests in the project. I have learned to accept that I cannot escape the connections to my own sense of identity as an African American woman or my intense desire to understand my own intellectual ancestry. In one sense, in typical fashion for scholarly endeavor, I operated intellectually with specific attention to scholarly conventions. However, when I acknowledged the personal dimensions of my intellectual engagement, I freed myself also to be emotionally and spiritually affected by the process. I do indeed care about this subject, and this caring has been a primary source of both motivation and inspiration as I engaged in the challenging task of exploring a subject area for which there have been no road maps.

My lessons in patience, on the other hand, have been of a different order. I have had to reconcile in my head and heart that I could very well have finished this project many times during the last few years. And by some measures, I certainly should have done so. In fact, there were several times when I thought I was doing just that, only to be reminded that the goal is not simply to know and say but to understand. I needed to see beneath the surface, to read between the lines. I needed to find interpretive lenses capable of accounting for these women's actions more thoroughly and more dynamically. As I reflect on my engagement with these tasks, the analogy that comes to mind is that coming to this moment of actually composing a seemingly satisfying text has been like sun-brewing tea on a partly cloudy day. The process has just taken time. At this point, I am confident that time on task with *Traces of a Stream* has been well spent, that my learning has been substantive, that there is much I want to say, although I know my thinking is not yet finished and that it may never be.

Time on task has meant also that many friends and colleagues have supported me along the way, some with acts of kindness and love; others by reading and responding to my words and by sharing their own; still others with advice, counsel, and words of wisdom. In recognition of this support, I extend special thanks to my students at Spelman College, the Bread Loaf School of English, and The Ohio State University. They have provided for me a stable discourse community within which I have been able to think, to try out theories, and to receive the most thoughtful feedback possible.

I am grateful to the ever growing collective of African American women scholars across the disciplines, particularly to those in history, without whose work my own would have been sorely lacking, if not altogether impossible. In this group of scholars, I include my former fellow editorial team members of *SAGE: A Scholarly Journal on Black Women* from whom I learned much and in the presence of whom I could feel myself growing as a researcher and scholar. I am grateful also to the archivists and librarians who helped me at various points along the way: Brenda Banks, Anthony Toussaint, Donna Wells, Dovie Patrick, Minnie Clayton, Roland Baumann, Beth House, and to other colleagues whom I met in archives, for example: Gwen Rosemond and Joan Maloney, who shared their work with me as I shared mine.

Within the field of rhetoric and composition (the arena that seems most appropriate for this project), I have benefited from the magnificent array of work generated over the last few years in literacy studies and related areas. I have particularly appreciated, however, the encouragement of David Bartholomae, who recognized the possibility of this project and, with his incredible style, said, "Why don't you think about doing what you really want to do?" I came to count on knowing that he and Jean Ferguson Carr had faith both in the idea and in me.

Also, I thank a small circle of colleagues who stepped in to read and respond to different versions of this manuscript at just the right times: Mike Rose, Beverly Moss, Courtney Cazden, James Phelan, Lisa Kiser. For many reasons, this project was difficult to share in progress, so the opportunities to discuss what I was trying to do were invaluable. Singular among such opportunities was an invitation in 1996 to speak at Spelman during the fifteenth anniversary celebration of the Spelman Women's Research and Resource Center. I counted it a special privilege to be able to share my work at the place where the whole process began. I will be forever grateful to my friend and colleague Beverly Guy-Sheftall for providing this signal moment of affirmation at a time when such affirmation was so clearly just what I needed. In the final stages of the project, I benefited greatly from several people: Lucille Schultz and Kathryn Flannery, for their careful and thoughtful reading of the full manuscript; Niels Aaboe, Ann Walston, Joyce Kachergis, Pippa Letsky, and Mark Jacobs for the time and care that they gave in making the text ready for publication; and the many other staff members at the University of Pittsburgh Press who helped to make this publication possible.

Last but not least, I am grateful for the women whose lives have made this work possible. They are a constant source of inspiration, as are my family, who are ever steadfast in showing me that my life and work are meaningful.

Traces of a Stream

Introduction

A Call for Other Ways of Reading

As the subtitle indicates, this book is about literacy, social change, and African American women. I chose the title because of reactions I have consistently received over the years when I have presented papers on early generations of African American women writers and their achievements. Without exception, after a presentation, at least one person—sometimes from surprise, or with an awareness of deprivation, or with indignation or embarrassment, or sometimes with a sense of what I have come to call deep disbelief[1]—at least one person will say to me, "I've never heard of these women." I have been compelled to tolerate this reaction as a truth, even though from my research I know quite well that African American women have actively and consistently participated over the years in public discourse and in literate arenas. They have conveyed in many forms their ideas, dreams, visions, and insights. I know quite well that their actions have made a difference in terms of their advocacy and activism within an array of both noble and ordinary causes. I also know quite well that the lines of accreditation, the rights of agency, and the rights to an authority to make knowledge and to claim expertise have often not been extended in a systematic way by this society to African American women. Quite the contrary.

On one level in addressing this reality, I have assumed a long-range view, with the intent of suggesting some trends about the general landscape of African American women's literate experiences within the context of systemic matrices of oppression. In this regard, what history demonstrates is that for many reasons (racism, sexism, ethnocentrism, political and economic oppression, and so on), barriers have been constructed within our society around many people's lives and thereby around their literate practices, with African American women being one clear example. African American women have been persistently subjected

3

to measures of value and achievement that have been set and monitored by others, who have not had their interests or potential in mind and who have been free historically to discount, ignore, and disempower them. These barriers, though variable, are socially, politically, and culturally defined, and the impact of them in this case is that they have cast the lives of African American women in shadow. The barriers have served as filters, screening from view the women themselves, systematically blocking out the very possibility of a substantial crediting of their achievements, such that these achievements, when they do seep into view, are typically considered exceptional rather than as part and parcel of a pattern. The presence of African American women as writers of worth has typically been neutralized and their achievements devalued.

Despite such constraints, however, my research indicates that African American women's resistance to sociopolitical barriers has been considerable and that, although their achievements may have been devalued, they have not been thoroughly neutralized or contained. From the beginning of their opportunities to learn, African American women have engaged consistently and valiantly in acts of literacy that have yielded remarkable rewards for themselves and for others. Periodically, therefore, these women have managed to surprise the world, to break out from whatever containments would seek to enclose them. Periodically, their talents have flowed past the barriers, reconstituted themselves, and become noticeable as "traces of a stream." Given impediments that serve to discourage recognition and accreditation, however, when moments of reconstitution occur, the world of letters and the society at large have tended to speak of these moments, quite ironically, as moments of "rebirth" and "renaissance," with the Harlem Renaissance and the African American women writer's renaissance of the 1970s and 1980s being two distinctive examples: times when talents and abilities that were in shadow trickled into the light. In effect, such labels indicate in an odd way that the society was reacting to resistance, that is, noticing the *presence* of those formerly unnoticed and unacknowledged as if to say, "Oh! There you are. I didn't see you before. How long have you been standing there?"

This view of reaction to *presence* provides a framework for understanding a follow-up question I sometimes hear as "Are there others?"— which I often interpret as "Who are these people really? Aren't they truly unique and exceptional? They're not typical or representative, are they? Shouldn't we just be surprised and move on? How did such success happen?" At these moments, I delight in the opportunity to say: "Yes. There were others. The list actually seems endless." And, "No, now that I know more about them, I'm really not surprised at all either by their numbers or by the quality of their achievements."

At such moments, I have the opportunity to acknowledge the stream that is visible as evidence of the sea that until now has passed unnoticed. In directly addressing the question "Are there others?" I explain that we are apparently experiencing in our contemporary world yet one more cycle of reconstitution, one more breakthrough of talent and ability. I explain also that, over the generations, African American women's achievements as language users have been surprisingly consistent. I suspect that, in being so, these activities have actually gained in both volume and momentum over the years. I explain that by many measures we have evidence in the current era of a renewal of strength within a less hostile context, a revitalization that seems to be giving rise, as we speak, not only to renewed strength but to new and unknown directions as well.

In this work I take into account this longer-range view. My intent generally is to view the acquisition of literacy as a dynamic moment in the lives of African American women, as people with desires for agency and authority in the use of written language. To facilitate this analysis, I have developed a theoretical framework within which to consider how early generations of African American women incorporated literacy into their lives and how they used literacy systematically as a variable tool. The theory begins with the notion that a community's material conditions greatly define the range of what this group does with the written word and, to a significant degree, even how they do it. The pivotal idea is that what human beings do with writing, as illustrated by what African American women have done, is an expression of self, of society, and of self in society.

Operating from this longer-range view of African American women's work, I seek to reconstruct a pathway to rhetorical prowess specific to their experiences, outlining a matrix of events drawn from the realities of African American women's history. In explaining the matrix, I present a framework and methodology for contextualizing the literate behavior of

African American women in time and over time. My intent is to underscore, at this point in our scholarship, that we gain in an understanding of literacy in general from views of literacy in its particulars, from placing the "thick descriptions" of the literate practices of a particular group in the company of similar descriptions of other groups. In other words, this analysis is rooted in the idea that we need a more concrete sense of human variety in the use of literacy in order to support the abstractions that we might very well draw more clearly at a later point in this analytical process as we place well-told stories of literacy next to other well-told stories of literacy.

From my perspective, however, it is not possible to render the complex story of African American women as literate beings in monodimensional terms. To interpret evidence more fully, we need not just a long view but a kaleidoscopic view. We need a sense of the landscape, certainly, but simultaneously we also need closeup views from different standpoints on the landscape. It has been crucial to this analysis, in fact, that I do not remain focused solely on generalities. My imperative has been to identify a specific set of women within the more diverse group of African American women and to consider this subcategory multidimensionally as a case in point.

I chose for this study elite African American women, focusing particularly on elites of the nineteenth century, an era during which the shift in educational opportunity after the Civil War gave rise for the first time to the development of a cadre of well-educated women. I assigned *eliteness* to this group based, not just on class privilege (though economic status is indeed one marker of eliteness), but more on the positions of status they occupied within their own communities. I chose to look at women who laid claim through their families and through their own actions to the label *well respected.*

Generally, in the African American community, *well respected* is not a term to which high economic status is always the first measure. Community status derives also from other measures. These women were well educated in communities that valued education. They were often professional women, particularly teachers, journalists, and community organizers in communities with critical needs, and they served these communities well. They were women from families of *good* reputation, and/or they were married to men of good reputation. Further, these women had also been diligent in building for themselves reputations as good and honorable women who demonstrated daily, in the face of hostility, that they were self-respecting, that they operated always with a sense of propriety, that they understood and accepted the requirement during this era that African American women needed always to be *ladies*.[2] They were perceived and perceived themselves to be hard-working, socially conscious, and ideologically committed to activism and advocacy. Perhaps more important, this combination of factors meant that, unlike many of their less fortunate sisters, these women had access to power and influence, and because of their elite status, they also had the luxury, the class privilege, and the time to use this access in their own interests and in the interests of others.

In addition to looking at a specific set of African American women, I also chose to look at one type of literate practice, rather than presuming I was able to consider all. Early groups of African American women writers wrote in many genres, and many of them wrote across genres. To localize the analysis, therefore, I chose to examine their nonfiction prose, concentrating mainly on the essay. In terms of form, the essay is variable, with unique potential for those who speak or might be compelled to speak against prevailing sentiments—in this case in the interest of social change. The essay among African American women is a long-standing genre of choice, such that focusing on essay writing as a specific literate practice offers a distinctive opportunity as an analytical springboard.

In bringing together these multiple viewpoints for an examination of African American women's literate experiences, my intent is to state unequivocally that African American women are not monolithic in terms of either personhood or literate practices. In making this statement, my goal is not to concentrate on building a place for African American women that is defined by a sense of essentialism. Actually, my goal is quite the opposite. I seek instead to acknowledge that I am looking generally at patterns of behavior, but specifically at just one set of women who vary even within the distinctive category I have assigned to them. My effort, therefore, is one of balance. While trying to resist essentialist analyses, I am trying at the same time to identify and to contextualize general patterns of literate behavior. The effort is to document and account for what was accomplished by elite nineteenth-century women as a cadre of educated professional women, and to suggest how their activities might connect, again multidimensionally, to the practices of others both before and after them in the making of various traditions.

In this regard, I am very much aware that comparisons between African American women and other groups are certainly possible, by gender, race, class, genre, purposes, and so on. There are some practices that connect well with the practices of African American men, or with women of other races and ethnicities, or with other writers of essays, and so forth. This analysis, however, does not seek to make comparison a central methodology, in either an intragroup or an intergroup way. Although such comparisons are instructive and ultimately critical to a full understanding of how literacy works, I prefer to take as a point of departure the analysis and interpretation of the particle (that is, elite African American women in the nineteenth century) in a definable and defensible context (literacy as social action), rather than taking on as an initial endeavor all that should be accounted for in a comprehensive analysis of the full wave of possible literate activity.

In making this distinction, I recognize that, to the extent that the experiences of African American women overlap with the experiences of others, so too is it likely that any conclusions I draw about their literate practices might well apply to the literate practices of others. Since my intent at this point is to make a case for clarity and understanding and not for separateness or uniqueness, I expect such possibilities. With this project, in fact, my view is that the task at this point is to reconsider the information base in specific ways and then to engage in a systematic process of re-formation and review in the interest of constructing dynamic analytical frameworks with more interpretive power, that is, a greater potential to account for variety and pattern and to explain them. The immediate challenge is to make visible many features, factors, relationships, people, and practices that heretofore were not visible—to articulate what is there and what seems to be going on. Further, the challenge is to resist a drifting toward speedy claims, static conclusions, or overgeneralizations. Although I believe we should expect theory and practice to shift in the ongoing accumulation of knowledge and understanding, my desire with this project is not to claim either distinctiveness or sameness but to make better sense. A preliminary step in making sense is learning to look, listen, and look again, to think well, and to speak as though knowledge is now and has always been in the making.

Given this attitude, I am making no claims in this book for the exclusivity of African American women's actions or the exclusivity of their importance as writers in the larger scheme of things. This statement indicates that, although I believe there are distinctions to be made, I accept that there is much work still to do in this area before hierarchical assertions of excellence and quality may need to take priority in either theory or practice. I also accept the reality that, although this book contributes to the knowledge base, it cannot be expected to do in its limited pages everything necessary to clarify all literate practices and achievements of all African American women.

Worthy of note in explaining the choices I have made is the organization of the chapters. There is an identifiable progression in thought presented across the chapters, but the progress is not always linear. It might be more apt to say that the chapters do indeed have a chronology that plots the experiences of African American women along a trajectory. For example, I start in the present, flash back to precolonial Africa, and generally build from there chronologically back to the present. However, in keeping with the need for a dynamic view, the pattern of development—though shaped by chronology—is more webbed than linear. I seek to enrich the vision of the reader as I render this account by bringing texture into the story—taking time to explore each piece as a distinctive dimension of the pathway to understanding. I have tried consciously to resist being driven by the desire to assure that each step is a forward movement. By contrast, the movement tends instead to be forward-looking, perhaps, but also somewhat meandering and recursive. The story of African American women's acquisition and use of literacy is complex; its rendering should, likewise, be guided by the need to complicate the reader's vision rather than simplify it.

In order to facilitate the reading process and to signal the way in which I see three basic viewpoints converging, I have organized the chapters into three sections: a rhetorical view, a historical view, and an ideological view. It is the combination of these three perspectives that constitutes what I am calling the "thick description" of the literate practices highlighted in this book. There are two chapters in part 1: "In Search of Rivers: Womanist Writers and the Essay" and "Toward an Analytical Model for

Literacy and Sociopolitical Action." In chapter 1, I use *In Search of Our Mothers' Gardens* to examine African American women's habitual use of literacy for sociopolitical action. I establish essay writing as the form of choice in these practices, and I contextualize the practices as part of the whole cloth of communicative experience. In chapter 2, I construct a model, designed to clarify literacy as a sociocognitive practice; to distinguish the sense-making strategies of African American women; and to establish the roles and functions of essay writing as particular to a systematic making of meaning in the habitual use of language for sociopolitical action.

In part 2, I focus on a historical view of African American women. I concentrate particularly on the acquisition of literacy and the development of rhetorical sensibilities. In chapter 3, "The Genesis of Authority: When African Women Became American," my intent is to reconstruct a historical pathway for literate behavior; to outline a matrix of events, values, and practices drawn from accounts of African American women's history; and to connect this matrix to the literate practices of African American women over time, in light especially of what these practices suggest about *ethos* (the formation and development of a writing self) and rhetorical decision-making. In chapters 4 and 5, I move to talk about literate behavior and social action. In chapter 4, "Going Against the Grain: The Acquisition and Use of Literacy," I start with the acquisition of literacy among African American women as the development of a new tool in a new context. I discuss the social and political environments of the late eighteenth and early nineteenth centuries as they shaped the contexts for literacy acquisition and language use and as they supported the identification of clear and present mandates for social and political action. I demonstrate how these contexts operated in the lives of specific women (among them Lucy Terry Prince, Charlotte Forten, Clara Howard, and Selena Sloan Butler), and I assert that these circumstances are significant to the process whereby African American women developed cravings to participate in public discourse and to effect social and political change. I use Maria W. Stewart, the earliest-known African American woman writer of political essays, as a case in point, to show how literacy becomes an instrument for change.

In chapter 5, "From This Fertile Ground: The Development of Rhetorical Prowess," I discuss how African American women enhanced their literate resources and developed rhetorical prowess as they acquired higher education and entered the world of both paid and volunteer work. I take into account the emergence of a cadre of professional women and how professional identities were incorporated into ethos formation and the creation of a writing self. I pay particular attention to the rise of the Black Clubwomen's Movement, a movement ripe both for the development of rhetorical expertise and for engaging in social and political action. In addition, I examine the African American periodical press as a primary arena for the participation of African American women in public discourse and thereby to some extent in public policy-making. I end this chapter with a discussion of the tradition of essay writing in order to acknowledge that essays, as an accommodating nonfiction form, have consistently held a central and vibrant place in the text production of African American women, in their use of language to speak out, and in fulfilling their desires to participate actively in establishing and implementing social and political agenda. I emphasize that an examination of nonfiction writing offers other benefits as well, pointing out the extent to which such texts offer evidence, not only of traditions of rhetorical prowess but also of traditions of intellectualism and community leadership. In chapter 5, I draw examples from a variety of essay writers, over time, to show through this type of textual analysis that the essaying practices of African American women have been both habitual and systematic.

In part 3, my intent is to concentrate more precisely on methodological and ideological perspectives. In the last chapter, chapter 6, "A View from a Bridge: Afrafeminist Ideologies and Rhetorical Studies," I narrate my own learning curve in carrying out this project. When I look back over the years spent completing the project, I realize I have indeed learned many things. I realize I have things to say (about methodology, for example) and that there are lessons I can share with others who may have common or complementary concerns. This chapter recounts the process of my research and attempts to extrapolate, in a more precise way, a methodology, using the term *historical ethnography,* so that this approach might actually be useful to someone other than myself.

In essayistic fashion, these six chapters tell a winding tale concerning the development of a tradition of rhetorical prowess and a rendering of this tradition in scholarship. Each section focuses attention in its own fashion: on the arena in which literacy happens, on the ways and means of a language use, on the art and artistry of a particular language user, on frameworks that offer interpretive possibilities. In creating this textured viewing of African American women's practices, I am in effect extending a call to readers for other ways of reading—a call that resonates with what I suggest in this introduction is a demand from the subjects of study (literacy and African American women) for a shift in paradigms in research and in scholarship, or for other ways of analyzing and composing.

From the perspective of reading (as compared with analyzing, interpreting, and writing), as experienced readers of scholarship, we have the habit of readily expecting to affirm, question, or dismiss claims, and to see evidence in a fairly predictable pattern of development, in keeping with the discourse expectations of a given field. I suspect that this book will disrupt these habits in what may ultimately prove rather peculiar ways. My suspicions raise questions about the extent to which our reading habits and preferences—like our writing habits and preferences—might be more culturally influenced than we acknowledge. I suspect that this book might work better if readers are willing to delay their desire for claims and assertions to be immediately and predictably resolved. My approach might be more satisfying if readers recognize a claim, certainly, but are then willing, in a sense, to "run a tab" for evidence, not just in waiting to see that there is indeed evidence but in working with me, perhaps more actively than may be their habit, to see how the evidence variously connects as the story unravels, viewpoint by viewpoint.

In light of this call for other ways of reading, this book is indeed an invitation to listen to a story. As a writer, my obligation in rendering the text is to be clear and accurate, as with all scholarship, and I do indeed seek to fulfill this obligation. However, in the case of this scenario, where so much is unknown and undocumented, a second responsibility is to hypothesize about what remains missing in a way that is reasonable and useful for further research. Moreover, given what we have managed to document to this point, yet another responsibility emerges. As I spend time explaining in chapter 6, because I identify so closely with the subject, I feel deeply obligated to be respectful of women such as Maria W. Stewart, Anna Julia Cooper, Ida B. Wells, and so many others whom they represent. I am obliged to assume that their lives and work as African American women were fully laden with value and that it is up to us, the researchers and scholars, to discover the nature and extent of that value.

The effort to be true both to the tasks of scholarship and to the task of respecting the subjects of the scholarship is the process whereby I have experienced the most compelling desire to connect myself, as an African American woman, directly to this story. This desire manifests itself most clearly in the voice I use throughout the book. Primarily, the stance I assume is the stance of the typical scholar. I position myself at a respectable distance and speak with an acceptable amount of dispassion, as required for scholarly voices—most of the time. In fact, I do so because I agree that such a stance is generally appropriate.

In spite of my acceptance of this scholarly role and responsibility, however, occasionally I find I cannot, nor do I want to, set aside the fact that the story of African American women and literacy is my story too. There are moments, even after close editing, when I use the pronoun "we" and quite clearly signal that this "we" is not literacy scholars, the community I ally myself with throughout most of the book, but African American women. In other words, I shift the viewpoint deliberately, consciously, and I intend for myself to be viewed as one among those who constitute the subject of this discourse. I consider these moments to be an acknowledgment of what Amy Shuman explains as strategic romanticism.[3] I acknowledge my connections at these points quite simply because it seems it would be disingenuous and inappropriate for me to do otherwise. I realized fairly early in the project that I had no desire to be totally dispassionate, nor to assume a "pseudo-objective" stance. To the contrary, I have come to see advantages in acknowledging connections, in considering the ethical implications of these connections, and in admitting the biases that must inevitably inform any scholarship that might be produced as a result of an acknowledgment of ethical space.

As a result, what I do claim is that, in terms of the intellectual enterprise, I have used methodologies and composing strategies that are well rooted in current literacy scholarship. At the same time, I make the case that being well rooted in the discipline does not automatically dictate that I must set aside the passion this work generates in me. I have come to believe that a scholar can be scholarly and still be ethically and pathetically connected to the subject. What, then, needs to be acknowledged (as opposed to being apologized for) is scholarly viewpoint and vested interests. Consequently, I openly and proudly acknowledge my identity with this story. My view is that my personal passion, in its openness, does not change one iota the realities of these women's lives. Despite the places where passion might seep through this text, the story does indeed speak for itself, which makes my alliance with its central characters virtually a by-product of its power to hold and to absorb the attention. Moreover, in suggesting that scholarly viewpoint and interests be treated as normal rather than abnormal, I remain confident of the critical abilities of readers. I believe that the readers of this volume will be astute enough to make their own sense of the details I present and the process whereby I present them, and I have faith that the sense they will seek to make, whatever visions of reality they hold, will be positively and productively affected by my rendering of these lives.

Ultimately, my goal in this work is to establish a suitable place in the world of words and action for the contributions and achievements of African American women writers. In the context of a nation where race, class, gender, and culture matter, these women have been not only innovative but also bold and courageous. Their contributions and achievements stand; I am pleased to pay tribute, with all that scholarship will allow, to the hands and minds that made it so.

Part 1

A Rhetorical View

Chapter 1

In Search of Rivers

Womanist Writers and the Essay

Only the Black Woman can say "when and where I enter, in the quiet, undisputed dignity of my womanhood, without violence and without suing or special patronage, then and there the whole Negro race enters with me."

Anna Julia Cooper, *A Voice from the South*

And when Celie comes through those doors, buffalo soldiers on one side, Shug and Natty Dread and a clutch of dreadlocked Rastas perhaps on the other, and only when Celie comes through those doors; when Celie comes in from the cold of repression, self-hatred, and denial, and only when Celie comes in from the cold—do I come in. And many of you as well.

Alice Walker, *Living by the Word*

I've known rivers;
Ancient, dusky rivers.
My soul has grown deep like the rivers.

Langston Hughes, "The Negro Speaks of Rivers"

Alice Walker and a Tradition of Essaying

In 1983, I discovered that African American women write essays, and it was then I began to notice features of this type of writing that served ultimately to shape and direct the writing of this book. What prompted these insights was my reading of Alice Walker's collection of previously published and unpublished essays, entitled, after the best-known essay in the group, *In Search of Our Mothers' Gardens: Womanist Prose.* First among the distinctions of this volume is that it was published during a time when works by African American women were being celebrated as a literary "renaissance." By the 1980s the world of publishing, in fact, had opened its doors to many African American women writers, including Gwendolyn Brooks (1949), Paule Marshall (1959), Kristin Hunter (1964), Adrienne Kennedy (1968), Audre Lorde (1968), Maya Angelou (1969), Sonia Sanchez (1969), Toni Cade Bambara (1970), Mari Evans (1970), Nikki Giovanni (1970), Louise Meriwether (1970), Toni Morrison (1970), Alexis DeVeaux (1973), Ntozake Shange (1977), and many others.[1] Walker herself had published also several volumes of poetry and three novels, including *The Third Life of Grange Copeland* (1970), *Meridian* (1976), and *The Color Purple* (1983), which was already infamous and drawing both acclaim and derision. These women were creating a steady stream of novels, short stories, poems, plays, all of which were receiving attention in a serious manner from both popular and academic audiences.

This "renaissance" marked a time when the world seemed inclined as never before to make room for the voices and talents of African American women. Literary critics—especially African American women scholars such as Barbara Christian, Nellie McKay, Deborah McDowell, Barbara Smith, and Mary Helen Washington, to name a few—were examining these new works and linking them to the past, as they began to recover a provocative history of ongoing literary contributions and achievements. Their work—along with other scholarship in women's studies, African diasporic studies, and other areas within cultural studies—began to shed light on lives, conditions, and achievements in ways that pushed the boundaries of knowledge and questioned former interpretations of what is valuable in human endeavor. Thereby, the base of cultural production to which Walker contributed as a creative writer, with *Search* being one title among several, was rich and rewarding.

In addition, however, *In Search of Our Mothers' Gardens* holds a second distinction. This volume, especially the title essay, received considerable attention as a signal publication in what was then the budding field of Black feminist studies. Not only was Walker perceived to be a writer who became an object of study, she was also recognized as an important contributor to Black feminist thought by the way in which this essay helped to shape the theoretical and political frameworks through which interpretations of writers like herself could be drawn. In particular Walker added the term, *womanist,* to feminist analysis, to characterize the proactivism of African American women. She offered the now much quoted statement, "Womanist is to feminist as purple to lavender" (*In Search of Our Mothers' Gardens,* xii). Before the popularization of this term in feminist studies, many African American women in academic and nonacademic worlds had been resistant to an alliance with the mainstream feminist movement, a movement racked both historically and in the modern era with ideological differences and political tensions between white women and women of color.[2] However, *womanist,* especially as presented throughout the essays in *Search,* participated in forging new pathways to ongoing dialogue about issues of gender, race, class, and culture.

In contrast to these two distinctions for Walker's volume, a third passed relatively unnoticed and unmarked. This book was not a collection of short fiction or poetry. It was a collection of essays. In 1983, as nonfiction rather than fiction, *In Search of Our Mothers' Gardens* stood apart from other praiseworthy publications by African American women, but it did not stand alone. It was very much in the company of others. In 1981, for example, poet June Jordan published *On Civil Wars* and political activist Angela Davis published *Women, Race, and Class;* in 1984 poet Audre Lorde published *Sister Outsider* and cultural critic bell hooks published *Feminist Theory: From Margin to Center.* These collections show that, as in the case of the other genres of poetry, drama, and fiction, the momentum for the publishing of essays by African American women was also increasing. Since the 1980s this group has been joined by others, among them Nikki Giovanni, Patricia Williams, Toni Morrison, Maya Angelou, and Pearl Cleage, to name only a few.

Walker and her fellow essay writers are consistent in demonstrating their keen abilities in this genre. Their tendency is not to switch from more dominant creative forms to essays, however, but to use more than one form, with the second or third choice being the essay. Their patterns of productivity indicate that, in each case, these women are engaging in other professional writing activities and also writing essays. They are poets, novelists, short story writers, playwrights, and scholars. They are also writers of essays in the public domain. On one hand, we might say then that these women are writing across genres, which suggests an inclination as writers to be multidimensional, to demonstrate a general commitment to productivity, and to evidence a specific desire not to limit their visions or their voices in any way by the form of expression. Another way of stating it is that the writers have an irresistible desire to write—and to do so by whatever form seems appropriate at the time. This flexibility suggests that these writers are operating not just aesthetically but also rhetorically. In using language and literacy across a matrix of communicative practices, they illustrate how highly they value the place and function of language in their lives.

If we accept this latter interpretation of African American women's productivity, then we can see a pattern emerging, regardless of the form of expression. These writers habitually focus on issues with sociopolitical import. They write about the world around them, raising for scrutiny the experience of living as people of African descent. They chronicle relationships of people in culturally definable places and under conditions that make visible the personal, social, economic, and political dimensions of these relationships. As poets, novelists, and playwrights, they amplify experience, focusing readers' attention instructively on dimensions of this experience that establish the unique viewpoints of African American women as a gendered, racialized, and economically defined group. They draw readers into their imaginatively rendered worlds, demonstrating their abilities variously, and in the 1980s with increased frequency they began to receive critical attention and praise.[3]

Typically, the viewpoints of these writers counter, question, or open new doors in the interpretation of experience—and engage readers provocatively in a consideration of other ways of seeing and understanding. As Mae Gwendolyn Henderson (1992) has suggested, in expressing their own perspectives and interpretations African American women writers engage in complex discursive practices that mirror the complex social, historical, and cultural positions from which they speak. They engage in a "simultaneity of discourse,"[4] speaking in the creation of a single text both in a plurality of voices and in a multiplicity of discourses. Through their characters and narrative personae, they "speak in tongues," a metaphor Henderson (1992) uses to explain not just multivocality but the gifts of prophecy and interpretation.

In a contrast between this sense of African American women's use of creative forms and their use of the essay as a nonfiction form, the first point to emerge is that these women are writers with specific motives, and if we take into account the purposefulness of their actions as writers, three features emerge. First of all, viewing African American women writers across genres reveals more clearly the extent to which they are deliberately engaging in the social and political conversations around them, with the essay revealing more clearly perhaps than other forms how their interests are not just in expressing themselves in writing but in using language in such a way as to affect the reader's heart, mind, and soul. Certainly, they seek to render an experience well, but when we raise questions about audience, purpose, form, agency, and voice, for example, what becomes clearer is that they also evidence a desire, although perhaps a secondary one, to "move" the audience, that is, to inspire change—in thinking, feeling, and behavior. Moreover, in the resonances between their essay writing and their writing in other genres, African American women writers exhibit the same multivocal abilities as they do in their other literate forms. In essays, they speak in a plurality of voices and a multiplicity of discourses. With the essay, however, they do not speak through the mirroring effects of fiction, poetry, and drama. They speak as themselves (whomever they imagine those selves to be), as speaking subjects, face-to-face, eye to eye with their readers, and, they construct themselves variously as "I."

I am not asserting an essentialism about African American women writers as essayists. Quite the contrary. Even a cursory examination of their works demonstrates a full range of variation in terms of both substance and style. Rather, I am saying that, despite this variety, there remain resonances, which become visible through the analytical lens of rhetorical decision-making. I am suggesting that the publication of *In Search of Our Mothers' Gardens* constitutes an occasion to consider the essay a distinctive form, which makes visible the connections within African American women's writing between literacy (in this case the use of written language) and sociopolitical intent. The essay as a generic form offers a unique opportunity to analyze how a writer foregrounds experiences, establishes a speaking self, and showcases a mind at work.

In the case of African American women, this generic focus makes visible the importance of literate flexibility. With the very act of choosing flexibility as a value—that is, in their writing in multiple genres—this group of women writers permits us to see the complementarity of their messages, audiences, and purposes. We can notice their tendencies to have not just more than one richly endowed voicing of an experience or point of view, but more than one means of rendering such a voice. They convey an intent to satisfy (more comprehensively than just one mode can do) two imperatives: to enact their own complex expressive purposes and to meet a range of audience needs. One might say that these writers embrace the notion that what they feel compelled to say is not only worth saying more than once but also worth hearing in more than one way. In using rhetorical analysis, therefore, we bring into bolder relief the many ways African American women exhibit, throughout their literate practices, an understanding (whether conscious or tacit) not just of "voice" but of "register."

Further, as a distinctive expressive form, the essay permits African American women to claim a personal speaking/thinking presence. The writers can assume positions in their texts as interpreters and theorizers of experience, not solely as people who render experience for aesthetic purposes in multivocal ways.[5] In other words, as creative writers African American women are typically characterized as storytellers and artists. As essayists, however, they can be viewed as intellectuals, as theorists, as women who think critically and creatively about the worlds around them. Through essays, they seize the opportunity to speak directly with their readers rather than indirectly through the mediating effects of characters. This feature of essay writing has been established by scholars in genre studies (see Butrym 1989; Freedman and Medway 1994; De Obaldia 1995; Heilker 1996) as a distinctive one.

Prominent among other features that consistently recur with the essay is that it is marked by indeterminacy. It is fluid and flexible. Researchers have argued, however, that there are enough other features to suggest a need to add a fourth genre category to the typical ones of poetry, drama, and fiction.[6] By this reckoning, the essay can be categorized as a nonfiction form, along with others such as biography, autobiography, personal narrative, creative nonfiction, and so on, all of which African American women have chosen to use. If we concentrate on just their use of the essay, however, rather than all nonfiction forms, the essay consistently shows the following features:

1. The writer is self-authorized.
2. The "I" perspective is foregrounded.

3. Knowledge and understanding are grounded in experience.

4. There is a sense of a mind at work.

5. The thinking is exploratory, unfinished, open-ended.

6. The writer recognizes a listening audience and expects response.

7. The writer invites skepticism and thereby situates the text as going quite appropriately against the grain of current practice.

8. The text is situated in time and place and is thereby responsive to its context—the material realities of time, place, and the person/writer.

9. The writer's knowledge, experience, and insight can intersect in variable ways.

10. The form itself is protean and lends itself easily to an incorporation of a full range of expressive and organizational devices.

Because of such features, the essay has tremendous flexibility across a range of rhetorical, ideological, experiential, and aesthetic choices. It is capable of serving multiple purposes, including informative and persuasive purposes, which can also include using the essay as an instrument of healing, that is, for purposes that are cathartic, purgative, and affirmative; that release and direct energy; that cleanse the heart, spirit, and physical body in order to harmonize the self; that speak "truth," in saying to oneself and to others what needs to be said in the interests of sanity, harmony, and balance. All of these features are evident in the collective body of African American women's essays.[7]

Many scholars in genre studies see the advantage of conceptualizing rhetorical analysis and literary analysis as being interrelated rather than as representing separate domains of analysis. So do I. This book centralizes, however, basic rhetorical questions concerning voice, vision, agency, audience, form, and so on. Even so, I do not wish to polarize this analytical frame in either binary or exclusive terms. Instead I am suggesting that, in the case of African American women's essay writing, rhetorical analysis is one mechanism for paying attention to both generic form and the "performance" of it. My focus is on the essay as one type of literate action. My intent is to pay particular attention to this form as a conscious act of language use that occurs in a specific time and space and that results from specific processes, including sociopolitical processes. Through this expressive choice, African American women present to the world their visions, values, and desires—with one of those desires, as illustrated by the

actual essays over time, being a desire to inspire advocacy and activism in
the interests of humanity and particularly of the African American community.

These writers often assert forthrightly a desire to change perceptions,
attitudes, and behaviors in themselves, their readers, and the world. They
often foreground by topic and purpose that they are writing with a specific interest in issues, impacts, and consequences. Their choices suggest
that, instead of looking at African American women's essays in an isolated
way as a nonfiction expression of viewpoint or at their use of literary genres in an isolated way as enactments of aesthetic sensibilities, this analysis
can make room for the merging of these two sets of interests (aesthetic
sensibilities and a social agenda) as we gain a broader sense of what constitutes their literate experience. With a view of literacy as landscape,
then, in this book I focus on ways to view kaleidoscopically the complex
relationships between the use of written language and a desire for social
action.

Social advocacy and activism constitute, therefore, an important analytical value (see chapter 3 for a discussion of the two terms *advocacy* and
activism). Through this measure, we note that in the 1980s there was a
convergence of two critical factors. The first one was not new. Walker and
others stepped from behind the veil of story and character or narrative
persona to say—as themselves—what was on their minds, and many of
their messages showed their social and political concerns. The second was
new and thereby the ingredient in the process that truly set the moment
apart. With the perception of a literary renaissance, these writers were
finding audiences as never before for all their writing, regardless of genre.
There was a convergence of productivity and opportunity for publication. The mass availability of African American women's writing opened
a space as never before, for anyone who is willing to look, to notice the
critical connections between their writing and their interests in social action. These women were publicly asserting themselves not only as writers
with skills and abilities but also as writers with intellectual, social, and
political intent. Their essays offer us prime examples of the will and capacity to use literate resources in order to participate in public arenas,
and also of the desire to generate, and not just participate in, sociopolitical action. With a clearer sense of the complexity of their expressive pur-

poses, we see a connection for the Langston Hughes metaphor cited at the beginning of the chapter. Among African American women there is the possibility of an ancient and dusky wisdom and the evidence of an ancient and dusky commitment to language and action.

If we consider the 1980s as a dynamic rather than a singular moment, the potential for understanding increases. First, we can assume that just as the writing of poetry, fiction, and drama link contemporary women with others who have gone before, so too are there historical connections for nonfiction writing. The recovery of the essay-writing practices of earlier women documents that over time the written word has been a well-used tool for sociopolitical activism, and that the essay, as a flexibly defined form, has constituted traces of a fully flowing stream of productivity and intellectual engagement. For this point to be established in a straightforward rather than an incidental manner, however, more substantive questions arise than those of simple recognition:

1. When we examine material conditions surrounding the acquisition of literacy by African American women, what do we notice about the impact of these factors on the choices they have made in using literacy?

2. How have these practices developed over time?

3. What is particular about this connection between writing and activism?

4. What differences have our analyses of African American women's writing, especially their essay writing, made in our understanding of language and literacy more generally or in our understanding of the practices and achievements of this particular group?

In Search of Our Mothers' Gardens, as a collection that was published at this critical juncture of productivity and broad publication and as a collection recognized also for expressive excellence, offers a useful place to begin in developing a theoretical view.[8] On a basic level, the collection provides an example from which to think about connections between language and action in a specific set of hands. On another level—in concert with Walker's second collection, *Living by the Word*—it serves also as a gateway for formulating an inquiry process and developing from it an analytical framework. With a framework designed to take into account connections between language and action, we can look beyond Walker's individual habits toward the patterns that connect her in meaningful ways to a whole spectrum of women across time, who, like her, have found their own ways to use literate resources in the interests of a sociopolitical agenda.

As well known as Walker is for her participation in the ongoing creative trust of African American women, as a writer of essays she remains recognized and to some extent described but still inadequately analyzed.[9] This situation mirrors the tradition of essay writing itself. Only in the last decade or so has the essay experienced a resurgence in scholarly attention as a respected subject of analysis worthy of study in its own right.[10] With the research that is ongoing, however, the yield to scholarship in terms of the nature, means, and measure of this form has the potential to be considerable. Using Walker as a case in point, two basic questions help to focus this generic approach more sharply and situate it within a frame of discovery: (1) By what values does Walker define her task as an essay writer? and (2) What are the distinguishing characteristics of her way of seeing and expressing in this form that would suggest a pattern of action that might be instructive for the examination of other African American women writers? The fundamental objective of such an inquiry is to read Walker's text with two assumptions: (1) that African American women write essays with specific and deliberate intentions; and (2) that even though their practices may vary in style and content, the material conditions of life and work for African American women significantly shape and inform the manner and means of their rhetorical behavior.

The Writer's Task

In "An Essay on Alice Walker" (1979), Mary Helen Washington concluded:

> From whatever vantage point one investigates the work of Alice Walker—poet, novelist, short story writer, critic, essayist, and apologist for black women—it is clear that the special identifying mark of her writing is her concern for the lives of black women . . . her main preoccupation has been the soul of black women. Walker herself, writing about herself as writer, has declared herself committed to "exploring the oppressions, the insanities, the loyalties, and the triumphs of black women." (132)

In an interview with Claudia Tate (1983), Walker stated: "Twentieth-century Black women writers all seem to be much more interested in the

Black community, in intimate relationships, with the white world as backdrop, which is certainly the appropriate perspective in my view" (181). In other words, Walker defined her general task as a writer to be the illumination and interpretation of the lives and conditions of African American people, especially African American women, with an awareness of the broader social context in which race, class, gender, and culture converge.

Since then, Walker has gone on to articulate her philosophical perspective more directly in her second collection of essays, *Living by the Word* (1988). In this volume, using the essay as amplifier, she makes four types of statements that collectively draw out in broad terms a rhetorical frame for language and action. In one essay, "The Old Artist: Notes on Mr. Sweet," Walker says:

He was an artist. He went deep into his own pain and brought out words and music that made us happy, made us feel empathy for anyone in trouble, made us think. We were taught to be thankful that anyone would assume this risk. . . . This was obviously my legacy, as someone who also wanted to be an artist and who was not only black and poor, but a woman besides, if only I had the guts to accept it. (38–39)

With this statement Walker inscribes the notion that one role for a writer is to be courageous enough to go deeply into one's own mind, heart, soul, and experience and to bring forth language with social and persuasive intent in the interest of touching, teaching, and deeply affecting others.

In another essay, "Trying to See my Sister," Walker chronicles her failed attempt to see Dessie Woods, who by a questionable application of the law had been convicted for theft and murder and incarcerated in rural Georgia. Walker says: "Because it is obvious that black women do not have the right to self-defense against racist and sexist attacks by white men, I realize I am in prison as well. In the prison visitors' book, under the date November 10, 1980, I sign my name as witness to our common oppression, and add 'Tried to see Dessie Woods,' as a witness for myself" (23–24). Walker recognizes the need for writers like herself to witness oppression, to see one's own connectedness to it, and to record it for others to see, to know, and by extension, to be spurred toward action. This view enriches a lesson she reports learning in the essay that precedes this one, "Father." In this essay, she discusses her relationship with and her understanding of her father. She explains: "he taught me not to bother telling lies, because the listener might be delighted with the truth" (15). Walker encodes here a concern and respect for the power of "truth," a term that deserves careful consideration in her work, as in African American women's writing generally, especially given the contemporary questioning of "truth" as an absolute or as a universal concept. Walker's view of truth, in contrast to a questioning of the viability of absolutes, appears to be connected more directly to experience; to naming the experience from a well-articulated and self-defined standpoint; to accurately representing it from that view; to using this viewpoint respectfully as a touchstone for ongoing interpretive needs; and to being willing to bear witness and give testimony based on the understanding that grows organically from it.

Walker presents, perhaps, her most compelling vision of language and action when we juxtapose two statements, one from each volume of essays. First, in *Search* she says: "It is, in the end, the saving of lives that we writers are about. . . . We do it because we care. . . . We care because we know this: *the life we save is our own*" (1983:14). Second, in *Living by the Word,* she says: "I learn that the writer's pen is a microphone held up to the mouths of ancestors and even stones of long ago. . . . The magic of this is not so much in the power of the microphone as in the ability of the nonhuman object or animal to be and the human animal to perceive its being" (1988:170). Walker embraces in these statements the power of a perception that is well rooted in knowledge and understanding of the past, and she embraces compassion. With this combination she places herself in context and makes a space for action, especially her own individual action, in the saving of lives.

As an individual, Walker presents herself as a person who has grown up a poor African American female in the rural South. Her circumstances set her apart, make her unique, as do the contours of her life and history as a writer. As writer, she accepts the risk of seeing and perceiving deeply, with the consequent obligation to speak eloquently her own perceptions of truth. Walker clearly acknowledges that she speaks for herself, often in meditative and intimate terms. In speaking, however, she demonstrates ultimately a commitment to do more than simply speak. She displays also an interest in touching others profoundly in whatever sense of humanity they hold, such that at the end of *Living by the Word,* she commands in a gentle, but nevertheless insistent voice, "We are *indeed* the world. Only if we have reason to fear what is in our own hearts need we fear for the planet. Teach yourself peace. Pass it on" (193; original emphasis).

By the time of the publication of *Living by the Word*, we see that Walker extends her concern for the issues and problems of the African American community in broad context to a concern for human and non-human beings in the broadest of contexts, the universe. She pays attention to the quality of perception, the need for compassion, the multiple ways in which everything in the world stands in relation to everything else. In this work, she merges basic concerns for perception, compassion, and broad context; she views herself as a person of the world and views her task as saving both the world and those of us in it in all of our variety.

The Writer's Choice

Establishing Walker as an example of African American women essayists carries with it the need to look at how she defines the scope and possibilities of her task as writer. Important also is the need to examine the distinguishing characteristics of her way of seeing and expressing in this form. First, the content of her essays shows a broad range of sociopolitical concerns, a matrix of issues related to personal growth and achievement, and her awareness of the many challenges of living and breathing in the presence of others—interests she obviously shares with other African American women writers. Second, equally instructive are her structure and style in helping us think beyond her participation in a lively collective conversation to the identification of patterns of engagement that might suggest a larger picture for language use.

Walker's practices as an essayist vary. What is striking across the range of practices is general characteristics that seem to offer a useful analytical lens. We can begin the analysis with Walker's own meta-discourse about what she is doing. In "The Dummy in the Window," Walker says:

folklore [storytelling, wise sayings, community rituals] is at the heart of self-expression and therefore at the heart of self-acceptance . . . in accepting one's own folklore, one risks learning almost too much about one's self. . . . My view is that we needn't pull away from them because of the pain. We need simply to try to change our own feelings and our own behavior so that we don't have to burden future generations with these same afflictions." (*Living by the Word* 32)

Walker confirms that she defines her task in terms of deep perception and compassion, and in terms of thoughtful action. She recognizes the power of specific experience, of being willing to know the self deeply, and of using this knowledge to function as an individual, who in her case happens to write for a living. She unburdens future generations by taking onto her own shoulders the challenge of envisioning how she can learn to live a better life so that others to come do not have to solve this problem from step one. By extension, her unburdening also includes the unarticulated agreement to be a model—as she explains in "Saving the Life That Is Your Own" (*Search* 3–14)—for someone yet unborn who may in the distant unknown future need one.

In following through with her task, Walker claims storytelling and also other creative forms such as poetry as available techniques. She sees them as critical to the whole sense-making process. It is inadequate to say in a simplistic way that Walker tells stories or writes poetry even though unquestionably she is a fiction writer and a poet. For this analysis what is more striking is the consistency with which she affords these strategies a place of honor and preference, even when she writes in a more expository form. In addition, Walker consistently uses classical arrangements that historically are more attributable in the African American community to oral practices than to literate ones. As noted by scholars such as Eric Havelock (1988), classical rhetoric is rooted in orality. Coincidentally or not, in African American communities, classical rhetoric has been most vibrantly internalized in community practices through oratory, such as preaching. In her essays, Walker demonstrates that classical arrangement is indeed a well-internalized organizational building block.

In order to clarify the import of both storytelling (narrative techniques) and classical arrangements and to connect them to similar patterns among other writers, we can turn to scholars, including Havelock, who study the convergence of oral and literate practices in cross-cultural communication. In "The Oral/Literate Continuum in Discourse" (1982), for example, Deborah Tannen underscores fluidity between practices.[11] She posits an oral/literate continuum that reflects the degree to which a communicator focuses either on the audience (a responsibility associated with oral traditions) or on the content (a responsibility associated with literate traditions). The implication here is that a communicator who has internalized values from a cultural system that holds oral practices in high esteem is likely to carry those values into her literate practices as well, such that sense-making strategies are perceived flexibly and the lines between orality and literacy blur, sometimes to such an extent that interpretive power comes not from separating the practices but from acknowledging the blurring.

Tannen also cites the work of Paul Kay (1977) who uses the terms *autonomous* and *non-autonomous* to explain the location of meaning in the process of communication and the mechanisms by which it is conveyed or signaled by a communicator. According to Tannen, the encoding of information autonomously (that is, in the language itself) is typically associated with literate practices, and the simultaneous encoding of information in channels other than linguistic ones (through paralinguistic or semiotic features, for example) is typically associated with oral practices. From this perspective, the merging of spoken and written discourse practices encourages a consideration, not of whether a practice is of one type or the other, but of how the relationships between communicator, audience, and message are negotiated by a communicator within a particular community.

In the case of essay writing, such negotiations contribute to the indeterminate qualities of the genre itself. In the essay, the triadic relationships between communicator, audience, and message function in a fundamentally non-autonomous way. Knowledge is grounded in experience; conventions and traditions can be treated with great skepticism; notions of truth and insight are rooted in the particularities of time and place and are thereby subject to revision. With such a protean genre, inevitably, there is the possibility—even the probability—of fluidity and flexibility in the meaning-making process. In other words, there is an opportunity for oral and literate practices to merge variously. Two of the values that seem most tested are (1) the extent to which the audience is allowed an active or interactive role, rather than a passive one, and (2) the extent to which pathetic and ethical arguments, as compared with mainly rational arguments, assume value in the sense-making process. By these means, rhetorical choices multiply and the triadic relationships themselves transform.

Given this set of features African American women essayists have access to a well-endowed range of options for language and action. The existence of this flexibility underscores the need for researchers to examine both context and ethos, while at the same time retaining a concern for the initially identified set of triadic concerns (communicator, audience, and message). In the case of the original triad, however, we need a new category—rhetorical action,[12] so the focus shifts from concerns about communicator, audience, and message to concerns about context, ethos, and rhetorical action, all with the analytical intent of examining both autonomous and non-autonomous locations of meaning.

Adding to the dynamism of this view is the work of Wallace L. Chafe. In "Integration and Involvement in Speaking, Writing, and Oral Literature" (1982), Chafe distinguishes between "detachment" (qualities associated with written language that serve to distance it from specific concrete realities) and "involvement" (qualities associated with spoken language that indicate relationships to and identification with the audience). Chafe isolates several features of spoken discourse that become useful in identifying features in written discourse that might signal a blurring of oral and literate practices. Among these are references to the speaker (or the use of "I"); references to the speaker's own mental processes (the unpacking of a mind at work, which would suggest that the essay is a particularly appropriate form); the use of devices that monitor the communication channel (that question, for example, whether an audience is listening and understanding); the use of emphatic particles (vocabulary that signals levels of enthusiasm and commitment); fuzziness (the use of hedges by which communicator and audience can engage in conditional involvement); the use of direct quotations (which, in effect, evoke a specific concrete reality); the use of memorable images (to help carry critical ideas and connect them meaningfully with experience).

Further, Chafe identifies parallel connections between ritualized spoken language such as storytelling and written language. He recognizes that both means of expression have the quality of permanence: the text is reread; the story is retold, albeit perhaps not always exactly so but with a degree of constancy that, as with written text, indicates high regard. The implications for Walker and other African American women essay writers is provocative. The question is not whether orality and literacy can be distinguished and isolated, but the extent to which these writers offer evidence of involvement, rather than detachment, and the ways in which they may have capitalized on composing strategies across genres—for example, in Walker's case, the use of poetry, narrative techniques, and arrangements from both oratorical and written discourse practices.

To summarize, in this analysis, the point of departure for a close analysis of Walker's essays is the way in which she merges oral and literate practices. Central among these strategies is her attention to the triadic dimensions of sense-making—that is, to a kaleidoscopic view of context, ethos, and rhetorical action, to the tendency to connect writer, audience, and message in specific and concrete ways. Further, Walker uses language non-autonomously, in that she signals involvement rather than detachment, and she uses narrative techniques, and occasionally poetry, in the making of appeals and the structuring of arguments that actually bring qualities of orality rather than literacy to the text. These characteristics serve to question provocatively "great divide" assumptions about literacy and orality and to support the notion that both oral conventions and literate conventions are part and parcel of a collective of communicative resources, regardless of whether we choose to speak or to write.[13]

Consider at this point "My Father's Country Is the Poor" (*Search* 199–222). Walker begins this essay with a passage from Angela Davis's autobiography, in which Davis describes the Cuban delegation at the 1962 World Youth Peace Festival in Helsinki. Walker proceeds to establish a contrast between Davis's political maturity and her own, beginning then to establish her own level of awareness and to chronicle her own move toward political enlightenment and a deeper understanding of the Cuban people. Right from the beginning, Walker chooses involvement rather than detachment and unfolds her own pathway to enlightenment as an invitation to readers to walk with her and listen.

Walker proceeds then to use two classical tropes, anaphora (where one word or word group forms the beginning of successive clauses) and antithesis (where contrasting ideas are juxtaposed, often in parallel structure):

Many Americans who visit Cuba complain that life there is hard. And it is. But they do not seem adequately impressed by the fact that poverty has been eliminated, or that nearly all the people can read: that a 300,000-copy printing of a new book can be sold out in days. They do not seem awed by a country that provides free medical care to all its citizens, and labors daily to provide decent housing for everyone. They do not say—as I feel—that a hard life shared equally by all is preferable to a life of ease and plenty enjoyed by a few. Standing in line for hours to receive one's daily bread cannot be so outrageous if it means every person will receive bread, and no one will go to bed hungry at night. (203)

The effect is intense. By this parallelism ("They do not . . ."), contrast ("life there is hard . . . life of ease"), and implied contrast (outrageous versus not outrageous), she stacks the deck to the extent that the reader might ask, "Can this be true?" Walker then says, "I went to Cuba" (203), which provides an introduction for a narrative digression, or for what could be called narrative support for her move toward enlightenment. In the next few pages the reader experiences Cuba as Walker reflects on her experience of it. There are descriptive passages, dialogue, excerpts from other writers, even a poem. She creates a literary quilt of the Cuba she came to know. Then she signals the end of the narrative by stating, "What Cuba teaches is that revolution is not a flash in the pan of injustice" (209).

At this point, Walker pushes forward but just a few pages later she halts once more. This time her digression is to tell a dream, which she artfully connects to her experiences in Cuba—not with an expository interpretation of the dream but by establishing descriptively that her father who appears in the dream looks very much like a man she met in Cuba. As it turns out in her essay, the man, who has other parallels to her father, is instrumental—through her observations of him—in clarifying her understanding of Cuba, and in establishing a personalized connection for her to the Cuban people.

At the end of the essay, Walker says: "In spite of everything that threatens to make them less than free to be themselves, I believe, with them, that they will continue to win" (222). With this statement she connects with a community, identifying in a meaningful way with the Cuban people. She does not say, "I agree." What she says is, "I believe with them," and somehow, having been taken through the essay as we have, we can accept this statement—not as universal truth but as genuine Alice Walker. She reflects inwardly and outwardly, and she tells the truth, her truth. From one point of view, we can say that Walker sees with a storyteller's eyes and that she presents her vision with the assistance of a storyteller's tools.

Further evidence of her use of this organizational and conceptual strategy appears in "Zora Neale Hurston: A Cautionary Tale and a Partisan View" (*Search* 83–92). Walker starts with a narrative of how she discovered Hurston. She establishes the point of the narration, pushes on, and then establishes her own point, her personal connection and the identification of how a deeper perception obligated her to act:

Eventually, however, I discovered that I repudiate and despise the kind of criticism that intimidates rather than instructs the young; and I dislike fear, especially in myself. I did then what fear rarely fails to force me to do; I fought back. I began to fight for Zora and her work; for what I knew was good and must not be lost to us. (87)

In the next few pages Walker expounds beautifully on Hurston and why she values her so. In a very moving passage, she identifies why this essay is a "cautionary" tale, using again the classical anaphora:

Without money of one's own in a capitalist society, there is no such thing as independence. This is one of the clearest lessons of Zora's life, and why I consider the telling of her life "a cautionary tale." We must learn from it what we can.

Without money, an illness, even a simple one, can undermine the will. Without money, getting into a hospital is problematic and getting out without money to pay for the treatment is nearly impossible. Without money, one becomes dependent on other people, who are likely to be—even in their kindness—erratic in their support and despotic in their expectations of return. Zora, was forced to rely, like Tennessee Williams's Blanche, "on the kindness of strangers." Can anything be more dangerous, if the strangers are forever in control? Zora, who worked so hard, was never able to make a living from her work. (90)

The anaphora ("Without money . . ."), the question ("Can anything be more dangerous?"), and the contrast of effort and reward build a powerful image. The reader is led to see helplessness, meaningless waste, and perhaps even tragedy. Walker ends this essay with: "We are a people. A people do not throw their geniuses away. And if they are thrown away, it is our duty as artists and as witnesses for the future to collect them again for the sake of our children, and, if necessary, bone by bone" (92). She acknowledges a community and her own obligations as a member of this community, and she ends with an abstraction, a generalization about people and artists. She reflects inwardly and outwardly and tells a truth—once again, her own deeply perceived truth.

These two essays are representative of Walker's tendencies to incorporate narrative techniques both conceptually and structurally into her essays. In these examples the lines are very fine indeed between storyteller and essayist, and the lines between oral discourse and written discourse are equally fine. The reader is easily struck by Walker's nonconformity to traditional literate practices, which value detachment. Walker uses her own experiences to forge direct connections with the reader. She takes advantage of oratorical qualities to connect both emotionally and ethically to values and beliefs, and she freely and easily uses descriptive detail and dialogue to weave her expository tale. This combination of rhetorical choices, however, is not always present in Walker's essays.

In "Nuclear Madness: What You Can Do," (*Search* 343–46) Walker evidently sees her task to be moderately different. This essay is a book review, and Walker gets right to the point without the benefit of descriptive or narrative elaboration: "*Nuclear Madness* is a book you should read immediately. Before brushing your teeth. Before making love. Before lunch" (343). This anaphora ("Before . . ."), a technique that may be a stylistic favorite for her, quickly establishes with some apparent humor that she has serious points to make about this book. After considering the subject (nuclear madness), though, the snappy fragments also evoke a sense of urgency and a need (indicated by the way she begins the essay) to get on with it. And moving on with it she does—while maintaining both the humor and the urgency, while making pathetic, ethical, and logical appeals, and also while using each of these techniques to forge, again, a direct and personal relationship with the reader.

After indicating the author of the book (Helen Caldicott), Walker asks a variation on the question in her title: "What can we do?" Her use of the first person pronouns ("I" and "we") creates a communal space for herself and for the reader as she makes a passionate case for responsible action. She then answers the question: "I do not believe we should waste any time looking for help from our legal system. Nor do I have faith in politicians, scientists, or 'experts.' I have great faith, however, in individual people. . . . As individuals we must join others" (345). Walker goes on to offer several solutions for individual and collective action: "Write letters to those senators and congressmen who are making it easy for the nuclear-power industry to kill us; tell them if they don't change, 'cullud' are going to invade their fallout shelters" (345). The reader can see her humor and her values, made even clearer by her final sentence: "But first, read Caldicott's book, and remember: the good news may be that Nature is phasing out the white man, but the bad news is that's who She thinks we are" (346). This short essay tells us about Walker as an African American, as a female, and as a person with a sense of humor, who cares about environmental issues—and about the obligation of human beings to hold themselves accountable.

One final example of Walker as essayist is "The Divided Life of Jean Toomer" (*Search* 60–5). In this essay she again demonstrates an interest in African American artists, in African American women, and in community. Her effort is to talk about the "Jean Toomer mystery," in light of two of his works, the novel *Cane* and a multigenre collection edited by Darwin T. Turner entitled *The Wayward and the Seeking*. Walker uses these two works to clarify the type of person she thinks the author is. She discusses Toomer's struggle with his own racial identity and his attitude toward African American men and women in *Cane*. Her manner in presenting these views reveals her concern with how African American artists respond to the experience of blackness and to the African American community:

> It will no doubt be hard, if not impossible, for lovers of *Cane* to read *The Wayward and the Seeking* (the title is from one of Toomer's poems) without feelings of disappointment and loss. Disappointment because the man who wrote so piercingly of "Negro" life in *Cane* chose to live his own life as a white man, while Hughes, Hurston, DuBois, and other Black writers were celebrating the blackness in themselves as well as in their work. (62)

Walker sets up an ethical dilemma, a situation where values contrast, but she speaks not as a person who seeks only to analyze but as one who also seeks compassionately to understand. By the process of her inquiry into the "mystery," Walker does indeed come to an understanding. The strategies she employs in this inquiry process and in stating her conclusion are probably the most striking aspects of the essay. In the second paragraph, she states: *Cane* "was an immediate hit among those writers who would eventually make the Harlem Renaissance . . . though Toomer himself had considered *Cane* the 'swan song' of that culture" (61). With "'swan song' of that culture," Walker plants an image in the mind of the reader. The culture that Toomer chronicled in *Cane* was, in his view, dying.

Walker spends the next four pages exploring the manner of man Toomer was. In a very moving paragraph (note again the anaphora, "They will . . ."), Walker states:

To many who read this collection Toomer will appear to be, as he saw himself, a visionary in his assumption that he was "naturally and inevitably" an American—a "prototype" of the new race now evolving on the American continent, "neither white nor Black." They will note that it was not Toomer who ordained that a single drop of Black blood makes one Black. Toomer, looking more white than Black, could as easily argue the opposite point: that several obvious drops of white blood make one white. They will think it heroic of Toomer to fling off racial labels and to insist on being simply "of the American race." They will not be bothered by the thought that, during Toomer's lifetime, only white people were treated simply as Americans. (63)

Walker raises positives and negatives, densely encoding a balance in her analysis in the face of an apparent conflict she feels with Toomer's values. She explores the possibility of the "death"—but she gives, and then she takes away. She acknowledges the position "they" may hold with regard to Toomer; then by implication she states what "bothers" her about holding this position. Through this type of structuring Walker encourages the reader to see that beneath the surface there is discontinuity, something somewhat—maybe even seriously—out of order, something illogical.

In the final paragraph, Walker acknowledges *Cane* as Toomer's finest work; but she also proclaims that he owes a debt to his grandmother, "she of the 'dark blood' to whom the book is dedicated" (65) and to his mother. Then Walker reminds us of her image and puts in two clever twists: "*Cane* was for Toomer a double 'swan song.' He meant it to memorialize a culture he thought was dying, whose folk spirit he considered beautiful, but he was also saying good-bye to the 'Negro' he felt dying in himself" (65). With the first twist, Walker presents the "reported death" and then she explains the other, which to her seems from the historical data more likely to be the "real" death. The second twist comes in the last two sentences: "*Cane* then is a parting gift, and no less precious because of that. I think Jean Toomer would want us to keep its beauty, but let him go" (65). Walker further extends the "death" image by presenting *Cane* as "a parting gift." Then she demonstrates her compassion, her generosity and goodwill. She includes Toomer as a writer who can exist, at least symbolically through the existence of *Cane,* within her community by allowing him the privilege of being different, by allowing him to operate by a different set of values. Although she might prefer him to be otherwise,

Walker does not demand that Toomer conform. She accepts the gift he offers and allows him to move on.

Form and Performance in Assessing Rhetorical Intent

In her essays Walker demonstrates she is a writer of note. She engages in her nonfiction-writing tasks with the same insight and caring for which she is noted in her creative works. She produces essays that can be appreciated for both substance and style and that offer evidence of both eloquence and elegance. Beyond these aesthetic qualities, however, Walker's essays also constitute a springboard from which to consider the ways and means of rhetorical performance—that is, the process of decision-making that results in the performance itself. Paying attention to how the rhetorical features suggest the formation of ethos and identity, the formulations of task and purpose, and the use of various sense-making and organizational strategies makes us aware that Walker's writing is a complex literate event, deeply encoded with values and desires. In the essays discussed here, for example, Walker establishes a frame of reference in which a sense of community is deemed valuable. She consistently forges connections between herself and her message, audience, and context. She uses these devices flexibly, with eloquence and with grace.

In terms of generic form, Walker frequently begins an essay descriptively, establishes a point smoothly and gracefully with an elaboration, but then she stops this forward press to interject a descriptive or narrative digression. She uses narrative techniques so often to support her assertions that they seem actually to constitute the evidence itself. The outcome, however, is that she succeeds in making both pathetic and ethical links between herself and the reader. At this point, Walker might fall gingerly back into her original cadence, to continue a carefully reasoned exposition, and then end this type of essay by moving to a larger view and articulating an abstraction, a generality. In essence, such strategies serve to isolate a territory, to frame it, so that a focal point can be drawn for sense-making. The ultimate effect is to personalize the idea, to show the reader how it grows out of Walker's own experience and observations and that, through this experience, she connects the idea to a community and to what appears "naturally" and organically to be a usable truth. Walker allows the reader to make meaning with her, which then permits the reader to see the point of view as genuine, as true to Alice Walker. Her ideas seem unassuming and profound; sometimes even prophetic.

Moreover, Walker operates as a social critic, in the sense that she engages in critical commentary on the fabric of our daily lives. She constructs a viewpoint that takes into account the simultaneous discourses of race, class, gender, and culture, a viewpoint easily available to women of color. With this womanist viewpoint, as Walker names it, she inevitably operates both outside and inside the discourses of white male, African American male, white female, and Euro-American cultural traditions. Such practices we now recognize as core to what critics in the 1980s were naming the "renaissance" for African American women writers. In Walker's case, her fiction expresses this multivocality implicitly by the depth, quality, and growth of her characters within the circumstances she creates for them. In her essays, on the other hand, Walker speaks explicitly through her awareness of being African American, female, and artist in a racialized, gendered, capitalistic society.

In terms of style, Walker does not always remain within conventional boundaries of exposition and argumentation. She weaves in and out of these modes—at will, as a master storyteller might well do—and operates as if there were indeed a fluid space in which both autonomous and nonautonomous rhetorical choices can be selected. Sometimes she uses narration, description, dialogue, poetry, and powerful images, not just as interest-generating opening devices but as elaboration, as evidence for assertions that appeal to readers in terms of logos, pathos, and ethos. Further, she consistently pays attention to the triadic relationships between herself, her audience, and the subject matter, referencing her personal vision and experiences and the context in which she exists. She engages in a process of critical questioning (in the case of the examples here), by contrast and implication, and she uses the voices of others to remind us to listen and to be compassionate.

In the same way that Walker sometimes quilts her stories, she also tends to quilt her essays, taking a piece here and a piece there, revealing a mind at work, unpacking ideas that are complex in what is typically a nonlinear fashion. She demonstrates a concern for content, for context, and especially for the beauty and power of language, in keeping with both literate and oral practices. Often, her words are not simply well reasoned and insightful but also well placed and well rooted in experience-bound images that evoke bodily response—in the head, the heart, the backbone, sometimes the stomach. The question lingers, then: How, after such treatment by a writer, does a reader actually resist a call for action?

In Search of Our Mothers' Gardens, as an example of nonfiction writing by an African American woman, opens a window through which to perceive such writing in the context of lived experience. Walker writes from her own life and vision. Through her essays she inscribes a concern for others and for the making of a better world for us all. When she writes with this agenda, she is not alone. She writes in the company of others. She lets us know, through the saliency of her work, that these others exist, if only we can notice they are there now and have been there all along— for as long as there have been women of African descent in North America, if not beyond. In moving toward an appropriate theoretical frame to connect literacy and social action, therefore, we must take into account who these others are, where they come from, and how they might have helped to craft the space from which contemporary writers such as Walker might be privileged to speak.

Chapter 2

Toward an Analytical Model for Literacy and Sociopolitical Action

If to speak in tongues is to utter mysteries in and through the Spirit, to prophesy is to speak to others in a (diversity of) language(s) which the congregation can understand. The Scriptures would suggest that the disciples were able to perform both. I propose, at this juncture, an enabling critical fiction—that it is black women writers who are the modern day apostles, empowered by experience to speak as poets and prophets in many tongues.

Mae Gwendolyn Henderson, *"Speaking in Tongues"*

My imperative in theorizing literacy in the lives of African American women is to account for how, within this group, literacy has been practiced and made usable, with emphasis on the essay as a particularly instructive literate form. I acknowledge that there are many variables in African American women's lives and work, which make their stories of literacy far from monothematic. Vibrant among these practices, however, is the use of literacy as an instrument for producing spiraling effects in both sociopolitical thought and sociopolitical action. Literacy has enabled African American women to create whirlpools in the pond of public discourse, such that educational opportunity became for them the epicenter by which change could occur. This image suggests that, with the acquisition of literacy, African American women were able to amass energy and concentrate it—deliberately and with persuasive intent—in support of sociopolitical action. The significance of literate practices grows richer and richer, not just at the critical juncture of acquisition, as literacy became more systematically available to African American women, but in terms of the momentum created by the circles of activity made possible by those moments of opportunity.

The challenge in fashioning a theoretical frame for this group is to account for literacy in such a way as to consider it not just an autonomous, objectified artifact of education and refinement but also a fundamentally subjective tool, made meaningful within systems of belief. This type of subjectivity indicates that my task as researcher is multiple: (1) to analyze and interpret the ways in which written language and action systematically converge; (2) to document the rhetorical habits and choices of individual writers, an effort that requires attention to ethos and context, as well as to message and medium; (3) to examine patterns emerging over time, not simply to suggest, for example, that African American women seem to have an affinity for essay writing but to theorize about what such rhetorical preferences indicate about connections between this group, a worldview, and their deliberate uses of written language to meet sociopolitical purposes. In this regard, acts of literacy are identifiable as subjective in a twofold way. First, they embody the rhetorical prowess of an individual vision and voice in a way that can be articulated in terms of eloquence or aestheticism. Second, they signal that language use even in a singular set of hands is still a cultural production, subject to the constraints of the sociopolitical arenas in which such use acquires meaning and purpose.

A General Review of Analytical Paradigms in Literacy Studies

In making a reasonable case for literacy as a subjective tool in generating action, we benefit greatly from shifting paradigms in literacy research. These shifts have permitted us to value in more sophisticated ways the blurring of literacy and orality.[1] This advantage is critical in examining the literate forms of African American women since their practices show evidence of such blurring. In her edited collection *Literacy Across Communities* (1994), Beverly Moss presents a basic trajectory for these changes. She explains that an initiative in early literacy scholarship was to place literacy and orality in opposition to one another, as distinctive and distinguishable concepts (Goody and Watt 1963; Olson 1977; Ong 1982), thus creating an apparently dichotomous relationship between literate and oral cultures or cultural groups and positing an equally dichotomous view of cognitive abilities that, in effect, placed literacy in a privileged position and orality in a deficit position.

Through the work of Scollon and Scollon (1981), Scribner and Cole (1988), and Heath (1983), however, these dichotomies were questioned, and focus was directed first toward positing an oral/literate continuum (Tannen 1982), and more recently toward linking literacy to social practices in more dynamic ways. Such studies have moved us away from the sense of clear distinctions between orality and literacy as discrete practices toward literacy as part of the whole cloth of communicative practices, in which orality, literacy, and other symbolic systems are all intricately entwined. For example, Brian Street explains, in *Social Literacies: Critical Approaches to Literacy in Development, Ethnography and Education* (1995), that technical skills as well as cognitive aspects of reading and writing are "encapsulated within cultural wholes and within structures of power" (161). With this view, we accept the notion that, amid a complex system of communicative practices in the general culture, there are multiple literacies across sites and language boundaries, as well as across perceived needs, purposes, and communicative norms (see Kintgen, Kroll, and Rose 1988; Scott 1990).

Recent studies, such as those presented in the Moss collection, demonstrate that when literate practices are examined as behavior or events within social and cultural context, dichotomies between literacy and orality blur, and so do hierarchies (see, for example, Farr, McLaughlin, in Moss 1994). The deepest insights concerning communicative practices, however, are sometimes the most obvious, those that we understand tacitly but do not always feel compelled to articulate. Concerning literacy, what often goes unstated is that engaging in literate practices is a peculiarly human thing to do. This statement somehow seems redundant, even in the saying of it, but it is especially useful when stated as a touchstone: Literacy is a human experience. This notion comes alive in literacy research through ethnographic studies, studies that tend methodologically to accept human complexity as a defining principle. The research projects vary tremendously across target groups and sites (Kirsch and Sullivan 1992; Street 1995; Mahiri 1994; Weinstein-Shr 1994), as well as in terms of the foci of exploration, but each problematizes literacy in such a

way as to insist that our definitions include qualitative measures of productivity and performance and that they make room for what Clifford
Geertz (1973) has called "thick description."

Much like viewing a painting by Salvador Dali, we have come to appreciate the creative and interpretive power of the landscape view of literacy
only as we have become aware of the striking and seemingly magical distinctions of the detailing within. This metaphor suggests that a fundamental task for contemporary literacy researchers is to find useful ways to
envision literacy in its particulars, in this case within the lived experiences
of African American women. In an examination of literacy within this
group, I underscore the idea that literacy connects profoundly, variously,
and inextricably with their lives in specific contexts as they have acquired
literacy, used it, and become entwined in it by its benefits and consequences—historical, social, economic, political, cultural (Graff 1991:3).

Literacy as Sociopolitical Action

Sojourner Truth, an African American woman categorized most often
as illiterate, offers a place to begin in understanding literacy as emanating
from lived experience. In 1867, in an informal response to a literacy requirement for the right to vote, Truth said: "You know, children, I don't
read such small stuff as letters, I read men and nations" (Loewenberg and
Bogin 1976:239). This comment suggests that literacy is a sociocultural
phenomenon, a use of language, a component of a complex system of
understandings and intents from which decoding and encoding texts
must inevitably get their shape, direction, and momentum. Truth's comment acknowledges that making meaning with language is at essence a
social act and suggests that it is also a political act, in keeping with the
analysis of Paulo Freire and Donald Macedo (1987) when they talk about
reading the word and the world.

Given this perspective, a useful definition of literacy is that it is a sociocognitive ability. It is the ability to gain access to information and to
use this information variously to articulate lives and experiences and also
to identify, think through, refine, and solve problems, sometimes complex problems, over time.[2] My intent in using the term *socio-cognitive*
here is to push beyond an examination of levels of social awareness and
ways of making judgments in order for this concept to encompass also

ways of knowing and believing (as crystallized, for example, in the work of Belenky et al. [1986] and Cook-Gumperz [1986]) and also ways of doing (as addressed, for example, by the work of Gardner [1993]). This more comprehensive view permits boundaries between orality and literacy to be questioned from an even broader range of language practices (which will not be addressed in this book), for example, singing, as a multilayered event; storytelling, as a tool of cultural indoctrination and instruction; and signifying, as a rhetorically complex gaming practice.

In moving from the flexibility of this definition toward a theory of literacy as sociopolitical action, language theorists from several disciplinary perspectives provide collectively a useful place from which to clarify how the complex of understandings that undergird African American women's literate practices might be revealed and interpreted.[3] Dell Hymes, for example, uses the term *communicative competence.*[4] In pointing out the social dimensions of communication, Hymes recognizes that, in order for people to use language as an act or tool of communication (in this case, to engage in an act of literacy), they need knowledge and understanding of how this language is used in the midst of a particular set of sociocultural norms, norms that also include political dimensions. The communicator must have internalized sociolinguistic knowledge and be able to use this knowledge to "read" a situation and to create meaning that can be conveyed to others.

Clearly Sojourner Truth, unlettered though she was, had the ability to understand sociocultural information and to operate with power and authority within the context of the communities in which she spoke. She was able to see what was there and what was not there, to grapple with complex situations, and to emerge as a rational and capable thinker who could articulate her visions and understanding of reality, albeit orally. Truth had internalized sociolinguistic knowledge. What she had not acquired were the tools of decoding and encoding text. She was able to make an awful lot of meaning. She was not able to read and write.[5]

Further, Hymes points also toward the dialectical and reflexive nature of the process of communication, in other words, toward communication as a cognitive process. My use of the term *cognitive* in this discussion is intended in its broadest sense—with a "small cee," that is, without specifying any particular cognitive theory. My intent is to focus unceremoniously on there being mental processes involved in languaging ability. The assumption is that whatever the mental processes are exactly, they happen, and what we have, in fact, is a human mind at work. Without specifying, then, the details of the processing, my point is that Hymes indicates that communicators (in this case readers and writers) use their abilities to process a reservoir of sociolinguistic information, gauging effectiveness and ineffectiveness continuously in order to construct meaning. He focuses on the ways in which communication is an exchange, a give-and-take process, with the opportunity for feedback, rethinking, and modification. This explanation underscores language use as a learning experience.

In Hymes's view, we learn by communicative experience and by incorporating both past and ongoing experience into current practice, even when the communicative event is actually an event in progress. The development of communication skills can be viewed, therefore, as a lifelong process, which allows us to incorporate sociolinguistic information and to adjust and readjust operational strategies continuously in the interest of meeting communicative needs and purposes. By this means, we operate within socially established norms, and we can be perceived as communicating appropriately with others.

Communicative competence, then, is at once the process and the performance of communication, whether spoken or written. This competence is what communicators use to negotiate the meaning space in progress. It is embodied in the actual shaping of the event and in the capacity of that shaping to accomplish goals as communicators designate and re-create these goals during the event itself. Communicative competence is tied, therefore, to a base of language experience. It is tied to the knowledge and understanding that an individual brings to the language event and also to her actual abilities to perform during the language act itself. Sojourner Truth demonstrated that she had acquired knowledge and experience, and that she understood what it meant to make meaning in the contexts in which she operated.

In this regard communicative competence clarifies the generative and reflexive nature of language use in social context and sets us up well to examine a particular language practice. The concern of this chapter is to refine communicative competence as a general process, and to focus more on the use of written language for persuasive purposes, that is, with the deliberate desire to change thinking, perception, attitudes, or behavior. To mark this transition, I have chosen the term *rhetorical competence*. In resonance with Hymes's view, this term suggests that writers have a base of sociocultural knowledge and language experience (as communicators generally do), which they use in the process of making meaning and conveying that meaning to others in the satisfaction of specific purposes. The task of the writer is to understand the world around her; to determine how she should face and negotiate literacy challenges, given her knowledge and experience; and to determine what she should actually do to perform in a way that produces desired effects, in this case the appropriate change in thinking, perception, attitudes, and behavior.

Scholars such as Brenda Dervin and Kathleen D. Clark (1993) have discussed similar concerns from both a macro-level and a micro-level analysis, with attention to how these two streams of analysis need to connect. They take into account at the macro level how power and resources are distributed, who controls what, and what messages are communicated. At the micro level, they take into account more ideologically bound practices and procedures, such as the means and mechanisms by which individuals connect to and make sense of self, other, society, culture, and institutions; they consider with equal concern how societies, cultures, and institutions connect with individuals and with each other. Their view encourages researchers to focus on the communicative mandates of particular language users and on how these mandates become the springboard from which communicators invent strategies, engage in sense-making processes, and thereby produce rhetorical effects. From this perspective, the essay as a literate form becomes one manifestation of how African American women respond to sociocultural conditions, as these conditions are defined by social, cultural, and institutional power systems and structures. Given this framework, the essay functions as a communicative invention. As an expressive form, it is employed by writers to serve specific needs at a particular time and place, in response to the construction of mandates for action.

In keeping with Dervin and Clark's analysis, if we focus on the essaying practices of African American women, we can see that one goal of communicative mandates has been to make obvious, visible, and flexible what has been hidden and assumed, in the interest of appropriate rhetorical effects. The essays of African American women demonstrate that the writers seek to make sense of lives and conditions that to them do not make sense. They reveal continuities and discontinuities and set up contrasts between what is there and not there and what should or could be there instead. Further, the desired effects of their sense-making cluster around their interests in making the world a better place for those who are not permitted to operate with power and authority in American society and who are systematically impacted upon so negatively by social, political, and economic forces.

Consider the following examples. In 1831, in an essay entitled "Religion and the Pure Principles of Morality: The Sure Foundation on Which We Must Build," Maria W. Stewart states:

This is the land of freedom. The press is at liberty. Every man has a right to express his opinion. Many think, because your skins are tinged with a sable hue, that you are an inferior race of beings; but God does not consider you as such. He hath formed and fashioned you in his own glorious image, and hath bestowed upon you reason and strong powers of intellect. He hath made you to have dominion over the beasts of the field, the fowls of the air, and the fish of the sea (Genesis 1:26). He hath crowned you with glory and honor; hath made you but a little lower than the angels (Psalms 8:5); and according to the Constitution of these United States, he hath made all men free and equal. Then why should one worm say to another, "Keep you down there, while I sit up yonder; for I am better than thou?" It is not the color of the skin that makes the man, but it is the principles formed within the soul. (29)

Stewart questions the oppression and enslavement of African Americans, expressing her views of the nonsensical ways by which white people during this era systematically dominated African Americans because of the color of their skins. In the remainder of the essay, she continues to cast light on the discontinuities of these actions (that is, the disconnections between principles of morality and the actions that were predominant in American society) and to offer educational, economic, and political solutions that support justice and empowerment.[6]

In similar fashion, over a hundred years later in an essay collection entitled *Technical Difficulties: African American Notes on the State of the Union* (1992), June Jordan states:

American delusions of individuality now disfigure our national landscape with multitudes of disconnected pained human beings who pull down the shades on prolonged and needless agony. But if we would speak the unspeakable, if we would name and say the source of our sorrow and scars, we would find a tender and a powerful company of others struggling as we do, and we would know we should show to the world, at last, that shame belongs with blame, not on the victim.

We would undertake collective political action founded on admitted similarities and grateful connections among us, otherwise needful citizens who now regard each other as burdensome or frightening or irrelevant. This would mean a great national coming out—a coming out of our cars, a coming out of our deadpan passage through the streets of America, a coming out of the suburbs, a coming out of our perverted enthusiasm for whatever keeps us apart. . . . But each American one of us feels so special and so different that none of us assumes the validity of his or her outrage or longing inside the mythical context of "the American Mainstream." ("Waking Up in the Middle of Some American Dreams," Jordan 1992:19)

Like Stewart, Jordan sees discontinuities, that is, concepts that we need to question more critically: "individuality," "mainstream." She reveals inconsistencies between what we uphold and what by contrast our upholding disables rather than enables. She posits that we live unnecessarily with delusions and myths; she proceeds to illustrate her viewpoint and to propose alternative ways of thinking and acting. Stewart and Jordan illustrate a continuity of rhetorical actions among African American women. Through their essays they demonstrate that their knowledge and experiences permit them to understand the world around them and to perceive a need for action. They also go farther. Using the essay as a mechanism for expression, these writers demonstrate that they see language/literacy/rhetoric as action, as a means of engaging actively with problems, as a strategy for presenting solutions persuasively to their audiences—who can in their own turn act accordingly.

Resonating significantly with this illustration of rhetorical competence and sense-making strategies is Lev Vygotsky's theory in *Mind in Society* (1978), which examines the convergence of speech and action in the course of intellectual development. Vygotsky's basic point is that the dynamic relationships between speech and action reveal the critical role played by socialization. In his analysis of the development of cognitive abilities, Vygotsky posits that we internalize social speech, which results in a dialogic dimension in monologic uses of language. In other words, even when we write alone (a monologic use of language), we do so—as

Mikhail Bakhtin (Holquist 1981) articulated it—with a sense of how language works in a discourse community. We engage in "conversations of the mind" (Bruffee 1984), a dialectical experience that allows us to function more effectively as language users who expect to be heard or read and responded to.

In Bakhtinian fashion, we think and write in conversation with ourselves (as "constructed" members of communities) around the text, beneath it, between its lines, and we make meaning through conventionalized, socially and culturally determined uses of language. Even when we are writing alone, we are still in community with others. My view is that we make meaning as sentient beings, but we do so within boundaries of tolerance created by our communities, or at the very least either proactively or reactively in relation to those boundaries. The task is complex. We envision a use of literacy and operate from our perceptions and experiences. We make meaning with whatever creativity we can muster and to the extent that contextual constraints will allow, and we demonstrate our abilities to operate not just as speaking subjects within community but as intellectual beings, capable of learning and capable of exercising the knowledge that we have acquired.

As Mae Gwendolyn Henderson suggests, what typically happens with African American women writers as they acquire knowledge and experience and engage in communities of discourse is that the texts they produce become multivocal.[7] Typically, the writers respond to communicative mandates that require them to engage with multiple discourses. Their strategies for responding include the use of plural voices—and frequently (I add) the use of multiple genres as well. African American women essayists are often also novelists, poets, playwrights, academics, or users of some combination of literate forms, indicating their desires to address concerns through more than one form (see chapter 1).

One example of how African American women display this type of complexity is the anti-lynching campaign of Ida B. Wells.[8] As an investigative journalist from the 1880s through the 1930s, Wells's purpose with this campaign was to uncover the truths of mob violence and to identify more accurately the nature of the problem so that more appropriate solutions could be identified and implemented. The editorial that started her down this pathway states:

Eight Negroes lynched since last issue of the *Free Speech*, one at Little Rock, Ark., last Saturday morning where the citizens broke (?) into the penitentiary and got their man; three near Anniston, Ala., one near New Orleans; and three at Clarksville, Ga., the last three for killing a white man, and five on the same old racket—the new alarm about raping white women. The same programme of hanging, then shooting bullets into the lifeless bodies was carried out to the letter. Nobody in this section believes the old threadbare lie that Negro men assault white women. If Southern white men are not careful, they will over-reach themselves and public sentiment will have a reaction; a conclusion will then be reached which will be very damaging to the moral reputation of their women. (Royster 1997:79)

In this short paragraph, Wells invokes multiple discourses. She references racist stereotypes and subverts images of barbarity that were evident in discourses on race; she references sexist stereotypes and questions images of danger and desire that were intricately imbedded in discourses on gender; she questions stereotypes of lawlessness for African American men and stereotypes of moral superiority for white men as these stereotypes often reigned in discourses on democracy; and so on. And she does all at once. Moreover, throughout her campaign, Wells held central in her sense-making strategies the need for multivocality, that is, the need to keep all participants in lynching scenarios in clearer relationship to each other and to the problem with particular regard for their actions and responsibilities: white men, white women, African American men, and African American women. Ultimately, in order to respond to her mandate to advocate for justice, law, and order by analyzing the complex problem of lynching, Wells complicated her rhetorical viewpoint with these types of simultaneous concerns. And she demonstrated, in keeping with Vygotsky and Bakhtin (whose theories address the socio-political negotiations required by language use), that she was keenly aware of living within a web of social and political forces that affected her capacity to use words with the consequence she desired.

Along these same lines, Vygotsky theorizes that, in continuing cognitive development, language becomes a valuable tool in thinking through, refining, and solving problems, and also in consciously planning (as in the act of writing), in order to engage in complex operations over time (1978:27–28). This view is similar to Hymes's view, insofar as Vygotsky acknowledges that literacy, as a planned use of written language, has social and cognitive dimensions. By this reckoning, rhetorical competence is enhanced by the ways language use over time becomes a continually generative learning experience. To put it more simply, through a process of ongoing learning and development, using written language—especially with the opportunity for feedback and reflection—begets better uses of this medium. As writers learn from their literate practices and continue to use writing, they release greater potential to engage with increasing expertise in the use of literate tools in actions and interactions.

The message is actually basic, in terms of trends and practices in composition studies. Teachers and scholars in this field generally accept the idea that experience counts. Writers gain comfort and confidence as they develop the habit of writing, not just with writing more but with the opportunity for response and reflection. As writers develop experience and expertise, they have the potential to affect their worlds through literacy, as they are continually affected by and have to account for the worlds around them. Without a doubt, African American women have developed the habit of writing; and with essay writing, as a nonfiction form, they have also found reading and listening audiences in public arenas (see chapter 5), a circumstance that has enhanced their success.

This view of the social context of learning suggests, as Hans-Georg Gadamer does, that understanding is the result of mediation—in effect, a trans-mediation—of past knowledge and experience into present situations, such that there is a "fusion of horizons" (1977:39), past into present. Gadamer recognizes the language-bound nature of this process, with language functioning as the medium by which the fusion proceeds. Language helps to make our knowledge conscious, visible, and knowable. It embodies and makes transformable the socially determined spaces in which we as linguistic beings create ourselves and a working sense of the world and its possibilities.

Moreover, Gadamer also uses the term *hermeneutical consciousness* to identify our ability to see what is questionable. This dimension gains significance when a bridge needs to be constructed (or in the view of Dervin and Clark [1993], when a communicative gap needs to be negotiated) between the familiar, or that which is close and understood (the past), and the strange, or that which is distant and unnamed or unfocused (the new and different). In this regard, Gadamer seeks to examine the material conditions that make understanding, and thereby interpretation, possible. In applying this notion of hermeneutic consciousness to acts of literacy, when a person seeks to engage in an act of literacy, to convey to others (who may understand the world differently) her knowledge, experience, and interpretations, the conditions for a hermeneutic problem exist. The writer is called upon to negotiate meaning, facing the challenge of how to build bridges, fuse horizons, and accomplish the goals of the task.

This hermeneutic problem is easily identifiable in the use of literacy by African American women for social change. As people who have been systematically constrained by issues of race, class, gender, culture, and so on, they have nevertheless been successful in questioning the world and constructing spaces from which to assert their viewpoints. Consider the passage below from "Duty to Dependent Races," a speech delivered in 1891 by Frances Ellen Watkins Harper:[9]

While Miss Fletcher has advocated the cause of the indian and negro under the caption of Dependent races, I deem it a privilege to present the negro, not as a mere dependent asking for Northern sympathy or Southern compassion, but as a member of the body politic who has a claim upon the nation for justice, simple justice, which is the right of every race, upon the government for protection, which is the rightful claim of every citizen, and upon our common Christianity for the best influences which can be exerted for peace on earth and good-will to man. (Logan 1995:36)

With her knowledge and experiences as an African American woman, Harper saw the world in a different way than did Miss Fletcher, the person who had spoken before her. With this vision she was able to question conditions differently, asserting that the claims of African Americans and others were the rights of citizenship and humanity rather than supplications for kindness and generosity. In order to articulate such an alternative viewpoint, Harper had to construct a space that bridged her view and Miss Fletcher's view (as representative of liberal expectations of the day) and that permitted a new horizon to emerge. From this new horizon, Harper could speak with agency and authority across chasms of systemic disbelief—if not always overt and direct hostility. Her imperative was to claim space and to use it well.

Another scholar whose work becomes significant at this point (that is, when the hermeneutic problem of creating space for action also becomes rhetorical) is Kenneth Burke, who expands yet another boundary of our thinking about language and action. In *Language as Symbolic Action* (1966), Burke distinguishes between "scientistic" and "dramatistic" approaches to the nature of language and indicates that the "scientistic" involves definition and naming and that the "dramatistic" involves stressing language as a mode of action. In clarifying this distinction, he situates language in the world of action and recognizes the importance of two rhetorical principles: identification and consubstantiation (which he discusses more thoroughly in *A Rhetoric of Motives* [1969]). Burke explains "identification" and "consubstantiation" by this example:

> *A* is not identical with his colleague, *B*. But insofar as their interests are joined, *A* is identified with *B*. Or he may identify himself with *B* even when their interests are not joined, if he assumes that they are, or is persuaded to believe so.
>
> Here are ambiguities of substance. In being identified with *B*, *A* is "substantially one" with a person other than himself. Yet at the same time he remains unique, an individual locus of motives. Thus he is both joined and separate, at once a distinct substance and consubstantial with another. (1969:20–21)

If we apply these terms to acts of literacy, perceived as essentially rhetorical events, we recognize that writers create a consubstantial space. Within this space they can interact with their audiences, and establish with those audiences mutual interests—from which the clarification of continuities and discontinuities of beliefs and viewpoints might begin, meaning might be created, and communication might take place.

To add to this analytical approach, Burke establishes the significance of the concept of a "terministic screen" and explains it in this way:

> When I speak of "terministic screens," I have particularly in mind some photographs I once saw. They were *different* photographs of the *same* objects, the difference being that they were made with different color filters. Here something so "factual" as a photograph revealed notable distinctions in texture, and even in form, depending upon which color filter was used for the documentary description of the event being recorded. (1966:45)

With this concept Burke suggests that we all live with filters, which screen our experiences so that we envision the world in a particular way. Given the terministic screens through which we make sense of the world, some things are revealed but others may be cast in shadow. Thus Burke offers a provocative way to view language use.

Speakers and writers, operating as human beings with a particular set of terministic screens, create consubstantial spaces, which, in Gadamer's terms, might be referred to as a fused horizon or, in accordance with Dervin and Clark, might be referred to as engaging in sense-making strategies. These speakers and writers engage in communication with others, which Vygotsky might identify as a space not only for language performance but also for cognitive development, and which Gadamer might identify as a space for mediation. They also have the potential to form or re-form attitudes and influence action, all of which Hymes might name as part of the process by which communicative competence or rhetorical competence is formed and exercised.

African American women essayists operate with their own terministic screens, certainly. They have demonstrated, though, an ability to help their audiences to notice and often to be instructed by their own terministic screens. Ida B. Wells offers an example in one of her essays, entitled "Lynch Law in All Its Phases," an address delivered at Tremont Temple in Boston, Massachusetts, on February 13, 1893:

> I cannot believe that the apathy and indifference which so largely obtains regarding mob rule is other than the result of ignorance of the true situation. And yet, the observing and thoughtful must know that in one section, at least, of our common country, a government of the people, by the people, and for the people, means a government by the mob; where the land of the free and home of the brave means a land of lawlessness, murder and outrage; and where liberty of speech means the license of might to destroy the business and drive from home those who exercise this privilege contrary to the will of the mob. Repeated attacks on the life, liberty and happiness of any citizen or class of citizens are attacks on distinctive American institutions; such attacks imperiling as they do the foundation of government, law and order, merit the thoughtful consideration of far-sighted Americans; not from a standpoint of sentiment, not even so much from a standpoint of justice to a weak race, as from a desire to preserve our institutions. (Thompson 1990:171)

Wells proclaims as paramount the defining principles purportedly avowed by the individuals in her audience, and she sets up as a given that the audience should use these principles as interpretive lenses for seeing the problem of lynching and identifying appropriate solutions. People who are intelligent, observant, and thoughtful (that is, not ignorant of what is happening in the world); people who believe in the ideals of freedom, justice, law, and order; people who are good citizens; people who are far-sighted Americans and who have the common sense to want to preserve our national values; all should listen to what she has to say and to act in good conscience based on this analysis. In other words, Wells had a politically contentious viewpoint, but, like other African American women writers, she was, by necessity, a bridge builder.

From a different area of intellectual activity, African American science fiction writer Octavia Butler addresses the consequences of bridge building or the fusion of horizons. In her *Dawn* trilogy, which includes *Dawn*, *Adulthood Rites*, and *Imago*, Butler presents a world in which the future of Earth as a viable planet and humans as vital and viable beings depends on a fusion with alien beings. What Butler works out in complex fashion is that the process of fusion signals gains, deep losses, and the necessity of negotiation in the interests of growth and survival. She hurls her characters into a new, radically different world, demonstrating the ultimate chaos and frustrations that inevitably accompany change, especially for people who, as she says, are both intelligent and hierarchical. She suggests that it is through fusion that we have the capacity to exist. Newness, she suggests, forms at the intersections, the places at which the building of bridges which once crossed cannot be re-crossed. In fact, she suggests to some degree that it is only through such processes of fusion that we do exist. The implication of the ideological position she creates is that, despite our fears and hesitations, chaos is normal and we can indeed survive amid it. We can enter unknown and uncharted spaces, and we can do so understanding the inevitability of forward motion within this space. We can appreciate what we bring with us, and we do not have to be intimidated by the fact that the negotiations permitting us a future inevitably include gains and losses. From this viewpoint, we recognize that, when fusion happens, the resulting fused horizon becomes a new horizon and leaves open unanticipated possibilities that can emerge when multiple subjectivities are recognized, respected, and allowed to participate in the fullness of their glory in the making of meaning.

African American women writers keep a hopeful eye on the future, not a pessimistic one. They bring past knowledge and experience to bear on present problems, with a social obligation to make whatever adjustments are necessary to bring a better world into existence. They demonstrate persistently a commitment to the power of belief in possibility. They model in various ways that a basic strategy in sustaining such a commitment, even in the face of unknowns, is to constitute a vision and a set of values based on past knowledge and experience. Using this perspective (a sense of self, agency, and responsibility to society), these writers define and interpret problems and identify and implement solutions. With this habit of language and action, change can be perceived in both positive and productive terms. In her collection of essays entitled *A Voice from the South* (1892) Anna Julia Cooper stated:

It is these magic words, "I believe." That is power. That is the stamping attribute in every impressive personality, that is the fire to the engine and the moter [*sic*] force in every battery. That is the live coal from the altar which at once unseals the lips of the dumb—and that alone which makes a man a positive and not a negative quantity in the world's arithmetic. With this potent talisman man no longer "abideth alone." He cannot stand apart, a cold spectator of earth's pulsing struggles. The flame must burst forth. . . . Who cheats me of this robs me of both shield and spear. Without them I have no inspiration to better myself, no inclination to help another. ("The Gain from a Belief," 1988:302)

Connecting literacy and sociopolitical action in the lives of African American women encourages us to use a multidimensional analysis. To summarize the operational terms:

1. *Communicative competence* offers an instructive example in fashioning a framework designed to examine *rhetorical competence,* the process and performance of rhetorical action. As an operative term *rhetorical competence* focuses on the use of sociolinguistic knowledge and sociocultural experience to set communicative mandates and to engage in a process of rhetorical decision-making—in this case, in the use of literacy with sociopolitical intent.

2. Using this basic framework, we can examine both *macro-level* issues, in terms of the *context* for rhetorical action and the systems and structures of power and control that operate in this context—in general and in various communities of discourse; and *micro-level* issues, with regard to the formation of a sense of self in society (or *ethos formation*), the construction of mandates for action, and the use of meaning-making strategies to carry out these mandates.

3. In this configuration of *context, ethos formation,* and *rhetorical action,* essay writing functions as part of a meaning-making schema, as a resource that the writers find useful in the implementation of communicative and expressive mandates.

4. As a useful literary form, essays operate as both *invention* (a tool in the process of making meaning) and *intervention* (a tool in achieving social and political goals).

5. In terms of a macro-level analytical perspective,[10] over time the lives of African American women have been constrained by various hierarchies of power, authority, and control, articulated often in terms of a convergence of oppressions—by race, gender, class, culture, and so on. The consistency of these oppressions in their lives has been paralleled by a consistency of responses, that is, by acts of resistance. Among these acts of resistance has been the use of literacy for social and political change.

6. In terms of a micro-level analytical perspective, African American women have exhibited a continuity in the patterns whereby they, in response to sociopolitical conditions, have formed ethos, identified communicative and expressive mandates, and chosen the essay habitually as an expressive form.

7. Analyses of literacy as sociopolitical action benefit from the merging of both macro- and micro-level factors. In the case of African American women, we can take into account the extent to which the material conditions of their lives form the backdrop against which they, as individual women, create a *working sense* of their environment and how to function within it. Differently stated, within their particular sociocultural contexts, these women form *visions of reality* and exercise their abilities to be perceptive. Through this process of learning to perceive reality within a materially definable context (that is, based on the existence of recognizable forces, conditions, and circumstances), they accumulate knowledge and experience. The combination of knowledge and experience in fashioning ways of seeing and being constitutes the process whereby they develop *terministic screens,* the habitual lenses through which the women make whatever sense of the world they can and gain the ability to discern what is questionable or does not make sense.

8. When *hermeneutical problems* arise, that is, when there are *gaps* between sense and nonsense, the mandate is to make sense, to adjust whatever needs adjusting in order to rebalance the sense of reality. The process of making new sense calls for a fusion of horizons and a bridging of communicative gaps. This hermeneutical space becomes a site for interrogation. We can question how the women bring past knowledge and experience to bear in articulating and solving present problems. At a

point of problem-posing and problem-solving (as in the use of essay writing for sociopolitical purposes), discontinuities become visible and so do strategies for addressing the resulting challenges. With language use as the primary instrument for instituting the adjustment or the change, the significance of a series of language acts becomes more evident.

9. The writers use language to name, filter, interpret, negotiate, mediate, amplify, and so on. They identify stakeholders or audiences for whom they construct a sense of sameness, that is, they engage in a process of *identification*. They draw for these stakeholders a *consubstantial space* and then use their rhetorical abilities within that space to construct new, more enabling points of view by which the world can make better sense. Toward this end, which they articulate often as "making the world a better place," they engage in various languaging acts: making problems visible; clarifying and amplifying imperatives; establishing more useful terministic screens or interpretive lenses; maintaining a sense of mutual interests or a common ground; negotiating and mediating differences. Communicative goals include the subversion of old ways of thinking, being, and doing; the conversion to new ways of thinking, being, and doing; the affirmation of fused horizons, newly negotiated and mediated spaces that bridge communicative gaps and direct us toward the future.

10. At the micro level, challenges to the African American community have been defined over the decades as issues of justice, equity, and empowerment. These issues constitute focal points in the essay-writing practices of African American women. The historical lack of status and privilege permitted women of African descent in American society has dictated that the hermeneutic space described above has functioned fundamentally as a rhetorical one. African American women have habitually recognized writing as their most available resource for sociopolitical engagement. Moreover, this lack of status and privilege has also dictated that their uses of language would not typically be within "mainstream" communities of discourse but within what Nancy Fraser (1997) refers to as "counter" discourses.

11. Paying attention to these types of factors in analyzing the literate practices of African American women enables us to see in bolder relief the consistency with which they have used literacy (with essay writing

being an instructive example) as an act of resistance to disempowering conditions and in support of agenda for positive action.

To return to Sojourner Truth's statement (quoted earlier), I assert that, in the hands of African American women, literacy has meant more than the mere deciphering and producing of little letters on a page. It has been the exercising of rhetorical competence—that is, the skill, the process, the practice of "reading" and being articulate about "men and nations." For African American women, becoming literate has meant gaining the skills to read and to write; it has also meant taking the power and authority to know ourselves, others, and our circumstances in multisensible ways and to act with authority based on that knowing. This process of the making and shaping of literacy allows us (as Mary Helen Washington weaves the notion throughout much of her analysis of African American women writers) to see the significance of using writing "to write ourselves into being," that is, to entitle our own selves. This process also allows African American women to take note of the greater significance, perhaps, of how accomplishing such a task has enabled possibilities for envisioning resistance, sociopolitical action, and sociopolitical change. What should be noted in particular is that, included in these actions, is the act of claiming creative and intellectual authority over information and experience and thereby, with a sense of vision and agency, using literacy both well and with persuasive intent.

For the first generations of African American women especially, literacy became a tool with which to empower themselves. It became an enabler that facilitated their abilities to operate with vision, insight, passion, and compassion in making sense of their lives and seeking to improve their conditions. Symbolically their lives became literacy in action, that is, an empowered use of literacy in the interests of action, social consciousness, and social responsibility.

An Analytical Model

This view of literacy as sociopolitical action takes into account three basic features of literate acts: *the context for literacy production; the formation of ethos;* and *rhetorical action*—that is, the meaning-making strategies actually deployed by the writer. These features constitute points of inquiry in an analytical model designed to interrogate the manner and means of African American women's participation within worlds of discourse. One point made by this model is that, in keeping with contemporary conceptual frameworks for literacy, I do not distinguish between literate sense-making strategies and oral sense-making strategies as being necessarily separate. These strategies merge in the literate production of African American women. I consider both oral and literate strategies to be part of the whole cloth of communicative knowledge and experience.

A distinction I do make, however, is the contrast between the acquisition of spoken language and the acquisition and development of literate expertise. On one hand, spoken language is considered a more naturally occurring process, in the sense that individuals learn and develop expertise in spoken language by living in a speaking environment. The acquisition of written language, however, is generally considered a more unnaturally occurring process, which typically demands more formal attention. This project, therefore, examines historical patterns of literacy acquisition, as well as opportunities for both formal and informal rhetorical training.

In considering the impact of formal education as it functions in tandem with more informal learning processes, I seek to underscore the importance of cognitive dimensions of language development in all learning opportunities, whether formal or informal. My view is that all language experience factors significantly into an individual writer's sociocognitive resources for rhetorical performance. Whether the source of knowledge and expertise about language use results from predominantly oral practices as speakers or predominately literate ones as writers, information from all sources constitutes an available resource—to the extent allowed by the talents and abilities of the particular language users. The sociolinguistic knowledge and sociocultural experience of speakers and writers become rhetorical knowledge, which supports their capacity to develop rhetorical expertise.

In an effort to examine how African American women writers have exercised their rhetorical competence, this model views rhetorical performance (in this case the use of essay writing to engage in sociopolitical action) in the threefold way articulated above, through analysis of (1) the context for production, (2) the formation of ethos, and (3) the use of rhetorical expertise to engage in action. These three sites of analysis merge, configure, and reconfigure themselves variously throughout the course of the rhetorical process. From an analytical perspective, therefore, each point of focus serves as a lens through which to examine and interpret competence and performance. Neither lens operates adequately in isolation to account for what is achieved by African American women. The interpretive power comes from the kaleidoscopic view, that is, from the merging of all three.

The Context of Literacy Production

Contextual analysis brings into focus the material conditions, forces, and circumstances that affect a writer's ability to perform and that influence the shape and direction of the choices made in carrying out the performance. In analyzing the context for African American women (see chapters 3, 4, and 5), I demonstrate this approach by showing how contextual factors over time have contributed to the establishing of general trends and practices in essay text production of African American women, especially with regard to the essay as an expressive form. The goal of this type of analysis is to enrich the viewpoint; to bring detail and texture to the sources from which writers draw in the formation of ethos and the identification of rhetorical strategies; and to clarify in light of this enriched view the manner and means of the rhetorical action itself.

To illustrate, chapter 3 starts with an acknowledgment that, in the main, the worlds of discourse into which African American women have entered have been systemically hostile and chaotic spaces, not designed with their interests in mind. An examination of the systems and forces that operate in these arenas, then, makes clearer the extent to which there is indeed a misalignment. As suggested by the analysis, for these women, we are primed to notice, for example, the absence of a predisposition to listen to this group of voices or to be accommodating to their needs and purposes. We notice the persistence, in fact, of a disregard of them. As people of low status or of no status or privilege, given the habitual hierarchies of power, in the discourse they are deemed unimportant and made invisible or non-entities. Generally, as speakers and writers in such contexts of disregard, by necessity African American women must not simply operate with rhetorical eloquence (which they have certainly demonstrated they can do), they must also create a space in which their eloquence can be heard. As bell hooks says:

Our speech, "the right speech of womanhood," was often the soliloquy, the talking into thin air, the talking to ears that do not hear you—the talk that is simply not listened to. Unlike the black male preacher whose speech was to be heard, who was to be listened to, whose words were to be remembered, the voices of black women—giving orders, making threats, fussing—could be tuned out, could become a kind of background music, audible but not acknowledged as significant speech. . . . Writing was a way to capture speech to hold onto it, keep it close. (1989:6)

In chapter 3, then, I take into account that African American women writers have traditionally been situated as marginal in society, and that any acts by which they claim agency and authority are necessarily defined, as going against the grain (see chapter 4), that is, against the dominant values and expectations of the general culture. By this schema the materiality of their daily lives has dictated that, in order for them to engage rhetorically, African American women must use their ingenuity and creativity to turn the gaze of their audiences, to reorient their reading and listening minds, and to reconfigure what constitutes sense and sensibility within the communicative environment. I suggest (see chapter 5) that the contexts for action evidence, then, a misalignment of interests, and these contexts have compelled African American women to question and subvert existing interpretive frames and to disrupt and shift habitual sense-making processes. By this means, their written language has functioned in a significant way as a transformative tool. With literacy, these women have created discursively "new" worlds, worlds that they instantiate through language, worlds that permit them a place to exist and to use their talents and abilities to engage positively and productively as they see fit.

The Formation of Ethos

Sharon Crowley (1994) offers two terms that are useful in positing a framework for the ways in which African American women, as literate beings, operate with a sense of ethos: *situated ethos* and *invented ethos*. With situated ethos, Crowley acknowledges the existence of power relationships within the environmental context, which bolster a communicator's communicative ability, or in the case of African American women, typically compromise it. She suggests that the greater the disparity between the situated status of the writer and her audience, the greater the gap that must be traversed in order to communicate effectively and, given this model, to construct effectively consubstantial space for rhetorical engagement.

In the United States, markers of status include race, gender, class, cultural origins, and language (among others), factors that, by historical practice, have operated as marks against rather than for African American women. Traditionally, such women have come to a rhetorical task with a reputation, that is, with a situated ethos more often than not deeply compromised, especially when they seek as one of their target audiences those outside their immediate home community. In such scenarios, African American women are called upon to define themselves against stereotypes and other negative expectations, and thereby to shift the ground of rhetorical engagement by means of their abilities to invent themselves and create their own sense of character, agency, authority, and power.

As writers, African American women are called upon to find ways to present themselves in textual space as intelligent, well-informed, well-meaning people of good character who should speak, who should be heard, and to whom audiences should respond. They spend time in their texts, therefore, acknowledging in one way or another perceived rhetorical distance and crafting carefully a consubstantial space that permits multiple opportunities for ears, hearts, and minds to be inclined in their direction. In keeping with Burke's view, they place their messages along a continuum of identification, bringing themselves and others to resting places that seem appropriate for productive rhetorical engagement. Two excellent examples of these strategies are the essays of Ida B. Wells (Royster 1997) and Anna Julia Cooper (1988).

The rhetorical prowess of African American women, as seen in particular texts over time, suggests that traditionally they have recognized that once they have crafted "identities" for themselves as writers and for their audiences in space and time, they can proceed to make their cases, whatever those cases might be and however they might be made, in ingenious and often eloquent ways. In fact, the essaying practices of African American women illustrate a variety of ways by which they negotiate triadic relationships between context, ethos (the identities they create for themselves and for their audiences), and rhetorical action. They assume a stance and craft relationships between themselves and others, and they take their chances in public discourse, typically as uninvited participants who boldly and courageously engage in rhetorical struggle to overcome disregard and dispropriation.

In inventing ethos, African American women writers draw variously from a richly endowed base of knowledge and experience, a base that includes also a wide array of persuasive strategies, useful in bringing their sense of writer position and audience relationships to life. In this model of analysis, therefore, the construction of ethos does not operate in the absence of rhetorical actions but in tandem with them and also with the way that these writers envision the context. The triadic relationships merge in the creation of a speaking self as the writers make rhetorical decisions and seek to satisfy their communicative mandates.

My view is that African American women use logical, ethical, and pathetic strategies with flair and style and that these markers manifest not only a sense of being in the text but also a sense of reaffirmation as the women connect each of the selves that they create in multiple ways to the others. Consider, for example, the long list of identities invoked by Audre Lorde in *Sister Outsider:* "Perhaps for some of you here today, I am the face of your fears. Because I am woman, because I am Black, because I am lesbian, because I am myself—a Black woman warrior poet doing my work—come to ask you, are you doing yours?" (1984:41–42). In the essays throughout this collection, Lorde gives a laundry list of identities she insists on claiming for herself. To some extent, she flaunts these identities, pulling them out at will as she reminds her readers who the speaking voice is and how she is bringing forth her viewpoint, and she makes this viewpoint credible as it is defined, shaped, and enriched by those very identities. Simultaneously, Lorde is facilitating an opportunity for identity-making by her readers ("are you doing yours?"). She claims who she is. She also makes room in the essays for others to claim their identities as well. In the room that she permits in her essays for identification, Lorde creates a consubstantial space that makes possible both conversation (the exchange of viewpoints) and action (both individual and mutual).

In terms of logical proofs, African American women essayists have a habit, as many essayists do, of fashioning arguments that appeal through reason. They sort through premises, facts, examples. They define, compare, and contrast argumentative positions. They identify patterns of thought and question old paradigms as they give birth to new ones. They create metaphors and analogies that permit readers greater ease in absorbing new and different ideas. They draw richly from wise sayings and proverbs that credit lived experience as an interpretive tool. They take the time, typically, to survey landscapes, often rugged ones, so that they can engage their readers in the identification of reasonable actions and in the charting of productive pathways to change. Such a use of rhetorical strategies certainly helps make a rational case, but these strategies also convey a sense of the writer as a rational being who should be respected. This presentation of self as sensible and thoughtful supports the idea that African American women essayists are seeking actively to fill traditional interpretive roles for the communities in which they live, that is, to help others think well.

Further, in terms of their use of extrinsic proofs, these writers have a particular regard for testimony and bearing witness, acts that blur in provocative ways the lines between logical arguments and pathetic and ethical ones. Testimony, for example, as it credits proximate experience, sets in motion the opportunity and obligation to actually give the testimony, or as typically phrased, to bear witness. In African American women's texts, bearing witness functions vibrantly in the creation of a "true" and honorable self. A valuing of "truth," "authenticity," and the "genuine" creates a pathway that is knowable, and it makes transformative power available for the writer and for her audiences. From this perspective, "truth" is not static, abstract, or separate from the individual. Quite the contrary. "Truth" is an accounting for the "genuine" knowledge and understanding that grows organically from experience, particularly when the writer and her audiences have taken the time to operate reflectively. From this sense of truth, we grow within our genuine experiences and become inspired by them to be perceptive, to live right, to act with honor, confidence, and authority from a knowledge that can be trusted, as the women who are speaking in this way can be trusted. In what may be a non-Westernized sense of the relationships between experience and truth—and between these two concepts and the social roles that such relationships support in one's daily life—African American women invoke "truth" or experience as a source of both passion and commitment in constructing and presenting the speaking self.

By insisting on a place for passion in argumentation, African American women writers on a regular basis privilege both ethical and pathetic arguments. They appeal to a sense of "good" character and "right" action.

They also appeal to experience, emotion, suffering, and imagination. They center their arguments, not just rationally and ethically, but in the body—in the head, the heart, the stomach, the backbone—in the interests, apparently, of inducing not just an intellectual response but a holistic one, that is, a whole-body involvement. The goal seems often to be quite literally to "move" the audience. Consider a quotation from Ida B. Wells in "Lynch Law and All Its Phases":

Do you ask the remedy? A public sentiment strong against lawlessness must be aroused. . . . When a demand goes up from fearless and persistent reformers[,] from press and pulpit, from industrial and moral associations that this shall be so from Maine to Texas and from ocean to ocean, a way will be found to make it so. . . . I am no politician but I believe if the Republican party had met the issues squarely for human rights instead of the tariff it would have occupied a different position to-day. The voice of the people is the voice of God, and I long with all the intensity of my soul for the Garrison, Douglas, Sumner, Whittier, and Phillips who shall rouse this nation to a demand that from Greenland's icy mountains to the coral reefs of the Southern seas, mob rule shall be put down and equal and exact justice be accorded to every citizen of whatever race, who finds a home within the borders of the land of the free and the home of the brave. (Thompson 185–86)

This passage contains logical appeals that connect the reader's head (lawlessness will stop when public sentiment insists that it stops); ethical appeals that connect the reader's sense of the backbone required for justice (fearless and persistent reformers—such as Garrison, Douglas, Sumner, Whittier, and Phillips, all righteous men of talent—from press and pulpit, pen and voice, will find a way to act, as they are obligated by duty as journalists and Christians to do); pathetic appeals that connect the reader's heart and soul (good people will passionately rouse the nation as they know it should be roused to preserve the glorious principles on which we stand). Of course, the major portion of the essay is devoted to reciting the horrors of lynching incidents, which have a high potential for turning, not just the head, heart, and soul, but also the stomach. The merging of these appeals—the intersecting ways they produce bodily effects—suggests that these writers are interested in holistic effects, leaving as it were no rhetorical holds barred.

Moreover, many of these writers spend time in their texts assessing the emotional states of their audiences, taking into account (that is, interpreting) what the audiences must be feeling and thinking, and what they need to know and understand, again in their minds, hearts, souls, and bodies. The writers draw empathetically from feelings shared by one human being with another. They acknowledge and arouse passion. They share options for using passion positively and productively. They evoke the imagination, seeking to create vivid images from which they, apparently, do not wish their audiences to escape. For example, in another essay in *Sister Outsider,* Audre Lorde speaks of our most deeply seated passions:

The erotic is a measure between the beginnings of our sense of self and the chaos of our strongest feelings . . . the erotic is not a question only of what we do; it is a question of how acutely and fully we can feel in the doing. Once we know the extent to which we are capable of feeling that sense of satisfaction and completion we can then observe which of our various life endeavors bring us closest to that fullness.

The aim of each thing which we do is to make our lives and the lives of our children richer and more possible. Within the celebration of the erotic in all our endeavors, my work becomes a conscious decision—a longed-for bed which I enter gratefully and from which I rise up empowered. ("Uses of the Erotic," 54–55)

The rhetorical effort to combine logical, ethical, and pathetic strategies in eliciting a holistic, whole-body response places the audiences on alert. There is engendered by such processes a distinct possibility that their heads can turn, that they will be persuaded, that sooner rather than later they—like the writers who are helping them to think—will be compelled to participate in positive action.

As contemporary critics have examined the essays of African American women, they have tended to consider the characteristics described above primarily in terms of content or purpose. They suggest, for example, that for African American women the essay is an instrument, "a weapon of choice" (Mittlefehldt 1993). I agree, especially given the use of warrior terminology by some of the writers themselves (such as Lorde, quoted above). Through the model presented here, however, I would like to deepen our understanding of what such images might mean. I suggest that, in naming themselves "women warriors," African American women are not simply manifesting a tendency to be direct and sharp-tongued in their use of words and their desire for change. In my opinion these images are emblematic of a long-standing habit of ethos formation by which African American women construct a sense of an empowered self amid disempowering forces and use the energy generated by this process to act. I propose that images of weapons or tools or other instruments for active transformation not only encode ways of doing—identifying focal points and choosing effective means of expression. They also encode ways of being—creating a speaking self, which operates from a particular vision of mission and power, thereby exhibiting both agency and authority. In essays, African American women present themselves as agents of change, who accept the responsibility of "saving the group" and themselves.

If we view the essaying practices of African American women writers kaleidoscopically, with an eye toward the merging of analytical lenses (with ethos in this case providing the primary lens), we can see that their uses of the essay cease to appear arbitrary or coincidental. We come to understand that these women are not simply appropriating in a rather interesting way a form that was designed for others. We understand instead that their uses of a protean and self-authorizing form[11] are womanist—that is, proactive, not reactive—and the essay as the "weapon of choice" shapes itself, as it does with other essayists, in harmony with the particularities of their negotiations of triadic relationships (context, ethos, and rhetorical action). Viewing situated and invented ethos in this kaleidoscopic way lays the groundwork from which to increase our understanding of African American women writers as they write themselves into the discourses of humankind. In the face of contending forces, they draw from all they see, know, and have been. They craft a space, a complex identity, and a set of relationships with others, and in their essaying practices, as one response to sociopolitical mandates, they read and write the world anew.

Rhetorical Action

To focus on the sector of the kaleidoscope related to rhetorical action, African American women transform the world they perceive into the worlds that they desire through the use of language. In the space between the perceived world and the desired worlds is a hermeneutic problem space, in which there are opportunities for individual writers to use language in a variety of literate acts: making problems visible; clarifying and amplifying imperatives; establishing more useful terministic screens or interpretive lenses; maintaining a sense of mutual interests or a common ground; negotiating and mediating differences. All these literate acts can be categorized as participating variously in the creation of a consubstantial space for the conversion or subversion of interests, for the affirmation of new horizons, and for the facilitation of changes in attitude, behavior, or belief.

In keeping with Henderson's view, the consubstantial space is often not writer-to-single-audience but writer-simultaneously-to-multiple-audiences in terms of the ways in which the writers must account for the converging of the various discourses in sense-making. African American women writers convey the impression, for example, of a shifting audience for direct address. Sometimes, even in one essay, a given writer will indicate that she is speaking to African American women, to white women, to African American men, to white men, to everyone or anyone, and so forth, all at the same time. Consider, for example, a passage from Maria W. Stewart's essay "Religion and the Pure Principles of Morality," which illustrates what might be called a process of "roll-calling," or a calling out of stakeholders who, by these identities, should be paying attention:

Where is the *parent* who is conscious of having faithfully discharged his duty, and at the last awful day of account, shall be able to say, here, Lord, is thy poor, unworthy servant, and the children thou hast given me? And where are the *children* that will arise and call them blessed? Alas, O God! Forgive me if I speak amiss; they go astray as it were, from the womb. Where is the *maiden* who will blush at vulgarity? And where is the *youth* who has written upon his manly brow a thirst for knowledge; whose ambitious mind soars above trifles, and longs for the time to come, when he shall redress the wrongs of his father and plead the cause of his brethren? (M. Richardson 1987:31; my emphasis)

Stewart speaks to many categories of people by race, gender, and social roles as she spins a web of participation, and she assumes that all these groups could and should be listening to what she has to say.

Differently stated, African American women writers may address several categories of listeners, to whom they do indeed speak directly. At the same time, however, they convey the sense that they assume or expect "others" to be listening along with the specifically targeted listeners. Such characteristics suggest that African American women writers credit their worlds as complex places—in terms of social, economic, and political forces and also in terms of their multiple relationships to power and privilege. In accordance with Henderson's theories, the writers can be described as engaging in a simultaneity of discourses; their texts can be described as multivocal; the writers can be perceived, as I suggest, as people who often choose to write across multiple genres, in satisfaction of a variety of expressive needs.

Further, as this analytical model indicates, African American women writers value experience as a source of knowledge, "truth," and credibility. To articulate this knowledge, they engage in a variety of language practices, including those listed earlier: naming, filtering, interpreting, negotiating, mediating, amplifying, and so on. They create consubstantial space in keeping with their sense of context and ethos. They use their sociolinguistic knowledge and sociocultural experience throughout these processes, make rhetorical choices, build bridges between themselves and others, all with persuasive intent in the interest of rebalancing reality and creating a better world.

The Kaleidoscopic View

The advantage of analyzing African American women's literate practices in this way is that rhetorical action becomes visible as a site of continuous struggle in response to an ongoing hermeneutic problem. This model permits us to display analytically their rhetorical competence—as we discuss, for example, the *writer's task* and the *writer's choice* as two ways of focusing the results of such an analysis. These two strategies for organizing data (an assessment of task and one of choices) permit us to see more clearly the extent to which these writers add complexity to the voices speaking, to the visions and experiences deemed worthy of sharing, and to those who have the capacity to act with consequence. We see more vibrantly how their rhetorical actions complicate the world, make it multidimensional, textured, and subjective. We perceive more clearly that African American women writers use the power of language to resist simplification, stereotyping, and other disempowering effects. They use language to resist value systems that would render their knowledge and experiences irrelevant and immaterial, or that would erase the specificity of their material conditions. They use language to convey eloquently their understanding of how such erasures make it impossible for African American women to be seen and acknowledged, to speak with power and authority, to have historical presence, to act with consequence. They use language to envision a world as crafted by their own minds and hearts.

Setting this model at the intersections of *context, ethos formation,* and *rhetorical action* permits African American women to emerge from the shadows, to become more than traces of a stream. From this perspective, they can exist proactively in terms of their literate practices having their own integrity and fidelity. In this regard, the kaleidoscopic view is designed to make the hidden and unrecognized visible. This view, by its very framing (that is, in being multi-lensed), encourages us, above all else, to complicate our thinking, rather than simplify it, in search of greater clarity and also greater interpretive power.

Part 2

A Historical View

Chapter 3

The Genesis of Authority

When African Women Became American

It's not that we haven't always been here, since there was a here. It is that the letters of our names have been scrambled when they were not totally erased, and our fingerprints upon the handles of history have been called the random brushings of birds.

Audre Lorde, preface to *Wild Women in the Whirlwind*

I begin this chapter with a statement of the obvious. African American women write. We also speak, often in public. We are, in fact, talented users of language who have demonstrated expertise across multiple measures of performance and achievement. However, for African American women the obvious has not always been treated as such. My intent in this chapter is to suggest that it has only been through the shifting paradigms of the past three decades that researchers and scholars in literacy studies and in other disciplines have been able to see more clearly that the uses of literate resources by African American women over time have not been merely "the random brushings of birds" but evidence of a full and flowing stream of creativity and productivity.

We have benefited in recent years from a series of archaeological projects in African American life and history, such as the fifteen-volume Carlson series, *Black Women in United States History* (1990) and the twenty-five-volume Schomburg *Library of Nineteenth-Century Black Women Writers* (1988). The projects in literature have identified and clarified a variety of literary traditions among African American women specifically and people of African descent in general. The goals of these projects have included the recovery of source writers, the people who were among the first to achieve, and also the recovery of writers generally across literary genres and across time. The projects have focused on the preservation of historical texts, in context, and have celebrated the unfolding stories of literary achievement. Analyses of both individual works and the collective body of texts have brought attention to themes, trends, patterns, and best practices, and have gone quite far in documenting who wrote what when, why, how, and with what immediate and long-term impact. This work has functioned to remold literary history and to redirect both methods of analysis and approaches to interpretation.

I bring this type of interest to the recovery of essay writing. I have turned to rhetorical analysis in order to pay attention to four specific concerns that seem useful: the text, the creator of the text, the process of production, and the context in which the writer has participated and from which the product has emerged. In viewing essay writing in this contextualized way, I began my inquiries with basic questions, focused primarily on the distinctiveness of the writers themselves: Who are these writers? What are the worlds of discourse they are entering? How do they perceive of themselves in these worlds? That is, what ethos do they bring to writing as an enterprise, to the composing of their texts? Given the recognition of ethos as a significant rhetorical concern, what is the genesis of their authority to write, their sense of agency, their sense of identity and purpose, even their sense of "womanhood"?

The basic premise for such questioning is that writers use language with a sense of self and with a sense of their authority to speak. Knowing the particular circumstances of African American women and the various ways in which self-worth and personal authority have been systemically undermined, I was especially curious about what might be the sources of a positive and productive self-concept, and how this sense of self might be usable in the formation of a writing/speaking self—in the formation of an ethos that would permit a sense of agency and authority to emerge and focus itself purposefully. What I tried to imagine was that this genesis of authority, identity, agency, and purpose could have a long trajectory of development rather than a short one. By this type of reckoning, my moment for beginnings could and should not be 1619, the symbolic moment of subjugation of Africans in the Americas. Nor could or should it be the nineteenth century, during which literacy acquisition became an opportunity for large numbers of African American women. I posit instead that this trajectory was actually in motion much earlier, during precolonial times, as evidenced by a configuration of precolonial experiences of African women.

In making this assertion, my goal in this chapter is to reach beyond a narrow envisioning of 1619 as the defining moment of historical presence for African Americans. I seek instead to present a broader vision. My intent is to historicize Black womanhood, and thereby African American women's writing, not from the small stream of our habitual ways of crediting and understanding these women, but from a much richer and much expanded sense of being. The imperative is to look beyond Euro-American experiences, as interesting as they may be, to an inclusion rather than an ignoring of the influences on women's lives in Africa as well.

Reading Between the Lines

In *African Religions and Philosophy* (1969:22–27), John S. Mbiti uses two Swahili words to represent an African sense of individual presence within time, words that become instructive for this analysis. *Sasa,* which we might mistakenly represent as "present," and *zamani,* which we might mistakenly represent as "past," actually situate individuals within a time-space continuum and help us to perceive a striking dimension of African systems of cosmology, which makes it possible to focus on history as a particular type of narrative within time (Ricoeur 1984, 1985, 1988). In this schema, sasa becomes personal time, the time during which individual people exist physically in the world and also the time during which they are remembered, even after physical death, by the living. In this way, sasa is the present, the immediate past, and also the immediate future. When a person ceases to be remembered as an individual by someone who is still living, then that person leaves sasa time and enters another part of the time-space continuum, the zamani dimension. In zamani time, a person joins the collective or the community of spirits and achieves collective immortality. In this way, zamani is the past, the present, and also non-time, or a macro dimension in time, which is beyond both before (past) and after (future). In this case, then, our normal sense of an individual within time, or even history within time, is inadequate to account for this multi-folded notion of individual presence, given the ways by which sasa and zamani in their somewhat simultaneous encompassing of past, present, and future seem to overlap and entwine themselves so interestingly.

With this model of a time-space continuum with its sasa and zamani dimensions, there is room to negotiate what constitutes history, or at the very least to negotiate what constitutes historical consciousness as a precursor for the "making" of history (Ricoeur 1988, 99–274). Somewhere between sasa and zamani dimensions, there is a story that references history as a sasa experience and references it also as a zamani experience, that is, as integrated in a non–individually articulated way into the cultural community. In this way, these two concepts can serve as a frame for thinking again about the relationships between achievements by African American women writers that have come to the attention of the dominant culture (the traces) and the achievements that constitute the continuities and distinctions of this work over time (the stream). From the practical perspective of what can be easily documented, building a case in sasa time for a specified precolonial African American women's history beyond 1619 is problematic. In overwhelming numbers, we have long since ceased to remember the individual women as they existed in their own time. We no longer call out their names. We no longer acknowledge their individual achievements and contributions. We have ignored the fabric of their daily lives.

Using a zamani perspective, however, we can change the base of assumptions. We can acknowledge our own ignorance of individual stories as a significant factor and not assume so arrogantly that our not knowing predetermines that they and their experiences were absent, deficient, or unimportant. We can set aside for a moment what we cannot easily know (that is, personal history) and proceed instead to look more carefully at evidence, even trace evidence, from "collective" experiences, from the "facts" and artifacts that whisper rather than scream, in order to see how else we might still come to historical consciousness and thereby to other renderings of this collective body of lived experiences.

To reemphasize the fundamental challenge, documenting historically the lives and experiences of women of African descent is not an easy task. The work of Black feminist historians over the past two decades illustrates well the care and attention that must be given to small details and a convergence of social patterns.[1] In the case of the focus here, a substantive documentation of African American women's history, especially as it extends beyond 1619, has been hampered by (1) European-centered biases in historical production and validation; (2) the dominance of European and male perspectives in the creation and interpretation of history and in determining what constitutes sociocultural achievement and contribution; (3) until recently (as marked, for example, by the relatively recent emergence of a cadre of women scholars of African descent), a specific lack of scholarly interest in the perspectives, lives, and experiences of women of African descent; and (4) the nontraditional historical sources of information that are necessarily part and parcel of this process of recovery and documentation. All of these factors contribute to the challenge of reconstructing experiences in a credible way and drawing conclusions about these experiences that can be supported by evidence.

At this point in time, we can know earlier periods of African American women's history mainly through reconstruction: by finding whatever pieces of this complex puzzle (both traditional and nontraditional) that still exist and then by hypothesizing from the evidence, however skeletal it might seem, about what else seems likely to be true. We can use traditional scholarship on African cultures as one lens that, unfortunately, has had the habit of paying little specific or direct attention to women's lives and contributions. We can also be grateful to contemporary Africanists, who have begun the long process of reenvisioning African cultures and history (see Mokhtar 1990; Bullwinkle 1989; Hay 1988; Diop 1974). As Heinrich Loth (1987) suggests, however, we are still likely to find this story preserved most often, not so much in traditional scholarship (as yet) as in the early travelers' reports of Arabs, Italians, Portuguese, Dutch, French, and British authors; in archaeological finds; in myths, chronicles, and legends; in the contemporary evidence of cultural remnants within the African diaspora, and so forth.

As the early historical linguists did, therefore, we must learn to read women's stories, between the lines and around the "facts" and artifacts. We must learn to shake out vigorously the observations and propositions that have been and are being set forth about social forces and conditions. We can concentrate on abstracting from this configuration African women's presence in a zamani sense so that we can reference and ultimately reinvent in a more full-bodied way the pathways of their lives, if not their actual lived experiences. What stands central in this heuristic is a twofold process. On one hand, the task is to use available evidence to reestablish ancestral connections; on the other, it is to establish within those connections something that is perhaps even more problematic in building a more comprehensive case for African American women as writers, that is, a sense of "ancestral voice."

Life in the Zamani Dimension

In *Ancestral Voice* (1989), Charles L. Woodard records a series of conversations with N. Scott Momaday. Early in the dialogue, Woodward and Momaday talk about *The Way to Rainy Mountain,* a book Momaday wrote about his Kiowa ancestry. In discussing the apparent hunger of many people to know their origins, Woodard asks:

But what are those people to do? Those people who, as you say, can't go back that far in time? Those who cannot re-create enough of their pasts to discover their cultural legacies?

Momaday responds:

Well, I think that they must imagine who they are and where they come from. Having the facts at hand is less important, in my opinion, than is having the desire to satisfy one's curiosities through imagining. And we also need some great mystery in our origins. That is, I would not like to know everything about my heritage. I want to be absolutely free to imagine parts of it. The facts are not very important. The possibilities are everything. When I look back, I see infinite possibility, and that's exciting to me. (Woodard 1989:4)

At this point, the conversation weaves along, moving across a variety of topics. Sixty-four pages later, it again turns to *The Way to Rainy Mountain.* They are discussing how a writer "creates" a place out of his or her rendering of it, even (as in the case of Rainy Mountain) when that particular place actually exists somewhere.[2] Woodard concludes, and Momaday agrees: "The fact of it [the place] is not the truth of it" (Woodard 1989:68).

This conversation seems a particularly appropriate place from which to begin discussing an alternative analytical paradigm with which to reestablish ancestral connections between African American women and our African women ancestors, even though the individual stories of these women now exist primarily in zamani time. Fundamentally, the strategy for inquiry is to access whatever we can, in terms of what Alessandro Portelli (1994) suggests as narrative modes of history-telling, that is, narrative patterns associated with institutional, collective, and personal points of view. In effect, we can engage in a process of using multidimensional viewpoints as a heuristic for historical reconstruction. The task in such a process is to keep the eyes and the mind open for the imaginable, that is, for opportunities to make connections and draw out likely possibilities. A basic value with this strategy is to reconstruct history with respect for the *long* view, a view in which the focus is not expected to be fine-tuned. With a long view, the historical narrative does not reference individual experience. It references instead institutional, collective patterns in broad scope. These patterns form a cultural landscape, the contextual backdrop against which to render a meaningful and perhaps even a representative story. In other words, given the case of precolonial African women's history, we know that a documentable history through a close-up and personal lens is yet to be fully revealed, if indeed it can be revealed at all. However, we also understand that historical narratives based on existing evidence are nonetheless beneficial in offering texture and substance in broad scope for lives that we may never fully understand.

When historical narratives are relegated to drawing more from a zamani than from a sasa experience, imagination becomes a critical skill, that is, the ability to see the possibility of certain experiences even if we cannot know the specificity of them. As Erna Brodber, sociologist and novelist from Jamaica, has said: "We must imagine the truth until a better truth comes along."[3] This strategy for inquiry claims a valuable place for imagination in research and scholarship—*imagination* as a term for a commitment to making connections and seeing possibility. So defined, imagination functions as a critical skill in questioning a viewpoint, an experience, an event, and so on, and in remaking interpretive frameworks based on that questioning.

In establishing a place for critical imagination, I am not suggesting that a commitment to seeing possibility relieves researchers of the responsibility to demonstrate also a commitment to accuracy, adequacy, and precision. The use of critical imagination does not at all negate the need to do the hard work of engaging systematically in theoretically grounded processes of discovery, analysis, and interpretation. We must still ground ourselves in a well-articulated theoretical base. Beyond this, the necessity is to acknowledge the limits of knowledge and to be particularly careful about "claims" to truth, by clarifying the contexts and conditions of our interpretations and by making sure that we do not overreach the bounds of either reason or possibility. The fundamental point is that this paradigm for the recovery and reenvisioning of experience recognizes not just the potential for knowledge-making but also the potential for an understanding that exists at the intersections of scholarship and creative imagination. For women of African descent, this space of convergence is perhaps the only place to begin an exploration of who we are, where we come from, how we have found and negotiated life's pathways. We must look at what we know and reconstruct with critical imagination the worlds that might have been.

The notion of ancestral connections, of course, is not a new concept in the Black intellectual and creative community. Scholars and researchers of African, African American, and African diaspora studies have acknowledged for several generations now the significant impact of Africa in the Americas. For example, the period we symbolize as the Harlem Renaissance marks a renewal of interest earlier in this century in African forms, values, and expressions. This movement toward ancestral connection gained momentum, from the turn of the century, to manifest itself boldly during the 1920s and 1930s in literature, art, music, scholarship, and sociopolitical action (see Huggins 1971; DuBois 1994; Woodson 1990; Rozelle, Wardlaw, and McKenna 1989). As Alain Locke said in "The Legacy of the Ancestral Arts":

But even with the rude transplanting of slavery, that uprooted the technical elements of his former culture, the American Negro brought over as an emotional inheritance a deep-seated aesthetic endowment. And with a versatility of a very high order, this offshoot of the African spirit blended itself in with entirely different culture elements and blossomed in strange new forms. (1925:254)

Locke's statement is the tip of an iceberg. In essence, even a cursory examination of the variety and amount of evidence that has been collected across the disciplines reveals that there is a tradition of belief in Black scholarship—that, despite the efforts of the slave culture to dismantle

and disintegrate African lives and belief systems, remnants and resonances of this belief remain and continue to this day to connect African
people throughout the diaspora. As Edmund Barry Gaither says:

> Groups of slaves as well as free Africans brought to the Americas were men and
> women who possessed a framework—religious, mythical, political, historical,
> psychological, and ontological—from which they drew the meaning of their
> lives. This framework with its myriad components provided a profound sense of
> relationship to their ancestors, nature and the world as they knew it. It consti-
> tuted their culture. Africans from many cultures found themselves in this hemi-
> sphere where they were confronted with the reality of having to remake them-
> selves; they had to change from being Africans in the Americas to being
> Afro-Americans. . . . Black culture, here defined as African cultural elements re-
> worked and expanded, helped to assure the survival of Afro-Americans in their
> new socio-political and economic conditions. (1989:17)

The basic substance of this idea is illustrated through elements of language, narrative structure, dance, art, philosophy, and religion as these
forms are consistently manifested across African-based cultures (see Herskovits 1970; Turner 1949; Thompson 1983; Holloway 1990; S. Walker
1990).

As Benjamin Quarles explains (1987), such evidence of African American culture lends support actually to two notions that deserve separating.
The first is that there are cultural retentions from the African context
within African American communities—as illustrated linguistically, for
example, in the vocabulary and language use of some African American
speakers. The second is that there have been cultural fusions between
African, European, and indigenous cultures in the making of what is
American. In other words, in some instances, African cultural traditions
have actually been blended with other cultural traditions and have in effect reached beyond African American communities to become national-
ized—as in the more obvious case of contemporary musical forms such
as jazz or rock and roll, and the less obvious case of food production, as
explained by the work of cultural anthropologists (see Yentsch 1995).
When these two perspectives of the impact of African cultural systems
converge, at the very least we recognize the complexities by which African
Americans have creatively forged identities and operational styles and,
likewise, significantly influenced the forging and the implementation of
what it means to be "American."

In "African Philosophy: Foundations for Black Psychology" (1991), Wade W. Nobles theorizes that African Americans as a cultural group derive fundamental self-definitions from premises shared with West African cultures. He posits that African Americans have used these beliefs in the development of an African-based ethos, a system of belief and action (1991:47–48). Among the principles that form this system are the following:

1. The "survival of the tribe," as an integral and indispensable part of nature, is paramount.

2. There is a sacred obligation to the genealogical line, both vertically, in terms of the succession of generations (past, present, and future), and horizontally, in terms of a matrix of relationships in sasa time. "Kinship," in other words, is binding.

3. To be human is to belong to the whole community.

4. Both responsibility and destiny are collective.

5. Deep connections exist between what we do and what we believe.

If we relate this set of beliefs to beliefs that can be extrapolated from the writings of African American women, patterns emerge. In their writing, African American women show direct and indirect evidence of the following:

1. They have broadened the sense of "tribe" to include a sense of "the race," or "the people," meaning African American people, such that there has been an abiding concern for "the survival of the race."

2. They demonstrate a belief that generations matter. They operate as though they "owe" the past, the present, and the future, and they enact this obligation by paying tribute to the past, providing support and nurture in the present, and thinking toward—that is, having a passionate concern for—the future.

3. Their sense of their own humanness is significantly defined in codependence with the community (both narrowly and broadly envisioned) rather than in terms of themselves as autonomous individuals who are separable and independent from others.

4. They consider working with others for mutual benefit to be a reasonable and productive strategy for action.

5. They defy the separation of self into body, mind, and spirit and embrace "wholeness." In other words, they connect what they believe with

what they do, demonstrating a preference for the integration of intellect, passion, and ethical action.

A comparison of this list with the principles drawn from Nobles's explanation brings considerable vitality to the position that African American women's basic patterns of belief connect in meaningful ways to beliefs that are identifiable in West African cultures. The comparison also suggests that, in general, these African ancestral connections have functioned systematically among African American women over the generations, in the formation of patterns of action that became directive for the use of a new technology—that is, writing.

To Hear an Ancestral Voice

If we can abstract patterns of belief and action from a reestablishing of ancestral connections, the groundwork is laid for articulating a process of "cultural imprinting" that would account, at least in part, for continuities from continent to continent, from Africa to North America. Cultural imprinting would explain not just a general continuity in terms of remnants and resonances but also a specific continuity in terms of the genesis of African American women's authority as writers and the emergence of what I am naming here "ancestral voice." To begin fleshing out the concept of ancestral voice, I turn to contemporary evidence. For example, on her dedication page in *The Color Purple,* Alice Walker says:

> To the Spirit:
> Without whose assistance
> Neither this book
> Nor I
> Would have been
> Written.

In "Writing *The Color Purple*" (1983:355–60), Walker explains how she communicated with the characters of the novel, who guided her, quite insistently and irresistibly, toward the place where she needed to write—toward the level of attention and concentration that she needed to guarantee for herself in order to be productive—and also left her (at least for a while until they reentered with her next novel, *Temple of My Familiar*) when the novel was done. In this dedication and in the accounting of how she produced *The Color Purple,* Walker articulates a spiritual connection with her characters as ancestors whose story she was rendering. Within this articulation is recognizable the concept of "ancestral voice," a voice that communicates, peculiarly perhaps, both sense and sensibility, ways of being, ways of doing.

If we can re-imagine precolonial African women's lives, if we can reconstruct the pathways taken by those who crossed the Atlantic in their transformation from African women into African American women, if we can trace ways of being and doing, then cultural imprinting seems an appropriate way to talk about a trajectory for the development of a sense of ancestral voice as experienced by African American women over time. The concept of a culturally imprinted voice is that, over time, this voice becomes so deeply imbedded in cultural practices that it may be transmitted from generation to generation to generation in many ways. One way this voice may be transmitted might be intuitively. The idea is that African American women have been subjected to a body of continuously resonant experiences, experiences that can be articulated in contemporary terms as the converging oppressions of race, class, gender, and cultural domination. Over the course of these accumulated experiences, we have acquired an intuition, an ability to "know," to understand tacitly a sense of self, place, and possibility. This consistency between conditions and response suggests that a sense of survival in being so consistently necessary might become automated and somehow coded into the bloodlines.

The idea that knowledge and understanding might become coded into the bloodlines suggests a second way this voice may be transmitted. Perhaps African American women have perceived ancestral voice instinctively. Perhaps habits of knowing might actually become so ingrained that such ways of knowing come to be grafted into the socio-bio system and passed along. Perhaps the intimacy between social practices and biological imperatives is considered so entwined that, in fact, habits seem "natural" instead of "learned."

Walker's quotation, however, suggests a third way this voice may be transmitted. The connection might be spiritual, indicating the possibility of a direct connection, that is, a direct line of communication to the zamani, or perhaps a space in which we might continuously "bump" into our ancestors and hear their voices.[4] In Walker's case, she indicates that the ancestral spirits "talk" to her.

Whatever the means of transfer might be, however, my hypothesis is that, across time and space, women in the zamani have helped African American women to understand—whether by intuition or instinct, through the spirit or by storytelling, or by some other process—who we are, how we should see the world, how we should perceive ourselves in it, and also how we might assume the authority to speak and to act as thinkers, writers, and leaders, even in the face of contending forces within a new geographical and cultural context. As Momaday says:

> I sometimes imagine that I am my ancestors. That as I write I am speaking what my ancestors spoke or would speak through me. . . . I think sometimes that my voice is the reincarnation of a voice from my ancestral past. . . . It is something that brings about great serenity. I think of it as being irresistible. It is the way the universe is ordered. (Woodard 1989:112)

In the ways the universe has been ordered historically for African American women, we begin with the remnants, imagine the reality that must have produced these remnants, and reconstruct, as Paul Ricoeur suggests, historical time (1984:175–230).

With a sense of ancestral connection and ancestral voice, the inquiry begins. Who were these women, these real, live, human beings who crossed the Atlantic as captives? What lives did they leave behind? What patterns of belief and action did they bring with them? What image or images of womanhood did they hold in their hearts, heads, and bone marrow? What did they pass along to their own daughters, and to other young female captives who became their daughters since, despite their geographical displacement, these girls still faced the task of coming into womanhood? What did they use to shape the new roles they must fill for these girls, these strangers who had no one else? How did their experiences as slaves, young and old, reshape their images of themselves, their identities, their sense of themselves as women, as human beings? How did they emerge from slavery? How did their sense of "woman's role" or "woman's place" inform their use of new tools or non-African resources? With particular regard for the focus of this book, how were their uses of literacy as a "new" tool the same in terms of their typical patterns of belief and action? How were their uses of literacy different?

In light of even the most simplistically stated sense of human development, it still seems reasonable to say that when African women and girls set foot in North America, they did not come as blank slates. Instead, they brought with them sensibilities that had been fired in African cauldrons, the communities they left behind. Accepting the basic common sense of this statement leaves open the probability of at least traces, faint or strong, of the historical connections between the lives of African women in their communities and the lives that African American women assumed in the United States. In this chapter, therefore, I operate from the position that African women translated—from one cultural context into another—spheres of power, influence, and work; that they transferred basic mechanisms for operating autonomously and in cooperation with others; and that quite probably they preserved (to some degree at least) deeply imbedded cultural notions of self-in-society that would be useful to them, or at least their progeny, in the construction of self and voice as users of written language.

History Begins with a Story

On the Island of Goree off the coast of Senegal, the westernmost point on the continent of Africa, there is a doorway through which untold numbers of African women and girls passed on their way to becoming African American.[5] Small, dark, sinister, and unwelcoming, this portal is testament to a catastrophic event in the lives of African females. On the African side of the doorway, across the broad landscape of a number of western, central, and southern African cultures, were their homes, their families, the collectivity of beliefs, values, and behaviors that had formed their worlds, their lives, and their possibilities. On the other side lay the Atlantic Ocean, the Middle Passage, the shores of North America, and the endless years of unimaginable degradation, drudgery, pain, and suffering that awaited them.

At Goree, they were torn from their worlds, abruptly and often brutally severed, and brought to this place that, but for the business there, would have been beautiful, warm, peaceful, exotic in its accoutrements. The business, however, was everything and made all the difference. Goree was not a place of peace and beauty. It was a place that finalized the process by which African women and girls became chattel. It was the place where the commodification of their existence was made paramount. Their hopes, dreams, and expectations were translated by horrific measure into their potential for production and reproduction. By abuse, debasement, and dehumanization, there was a campaign to disintegrate and destroy their human consciousness, a process that often began at their capture and crystallized much too often, whatever their ages and whatever their social status, in the raping rooms of their Goree prisons.

No matter how much they fought back, cried, moaned, or wailed, there was no relief. No matter how many times they wished and prayed for compassion or salvation, none was forthcoming. No matter how much they longed for normalcy and the loving arms of their family members, friends, and neighbors, if such people came at all they came, as the women had come, in ropes, leather thongs, and chains. As in the case of Olaudah Equiano's sister, they saw the men to whom they had looked for protection killed, or stripped of power, status, and the resources to fight either for themselves or for the women. Much of what we know about these women, however, we must filter through and figure out, as we might tiny bits and pieces through a sieve.

We know Equiano's story, for example, from his narrative, *The Interesting Narrative of the Life of Olaudah Equiano, or Gustavus Vassa, The African,* first published in 1789. We know only remnants of his sister's story as we see for her a life within his life. She is nameless, existing only as "Equiano's sister," the only daughter of a "numerous family" (Equiano 1987:25). In telling his own life, however, Equiano succeeds also in shedding light on "Sister." Their father was a man of means and their lives as his children were comfortable. Equiano explains, however, that at age eleven he and his sister, whose age he does not give, were kidnapped. We can hypothesize that the two were close in age since they were left at home alone to play in the compound while the adults went to the fields to work, and since there is nothing about his references to her or about his poignant descriptions of the events of their capture to indicate that she was "unequal." Equiano states:

without giving us time to cry out, or to make any resistance, they stopped our mouths and ran off with us into the nearest wood. Here they tied our hands, and continued to carry us as far as they could . . . the only comfort we had was in being in one another's arms all that night, and bathing each other with tears. But alas! we were soon deprived of even the small comfort of weeping together. (1987:26)

The two were separated, to see each other only once more before the final separation when Equiano manages to make his way into history and Sister is left to enter the zamani dimension.

At the hands of captors without conscience or compassion, Sister and so many other unnamed but not unknown women and girls were made to know death, danger, destruction, violence, and despair as never before. Even without their names or the details of their individual lives, we still know these women. They were the victims of aggressors, foreign and African-born, aggressors who closed their hearts and eyes to inhumanity and their ears to human protest and suffering. Their oppressors tolerated no resistance or revolt; punished, tortured, and killed without hesitation or remorse; and operated with amazing fidelity to the insatiable gods of profit and power.

The Goree door took the women and girls by planks across a rocky shore to ladders made of ropes that swayed as body after body was made to climb them. To the smells of seared, rotting flesh that had been branded with the markings of the enslaved, they moved. To the sounds of hostile voices and the cracking of whips, they moved. To the sounds of their own anxiously beating hearts and the screams, moans, and protests of their fellow captives, they were herded like cattle into the bowels of the slave ship.

Longing for the past and fearing the present, the future, the unknown, surely among some of these women and girls there was a sense that they were moving in a dream, a nightmare from which they would awaken, if only they could. Among some, there must have been an intense moment of disbelief, a space in time when they felt mystically separated from the horror of this disruption to their lives, only to be brought back to this reality constantly by the ever present tyranny of their captors. I imagine that their senses were sharply attuned, not dulled, as they experienced a density of sensations with each moment. Their nostrils must have been filled to distraction with the stench of torture chambers, and their skins must have tingled with fear, anxiety, and desperation. They must have been horror-stricken by the sight of the lurking vessel that would transport them. Their bare feet must have felt the coolness of the stone door as they walked out of the holding place, and the roughness of the wooden boards as they walked across the planks to the rocky shore where the ship loomed before them. Their hands, large and small, must have felt every inch of the knots and braids along the ropes as they climbed to the ship's deck. Their souls must have reeled from the recent memories of their humiliations and the anticipation of more that they must surely have known would come. They must have wondered with an undescribable sense of confusion and disorientation what was happening to them and why.

They entered cramped, unlighted, disease-infested, filthy spaces unfit for human occupation, but prescribed on this journey just for them. They had little chance of escape, and even less of escaping alive. As they were pushed along, taking one step and then another, surely some, if not most, must have sensed from the very depths of their intuitive spirits that, not by choice but by the power, will, and mandate of their captors, they would never, ever see their homes, their families, or their African homelands again.

Such are the details, the "stuff," the fibrous realities of the critical space where scholarship and imagination meet. From this spot, we have a place to begin. What we know from the evidence in hand is that there was life and culture in Africa before the intervention of Europeans. What we also know is that, once African women reached North America, they were compelled to remake themselves in this new world. Among the mechanisms available to them for survival, they embraced writing as a new cultural element and they blossomed. What we have not adequately accounted for is the matrix of African sensibilities they might use to envision, shape, direct, and perhaps even inspire, that blossoming.

The Worlds They Left Behind

The growing scholarship on precolonial and postcolonial Africa clearly reveals the wide diversity of communities that populate the African continent (see Bullwinkle 1989; Hay 1988; Robertson and Klein 1983). There is little factual basis, therefore, for assuming that a reconstruction of African women's history would have a single line of development for African women's experience, either in ancient days before the intervention of Europeans or now. Acknowledging this diversity, my purpose here is not to make a case for cultural unity in any polarized way or to suggest a tunneling of vision to discount differences and embrace only sameness. Quite the contrary. My purpose is to accept the twofold reality of both cultural distinctiveness in African communities and complementarity, if not sameness, across particular cultural practices. My purpose is to see and seek to understand both distinctiveness and complementarity, so we can extrapolate at the highest level possible an aesthetic sensibility, a belief system, an ethos, as such notions may have formed a basis for survival in a new and hostile environment.

My sense of this situation is that newly enslaved Africans faced special and unusual circumstances. As they transformed identities from being African to becoming African American, I suggest that a dialectic between variant beliefs and practices permitted African peoples to construct a regionally defined worldview, that is, a West African–based ethos, despite the distinctive influences of the multiple community sites from which they came. Again, my intent here is to make a case for how a matrix of complementary beliefs probably converged when people from across communities were displaced and their lives severely constrained by the conditions and forces of African enslavement in North America.

To start from an acknowledgment of difference, the lives of African women show considerable variation across time and across territory. Differences arise from many sources, which have become clearer to us through the work of researchers in fields across the disciplines: history, political science, economics, anthropology, sociology, psychology, philosophy, religion, the arts, feminist studies, Black feminist studies, and other interdisciplinary fields. In fact, the cultural variety among African communities seems to become richer and richer if we use a multiplicity of disciplinary perspectives as we move from community to community across and within the geographical regions. The result is that, while much is still missing, we can paint a better picture of precolonial women's lives today than ever before.

First of all, from the time of the ancient African empires that date from the first century B.C., there is evidence that societies operated along a matrilineal-patrilineal continuum in terms of a complex of kinship, family, and lineal relationships (Bohannan and Curtin 1988; Loth 1987; Robertson and Klein 1983; Rodney 1972; Diop 1967). The placement of particular communities along this continuum relates most directly to how they determined succession to seats of power, inheritance, and the identity of children (that is, the parent to whom the children "belonged"). Scholars recognize that their categorizations of African communities in this manner should not be considered static. As Africanists examine how societies developed over time, their work suggests such categorizations simply do not remain neatly ordered. Instead, the call seems to be for a more fluid model, in which categories can be reasonably modified in one direction or another as a given community might vary over time, being more matrilineal or less, or more patrilineal or less.

When a community is categorized, at a point in time, as matrilineal or patrilineal, such categories do not directly translate into that community's falling into a corresponding matriarchal or patriarchal pattern. Whether matrilineal or patrilineal, formal power was probably in the hands of men, regardless of whether their access to it was through a female ancestor or a male ancestor. Viewing this schema dynamically, rather than statically, makes the legal and social status of women in the community more easily discernible. We can see more clearly, for example, their rights to their children, to landownership, and to participation in political, social, and economic systems.

As explained by Robertson and Klein (1983), for example, the power and authority of African women was tied less to a specific kinship and lineage system than to economic structures. By their reckoning, women's status and power were tied to the degree of dependence, independence, and interdependence between men and women, such that the type of economic development serves as a clearer measure of such relationships than just kinship or lineage patterns. Variations in women's experiences, therefore, do not pivot so much on a dichotomous male or female domination (as women's experiences are interpreted in European-based cultures) as on African women's formal and informal access to power and authority, and on the roles that a given community assigned for women in sustaining the economy—with such roles dependent often on whether the community was nomadic or agricultural, urban or rural, and so forth.

A second source of variation—as African societies changed over time and territory—was religious beliefs. As Ali A. Mazrui (1986) indicates, modern Africa is a product of three major cultural influences: indigenous, European, and Islamic cultures. By the second century, Christianity had developed in North Africa; by the seventh century, Islam had also taken root. Both had a negative impact on the social status and legal status of women (Loth 1987; Robertson and Klein 1983), in the ways these cultural institutions defined family roles and responsibilities, prescribed a woman's conduct and behavior, and determined her place or lack of place in the public sector.

A third source of variation was in agricultural development, urbanization, and the development of social class systems (Hay 1988; Loth 1987; Robertson and Klein 1983; S. Walker 1990). As some societies settled into stable agrarian communities rather than nomadic ones, the men spent less work time hunting or fishing and assumed more authority for maintaining the social fabric of the community—as well as for farming and animal husbandry, both of which at other times might have fallen to the responsibility and authority of women. The presence of men and their increased participation in the local economy often meant a negative change in status for women's legal rights, and a shift for women from positions of power, control, and decision-making to positions of influence. In other words, with agricultural development, the women often still had to work to maintain the life and livelihood of a community, but their work was sometimes tied less directly to their own status and power than to the status and power of their fathers, brothers, husbands, and sons.

As communities grew up around a more agrarian economy and moved toward urban development, the most obvious impact was social stratification. For women in privileged families, economic resources permitted them to be released from some household and field duties because of the slave labor (typically of women) that their families could afford. However, as Sheila Walker suggests with regard to contemporary African women in "Walled Women and Women Without Walls Among the Fulbé of Northern Cameroon" (1990), sometimes a privileged status had less of a liberating consequence for women than a cloistering one, especially in Islam-influenced communities.

With regard to enslaved women, as Rosalyn Terborg-Penn (1986) points out, the enslavement of women across the African continent was a familiar experience, not an unfamiliar one, and sometimes distinctions between wives and slaves in a given household were essentially in terms of prestige, not daily experience. Also, women in the cities, as compared with peasant women in rural communities, were able to provide special services. A professional class developed—including, for example, the women who carried water from peripheral areas and sold it in the city; the women who became the market women, selling food, cloth, and crafts; the women who prepared food commercially; and the prostitutes. All of these models of womanhood in society existed in one configuration or another, but as Herbert S. Klein (1978; 1999) reports, regardless of how experiences varied, women were highly valued for their roles in economic production and as vessels of life.

As specific examples of cultural variation, what these three sources of difference seem to indicate for women's experiences is that there were axes of power. The extent to which women were "dominant" or not in social, political, and economic systems varied along all these lines—matrilineal or patrilineal societies; matriarchal or patriarchal societies; indigenous, European-influenced, Islamic-influenced cultures; rural or urban setting; socioeconomic status, and so on. To be underscored is that precolonial African women were far from monolithic. They varied in social class in terms of family and community resources. Their slate of activities varied in terms of what in a specific community constituted women's roles in economic survival and prosperity. The degree of autonomy varied with regard to personal decision-making and so too with regard to the degree of authority, power, and influence in community decision-making. The majority of women lived in rural communities. Others lived in more urban environments. Some were Christian or Islamic, or were women who still operated within indigenous African belief systems. Some women were already leading lives in slavery, sometimes as field workers, sometimes as members of privileged households.

What seems constant is that all these women had internalized a sense of place within these environments. It is probable that, whatever the specific details of their day-to-day lives, women across all communities had internalized a sense of being an integral and essential part of the "natural" order of the universe, a sense of belonging to their group, a sense of being responsible to and for this group. Their experiences engendered in them a set of values, beliefs, attitudes, expectations, and behaviors by which they forged a sense of womanhood in the world. We can set aside questions of whether cultural connections among the women were strong—as demonstrated, for example, from an examination of the linguistic evidence that has established African language families (Welmers 1973; Pyles and Algeo 1982). We can set aside questions of whether connections were weak—as suggested, for example, by an examination of social stratification and the variability of religious practices. What we cannot set aside is that women in all sorts of categories fell victim to the slave trade. All manner of women were subject to siege and capture by those who sought to enslave them for trans-Atlantic markets; all manner of women found themselves imprisoned together without distinction on the Island of Goree and in other enslavement stations that would ultimately place them on slave ships bound for the western hemisphere.

According to Herbert S. Klein (1978; 1999), although the limitations of the data constrain the ability of scholars to draw definitive conclusions, available records suggest that approximately 38 percent of the captives who arrived in the Americas during the height of the trans-Atlantic slave trade by Dutch, Danish, and British ships were women and girls.[6] Records indicate that the captives came from western, central, and southern Africa. Klein's data also indicate that, to the extent that records were kept and are available, the captives were divided into three age groups: women (eighteen or older); teenagers (between eleven and seventeen); girls (from about seven to ten). He reports, for example, that from 1790 to 1820, of the group of female captives arriving in the Port of Havana, Cuba, approximately 50 percent were women; 21 percent were teenagers; 29 percent were girls.

These data, to whatever extent generalizations may be drawn, indicate one likely truth. The overwhelming majority of African women and girls who crossed the Atlantic Ocean as captives were old enough to have cultural memory. Specifically, at least 70 percent of them (those eleven and older) were already likely to have had a significant number of acculturation experiences. Quite likely, their communities had already demonstrated to them—both informally by role models and social practices and formally through puberty rites and other ceremonies, as well as through work experiences—who and how they should be as human beings, as women, and as members of a cultural group.[7] In fact, even the seven year olds would have had the time to accumulate and internalize experiences, images, even some preferences, habits, or patterns of belief. All of the women and girls would have had time to be socialized to some degree as African females within particular African communities.

The point of inquiry, then, is rather straightforward. Each of these women and girls brought with them to North America a sense of self and society. There were certainly cultural differences, but the question is whether there were enough resonances among cultures for some kind of complementary, perhaps even aggregate, sense of womanhood to emerge. The question is whether these women might have been able to see themselves and to operate, not just as individuals alone but as human beings in community, albeit a displaced and reconstituted community. My hypothesis is that these females found strength and affirmation in the company of other women who were in actuality more like themselves than different. The assumption is that among these displaced women a newly constructed community developed, largely because of their collective efforts to recover balance and stability in their lives—a role that I suspect at a general level was a traditional one, given the typical women's responsibilities for caring and nurture in their African communities. Stated differently, my assumption is that these women redefined community by using as a primary resource the matrix of cultural constructs, complementary in design, that they brought with them from Africa with the intent of keeping themselves and each other alive and sane.

Contemporary scholars emphasize that African women's experiences were different enough to demand that as historicizers we operate quite certainly with a clear and present need to resist overgeneralization. However, scholars also acknowledge that at some general level human beings, in their humanity, develop in a fairly patterned way, despite certain variations across cultures. They acknowledge the possibility that connections exist in a small stream at higher levels of abstraction. There are two obvious examples: one is that humans have the tendency to use language; another is that in human society children are dependent on adults in the community for sustenance and for an understanding of the world around them, whatever that world is.

Indeed, such abstractions offer evidence that a sense of community for displaced African women might quite reasonably have been extended beyond a local sense of self and society to a broader, reconstituted one. I add also that such a reconstituted sense of being would possibly have been continually renewed at the root by the constant influx of "new" slaves into the Americas for two full centuries. I suggest that much of the notion of Pan-Africanism, negritude, the African diaspora, and afrocentricity seems to draw significantly from such ontological possibilities. Gilroy (1993) offers an explanation of such ways of being and knowing in contemporary contexts. At a fundamental level, my sense is that scholars of African descent, and others interested in such issues, have found deeply compelling a lingering question: How else can we account for contemporary continuities across the African diaspora after all this time and after such extended moments of separation from the source?

Recognizing the limitations of our ability to substantiate with traditional documentation this type of ontological perspective, however, I have chosen, as Momaday and Brodber suggest, not to be constrained by just the facts, although certainly in this case there are many. I have chosen instead to use the community of discourse, invigorated by available documentation, to look imaginatively at the points at which women's lives, in all their variability, seem to have converged. The task is not so much to examine the variations on themes, in the interests of establishing truth for all time, but more to examine the themes themselves, in the interest (as Brodber indicates) of suggesting where a pathway to truths might reside. My specific intent is to extrapolate (from what at minimum are points of curiosity and at maximum are actual points of convergence) inferences that seem fruitful in positing an explanation for beliefs and actions from which African American women could form a sense of community and ethos. From this base, my view is that African American women have been enabled to act as literate beings, privy to ancestral connection and ancestral voice.

The Emergence of Literacy as a Sociopolitical Tool

The challenge at this point is to account for how identity and belief might have formed among African women from this cross-community perspective. As suggested by several scholars (for example, Ladner 1971; Meier and Rudwick 1970), wherever an African community might fall on the matrilineal-patrilineal continuum during the precolonial era, the "family" (that is, the kinship group that descended from a common ancestor, whether male or female) was the central political unit. Women's identity, therefore, was situated fundamentally within a kinship network. Their autonomy was defined not so much as individuals, but (since the women existed in relationship to others) as mothers, sisters, wives, and daughters, with the most central kinship being the bond between mothers and children.

In his groundbreaking work of 1941, Herskovits (1970:65) observed that in West African cultures there was a specific closeness developed between mothers and children. He suggested that this closeness seemed reasonable since typically each married woman had her own house within which she lived with her children (male and female) until they moved into their own homes. The children, sometimes depending on whether a culture was polygamous or not, may have shared their fathers with siblings by other mothers (who became their plural mothers) but they shared their own biological mother only with her children. It seems reasonable to assume, then, that the closest tie in kinship networks across various cultural models would be between mother and children, a relationship and measure of community status that African women in North America were able to retain, albeit precariously, during slavery.

Researchers since Herskovits (for example, Robertson and Klein 1983; Steady 1985) have documented that African women have traditionally held a secure place within the kinship network—in at least three ways. One, as indicated above, was as mothers, vessels for life. They gave birth. Another was as the nurturers and teachers of children. Third, they grew and prepared food and provided for the basic health care and well-being of the community. In the earlier years of childhood, women were responsible for introducing girls and boys to community values, expectations, and practices. They identified and taught appropriate behavior and action, assuming in some communities the voice of the community conscience. Their role in the latter case was to signal truth and to encourage ethical behavior, often as such lessons were imbedded symbolically in stories told around evening fires—a scene illustrated, for example, in Chinua Achebe's *Things Fall Apart* (1959). The women were not the griots (the historians), but they were storytellers, members of the community who taught with parables. They were the interpreters, the community members whose responsibility it was to think through and bring meaning to what was happening to the community and to suggest, directly or indirectly, ethical possibilities for action. African women were intrinsically valued for these roles, and through these responsibilities they participated actively in community life and gained access to power, their own authority, and autonomy. In North America, these roles continued, especially within the confines of their own quarters, and the women continued to be valued for their success in fulfilling these roles for "the race," the reconstituted community.

Further, in being heads of their own households in their African communities and having the responsibility of feeding, housing, and clothing their own children, they developed patterns of action. Prominent among these patterns is that they operated fairly autonomously and developed habits of hard work and self-reliance. They often formed alliances with co-wives or other women in the group—to take care of their broad responsibilities, including the feeding and care of husbands, the production and processing of food, the teaching and nurturing of children, the managing of the community conscience, and so on. Across West African communities, from which the majority of captives came, all these tasks were significantly defined as women's work.

In this view of precolonial Africa, such activities signal that women engaged in productive labor, not just reproductive labor, and they were accustomed to pooling time, energy, and resources in the interests of getting critical jobs done for themselves and for their communities. They expected to participate actively in these communities; typically they were able to use their organizational skills and their skills for working cooperatively as mechanisms for political and economic influence, at least, if not also for the attainment of actual power in their own right. In North America, African women continued to be perceived, though with increasing personal pejoration, as valuable in both productive and reproductive labor; they continued, as far as they were allowed, to work cooperatively with other women in the fields and in the plantation households to get assigned duties done; they continued to use whatever resources were available to sustain themselves and their reconstituted communities.

In considering woman's place in precolonial African societies in this way, I am suggesting the possibility of a sense of African American womanhood—shaped by the resonant experiences of African women first in Africa and then also in North America. I am suggesting:

1. that the ancestors of African American women held a sense of autonomy, tied to a sense of personal value within their kinship networks;

2. that in a general but relatively consistent way, African women brought with them to North America a sense of:

   a. ethos, or a system of belief and action that informed a positive redefinition of self and self-in-society once they reached North America;

   b. female power, autonomy, and authority;

   c. women's "rights," roles, and expectations in society;

   d. what constitutes the "work" of women, that is, a sense of the obligations and responsibilities by which women should help take care of what continued to be defined as the critical task—assuring the "survival of the tribe" or the people;

   e. how complex tasks can be addressed through cooperative strategies.

I am suggesting the possibility that this sense of woman's place in the world—with its incumbent expectations, obligations, and responsibilities—was passed along to subsequent generations, even in the hostile environment in which the first generations of African women and girls found themselves in North America. It seems reasonable to assume that these legacies of "place" helped shape the paradigms by which African American women have perceived, interpreted, and carried out ongoing and new sociocultural responsibilities. It seems quite possible that such legacies, within the context of slavery and afterward, actually shaped and nurtured African American women's sociocultural development—especially in the remaking of African womanhood as African American womanhood. The central point is that, amid a continuity of experiences occurring between the arrival of our African women ancestors and the emergence of identities among African *American* women as "new" world women, the "new" women had the opportunity to internalize variously a definable core of notions about self-in-society based on the convergence of old and new identities across contexts.

Advocacy and Activism

Imbedded in this assertion is another idea. My view is that, as if by voices from across time and space, continuities of experiences in identity formation contributed to a comparable development of continuities in response to those experiences and subsequently to continuities in actions. In my estimation these continuities formed patterns and constituted paradigms for ways of being and doing. Through these paradigms, African American women have consistently taken advantage of specific technologies and opportunities for action. One set of technologies has been those that support writing. One set of opportunities has been the ongoing need to address critical problems and issues in the African American community. In other words, the material circumstances among African American women (acknowledging the multiple variations of these circumstances) have consistently elicited responses (in this case, the use of writing) that can be viewed as demonstrations of their commitment to social advocacy and activism.

In using advocacy and activism to interrogate the literate practices of African American women writers, I am actually making several claims. One is that the very act of writing, especially for people who do not occupy positions of status and privilege in the general society, is a bold and courageous enterprise rather than simply a demonstration of the ability to express oneself. A second claim is that African American women have consistently included social, political, and economic problems and interests as focal points in their writing. They have addressed all manner of concerns, from issues of their own agency as capable and intelligent human beings to the impacts and consequences of various conditions of life for African Americans and others, to the implications of economic and political power, to the importance of peace, justice, and equity, and so on. A third claim is that the arenas in which they have participated as writers have consistently been "public" arenas. They have written for and spoken to many audiences within various social and professional networks, as well as to many general (that is, cross-community) audiences, including national and international groups. A fourth claim is that for most if not all of these writers, their acts of writing function locatively. In a manner of speaking, this function indicates that acts of literacy become a homing device for locating a more general pattern of work. I am suggesting that African American women have written in the interest of social, political, and cultural mandates. Looking at their written texts, therefore, permits us to articulate the consistent ways (large and small, local and nonlocal) in which these women have participated energetically in change processes.

To see the use of literacy in the interests of social change as an analytical value rather than as a label benefits from a specific consideration of connotations of the terms *activism* and *advocacy*. According to the online *Oxford English Dictionary*, *activism* is a twentieth-century term, first recorded in 1907. The dictionary lists two definitions: "1. A philosophical theory which assumes the objective reality and active existence of everything. 2. A doctrine or policy of advocating energetic action." These definitions draw from the word *active*, which has a longer history, with the first recorded use being in 1340. The dictionary lists several entries for this term. The most relevant for this discussion include:

A.1a. Opposed to *contemplative* or *speculative:* Given to outward action rather than inward contemplation or speculation; practical; esp. with "life."
A.1b. Practical, as opposed to *theoretical.*
A.2. Opposed to *passive:* Originating or communicating action, exerting action upon others; acting of its own accord, spontaneous.
A.4a. Opposed to *quiescent* or *extinct:* Existing in action, working, effective, having practical operation or results.
A.5. Opposed to *sluggish* or *inert:* Abounding in action; energetic, lively, agile, nimble, diligent, busy, brisk. (Of persons and things)
B.1. A person devoted to the active life.

In like manner, the OED lists 1340 as the first use of the word *advocate* and lists three definitions that seem relevant:

1. One called in, or liable to be called upon, to defend or speak for.
2. One who pleads, intercedes, or speaks for, or in behalf of, another; a pleader, intercessor, defender.
3. One who defends, maintains, publicly recommends, or raises his voice in behalf of a proposal or tenet.

Finally, the OED lists one definition of *advocacy* that relates to this analysis: "1. The function of an advocate; the work of advocating; pleading for or supporting."

In the context of these definitions, the space to envision African American women writers emerges. Their writing indicates a propensity to work energetically to achieve political, social, and cultural goals. These writers are dedicated to an active life—in this case, a life of productivity and creativity in writing. While there is no evidence to suggest that any of them actually oppose contemplation and speculation, given their work as writers, there is considerable evidence of their desires to apply contemplation and speculation toward practical purposes. They write and speak, conveying a passion for the causes they define. They plead these causes before literal and metaphorical "bars of justice," operating as defenders with deeply rooted interests that are articulated typically in both personal and altruistic terms. In this case, then, they apparently do not see themselves to be speaking for others. In essay writing, especially with the use of "I," they speak for themselves and for the principles for which they stand. They raise voices for their various audiences, and they do what they feel passionately and compassionately compelled to do.

To be noted is that this assessment is not a process of labeling. It is a process of analysis. From my point of view, the goal is not to claim that African American women writers define themselves—either personally or professionally—by the values I use to analyze their work. My imperative is to make sense of their work within a context specific to their lived experiences. The twofold frame I have specified is literacy and social change with the assumption that all these writers were operating intellectually and expressing themselves actively in writing with particular interests in social, political, and cultural mandates.

In shifting the view of African American women's writing in this chapter to focus on a genesis of authority, I am emphasizing the importance of noticing the extent to which their perceptive, interpretive, and productive sensibilities have systematically operated as they have acquired and used written language, and I am suggesting that therefore, we can search for evidence of the consistency with which they have chosen literacy as a mechanism for operating effectively within their own communities—whether those communities are narrowly or broadly defined. We can identify ways to document their practices as writers who envision both problems and solutions and who use their rhetorical abilities to participate in setting and implementing a sociopolitical agenda. We can chart direct and implied relationships between the lives they have been compelled to lead and their literate behavior. Ultimately, we can gain a clearer sense of African American women as active users of language and active producers of varieties of "texts."

As this book bears witness, my own analysis of African American women's writing using rhetorical methodologies has yielded the following general conclusions. Over the years:

1. African American women have internalized a keen sense of social responsibility.

2. They feel compelled to interpret the world and to tell the truth as they see it, despite in many cases the personal cost. They define and name problems, interpret these problems, and identify courses of appropriate ethical action for themselves and others.

3. They accept the burden of survival for "the race," typically by hard work and self-reliance.

4. They mother, nurture, and teach others.

5. They embrace working in groups as a useful strategy for meeting community needs.

6. They use literate resources to continue filling long-standing commitments for getting critical community (variously defined) tasks done.

In effect, African American women have acquired and mastered variously a new tool for a new day. We have done so with an apparently ageless set of tasks, all of which seem to pivot on notions of belief, identity, and social responsibility.

Chapter 4

Going Against the Grain

The Acquisition and Use of Literacy

O, ye daughters of Africa, awake! Awake! Arise! No longer sleep nor slumber, but distinguish yourselves. Show forth to the world that ye are endowed with noble and exalted faculties. . . . And where is the youth who has written upon his manly brow a thirst for knowledge; whose ambitious mind soars above trifles, and longs for the time to come, when he shall redress the wrongs of his father and plead the cause of his brethren? . . . Their souls would become fired with a holy zeal for freedom's cause. . . . Able advocates would arise in our defence. Knowledge would begin to flow, and the chains of slavery and ignorance would melt like wax before the flames.

Maria W. Stewart, "Religion and the Pure Principles of Morality:
The Sure Foundation on Which We Must Build"

Maria W. Stewart was the first African American woman known to have written essays.[1] The passage above, written in 1831, suggests that African American women have understood with great clarity two things: the power of language and learning and the inherent hostility of the context within which people of African descent must live in the United States. It is useful to our discussion to view this understanding of condition and instruments of power in light of Harvey J. Graff's assertion concerning literacy acquisition: "the environment in which students acquire their literacy has a major impact on the cognitive consequences of their possession of the skill and the uses to which it can be put" (1987:5). The history of African American women's acquisition and uses of literacy illustrate just how significant this connection can be.

Primarily, African American women's literacy has been the subject of scholarship within accounts of the history of African American education in the United States as a more general phenomenon.[2] Quite predictably, however, we are yet to bring full meaning to the women's stories. Their experiences often flow between the lines of the more comprehensive view. Although over the years there have been occasional attempts to see the distinctive pathways of women's achievements (through a number of master's theses and doctoral dissertations, for example, that have not typically been published for broader audiences), social changes in the last half of the twentieth century have laid the groundwork for a better understanding of these experiences (see Noble 1956; Willie and Edmonds 1978; Jones 1980; Fleming 1984; Anderson 1988). The modern civil rights and women's movements, the welfare rights, labor, and anti–Vietnam War movements, and other organized activist efforts have opened channels for hearing the voices of women, ethnic groups, lower socioeconomic classes, and others who have in one way or several been systematically discounted in this culture. The accruing record offers testimony that the dismantling of barriers to educational opportunity for such groups has been tedious, and that the struggles for opportunity and achievement have had to be constant, with African American women's efforts being no exception to this rule.

Since the beginning of Africans' lives in the Americas, African American women have been encumbered by racist, sexist, class-bound ideologies. This oppression has given rise among them to mandates that demand a questioning of power structures—in the interests of a desire for justice, equity, empowerment, and entitlement. Their resistance was basic. First of all, they were required to define themselves as human beings, rather than as animals, in order to establish a place for themselves under the law as rightful holders of the entitlements of citizenship, including opportunities for literacy and learning. Further, in facing disempowering images of themselves as amoral, unredeemable, and undeserving, they have had to carve out a space of credibility and respect as women.[3] Activism at such a basic level helped to fire their spirits with passion and to direct the means and mechanisms for acquiring and using literacy. The quest for literacy was a symbolic manifestation of their desire for agency and autonomy—as human beings and as citizens who should have rights and privileges. In this quest they also accepted personal responsibility for securing their own rights and perceived their opportunities to learn to be an obligation to use the benefits of those opportunities for *good* and *righteous* work in solving an array of problems, not only for themselves but for the race as a whole.

In looking more closely and directly at what these first generations of women managed to achieve, we see the extent to which they set their minds to the task, in the face of opposition. Not only did they envision wide-ranging possibilities for the worlds around them, they also quite successfully put that thinking into language and action (Royster 1990:108). These women played critical roles in their communities. They were the interpreters and reinterpreters of what was going on. They were the transmitters of culture as mothers, actual and fictive, as teachers, as social activists. They worked tirelessly as problem-solvers for both immediate and long-range concerns. They observed their worlds carefully and caringly. They articulated viewpoints that made work see-able and do-able. They worked persistently to get things done.

The basic assertion in this chapter is that the history of African American women's literacy is a story of visionaries, of women using sociocognitive ability to re-create themselves and to reimagine their worlds. Being fully aware of the material conditions of their lives and equally aware of the public discourses swirling around them, the first generations of literate African American women in the eighteenth century (and, in larger numbers in the nineteenth century), acquired literacy within an environment of activism, advocacy, and action. African American women were inspired in a context of resistance, as Stewart implores, to "show forth to the world that ye are endowed with noble and exalted faculties." They sought to learn, to better themselves, to change their worlds. In their hands, literacy became a tool for inserting themselves directly and indirectly into arenas for action and for doing whatever they could to mediate and manage the critical process of change. To their credit, they consistently used their language abilities and their intellectual powers to change hearts, minds, and conditions. Their legacies are there to behold, and they are distinctive, far-reaching, and filled with inspiration for others.

An Affirmation of Ethos and Identity

Since my focus here is on the history of literacy among African American women, and not on history in general, I do not wish to labor over the familiar ground of the "peculiar institution" of slavery and its impact in the lives of African peoples. Instead, it seems more productive for this analysis to focus, rather, on how the context of slavery dictated and strengthened certain patterns of action and belief for African American women and on how they would acquire and use literacy both before and after Emancipation. Drawing from the explanation of precolonial West African women's identities (see chapter 3), I hypothesize a trajectory for the formation of ethos in literate practices, which begins with an opportunity for continuity in self-esteem and in the definition of women's roles. Despite the displacement and oppressive circumstances African American women experienced in the slave culture, they could retain a sense of self that resonated with women's roles in West African communities.[4] Most certainly the slave world as described by several scholars (Harding 1981; Franklin 1980; Blassingame 1979; Gutman 1976; Genovese 1969) was gruesome and barbaric. Even so, African American women still found opportunities to maintain images of themselves as integral to the "community." Within their own racial group, they could envision themselves still in a traditional way, that is, in relation to others. They were daughters, sisters, "wives," mothers, with mothering still being a central identity marker, although in their case it was no longer allowed to be a sacred one. Despite their enslaved condition, the women could function in a familiar way without conflict with prevailing sentiment or practice.

In addition, as enslaved women, African American women were positioned in the social order as workers and breeders and were thereby central to the slave economy—a degraded status, certainly, given their former place of economic centrality in African societies, but central nevertheless. In this case, as Angela Davis (1981:3–29) points out, the "place" of slave women as workers was determined, not by a typically gendered system, but by expediency. They were treated in a genderless way as they were called upon to work side by side with men. They were treated as "females" when it was to the advantage of slaveholders to exploit their reproductive potential or to intimidate them in ways best suited for females. Sexual abuse and harassment were a primary mechanism, not only for capital enrichment, that is, for increasing the number of slaves through compulsory "breeding," but also for the punishment and terrorism of a whole community by means of the free and indiscriminate use and abuse of its women and girls without accountability or ret-ribution for the terrorists. As Davis points out so insightfully, however:

> While it is hardly likely that these women were expressing pride in the work they performed under the ever-present threat of the whip, they must have been aware nonetheless of their enormous power—their ability to produce and create . . . perhaps these women had learned to extract from the oppressive circumstances of their lives the strength they needed to resist the daily dehumanization of slav-ery. Their awareness of their endless capacity for hard work may have imparted to them a confidence in their ability to struggle for themselves, their families and their people. (1981:11)

In terms of how such material conditions might affect the formation of ethos, the fact of their holding such a clear place of "value" in the eco-nomic order, despite the experience of pejoration that actually accompa-nied that place, permitted the women to construct a view of themselves as durable. They could survive and help others do the same. This view sup-ported an ongoing commitment to long-standing cultural mandates—women's roles in assuring the survival and well-being of the community.

Further, in West African communities, while women may not have been the griots or community historians, they were storytellers. Within the slave community, African American women could continue during precious moments with their families and others to fulfill these roles, as well, imparting words of wisdom, understanding, guidance for self-suste-nance, and love. Storytelling remained a primary medium for cultural preservation and for the transmission of beliefs. Through a variety of communicative practices—stories, metaphors, wise sayings, proverbs, and so forth—the women used language to "instruct" their listeners in ways of believing and ways of doing. Constructing meaning through ac-cessible symbols, images, and thought patterns, African American women could sustain perhaps their most important traditional role—as the in-terpreters and reinterpreters of the world.

In this role they were called upon to "read" new experiences, to decode them, and to interpret them more deeply, given all that had to be contex-tualized in this new and hostile environment. In all probability, these cul-tural tasks were actually intensified during the slavery era. As Jacquelyn Mitchell (1988) suggests, African American women, especially in their verbal strategies, had to "read," name, then "paint" the world so that others could see it, understand its truths and consequences, and be compelled to act in the interest of the preservation of the community or "the race." Many of these women became (even more clearly than their counterparts had been in Africa) carriers of culture, and also "healers," women called upon to minister to the mind, the heart, the soul, sometimes to the body as well. They were responsible for taking care of illness, seeing it, naming it, identifying its remedies, especially when the illness was one of the heart, the spirit, or the head, that is, of the ways of thinking. They nurtured and cared for their people. They loved them—especially when love became the only answer that could reasonably be provided.

In resonance with these types of traditional roles in West African cultures, African women became American. This fusion permitted them to defy outrageously the system of slavery at its most fundamental point. Slavery was intended to break their will and their spirit. It tried to impose a sense of womanhood that defined women of African descent as inventory, chattel, capital. It positioned them as compulsory workers, beasts, breeders and suckers, without gender, without humanity. The conceptual frame within which these women were dictated to stand did not allow for a positive and productive self-concept. As Davis points out (1981:29), they were indeed beaten down, but they were not broken, and they actually managed to accumulate strengths and to re-create themselves under the lash, such that they emerged from slavery more whole than anyone could ever have expected.

African American women came out of two hundred years of legal oppression with a sense of self-worth as capable, tenacious, and self-reliant. They were confident in their abilities to work hard and to hold themselves and others together in the face of opposition. As Loewenberg and Bogin (1976) suggest, they were able to sustain a "wholeness"—a "psychic wholeness" forged at great cost but in the interest of the health and prosperity of a community for which they felt responsible. Hard-won strengths of spirit became a well-spring for activism, advocacy, and action. Within an environment of domination and oppression, African American women were able to form an understanding of "readiness from within."[5] This legacy of resiliency, of psychic and spiritual strength, served as a foundational element in individual and organizational action. It helped shape and define the lenses through which African American women would acquire literacy, present themselves in writing, and choose language and written expression as a tool.

Forced to redefine themselves within the context of a slaveholding society, African American women reendowed in large measure their passion for survival and established in the process the mechanisms by which they would form ethos and identity. By this reckoning, their ways of being, seeing, and doing were shaped, at least in part, by traditional habits within the context of new imperatives, which supported their desires for autonomy and for agency. They wanted to ensure—for themselves and the community or "race"—survival in the present and prosperity in the future. They recognized that literacy was a skill, a talent, an ability appropriate to their new environment. Their mandate, therefore, was to learn, to enhance talents, and to maximize abilities, with many of them holding deep-seated desires to participate proactively in both the making and the implementing of an agenda for new world survival.

Despite such focus and determination, however, the acquisition of literacy by African American women is very much a story of struggle, resistance, and resiliency. Theirs was an effort to learn, to affirm their own potential and the potential of others, and to act with authority and power as intellectual beings. Each movement toward literacy was a signal that these women were going very much against the grain of prevailing cultural beliefs, practices, and expectations. Their resistance to contending forces was by necessity noteworthy as they created a substantial record as advocates and activists for justice, empowerment, and change.

A Spirit of Activism

The African American women in the nineteenth century who come to mind first when we use such terms as *advocates* and *activists* are typically Harriet Tubman, conductor of the Underground Railroad, and Sojourner Truth, spokeswoman for the abolition of slavery and for women's rights. As we learn more, however, this first generation of activists can be extended to include others: such as Frances Ellen Watkins Harper, Charlotte Forten Grimké, Mary Shadd Cary, Ida B. Wells-Barnett (and a long list of others whose names are now gradually being read into history). Resistance leadership among African American women began well before Tubman and Truth. The very existence of this steady stream of examples within this group suggests long-standing desires for freedom and agency, that is, the privilege of doing whatever was commanded by an ethos reconstituted within the constraints of a slave culture.

Many scholars—among them William Preston Vaughn (1974), Jacqueline Jones (1983), Angela Davis (1981), Dorothy Sterling (1984), James D. Anderson (1988), Joanne M. Braxton (1989), and Thomas Holt (1990)—cite instances of the resistance of women who had faith in the law and were willing to take their cases before the bar of justice. One of the earliest incidents occurred in 1782, only six years after the founding of the nation, when Belinda, an enslaved woman, sued the legislature of Massachusetts for her freedom ("Belinda, or the Cruelty of Men Whose Faces Were Like the Moon," 1787). Another striking example is Lucy Terry.[6]

Terry was born in Africa, kidnapped as an infant, and brought to Rhode Island where she was purchased at the age of five by Ensign Ebenezer Wells of Deerfield, Massachusetts, to be his servant. Terry is recognized for being the first woman of African descent known to have written a poem, "Bars Fight, August 28, 1746." At the age of sixteen, Terry wrote about an incident in which sixty Native American warriors attacked two families who lived in an area of Deerfield known as "the Bars," a colonial word for "meadows." Terry's poem predates Phillis Wheatley's first published poem (1770) by several decades, even though Terry's poem was not published until 1855 by Josiah Gilbert Holland in *History of Western Massachusetts*.

In 1756 Terry married Abijah Prince, a former slave, a large landowner, and founder of Sunderland, Vermont. Prince bought Terry's freedom, and until 1760 their family, consisting ultimately of six children, lived in Deerfield. The Prince home was a favorite gathering place for people who enjoyed the famous storytelling of Lucy Prince, who came to be known in the area as "Luce Bijah." In 1760, when Abijah Prince inherited a one-hundred-acre plot in Guilford, Vermont, the family moved to Guilford, a village that was the home of several writers and poets but also the home of white neighbors who began to threaten the family. In 1785, Prince confronted the governor's council about the threats and demanded protection, which she received when the "selectmen of Guilford" were ordered to defend her home.

Prince's use of legal means in the securing of rights did not end there, however. In 1793, Prince petitioned the trustees of the newly founded Williams College in Williamstown, Massachusetts, in the interest of her son whom she wanted to attend there. Prince lost this appeal, but two years later she defended herself successfully before the Supreme Court of the United States. Prince had brought a suit against Colonel Eli Bronson in order to protect her property rights in Sunderland. Bronson had claimed part of the Prince lands and fenced off the disputed area as his own. When the case went to the Supreme Court, Prince was represented by Isaac Ticknor, who later became the governor of Vermont. As the trial developed, Prince became dissatisfied with Ticknor's arguments and decided to argue her own case. The presiding judge, Justice Samuel Chase, is reported (Greene 1959:315) to have found her appeals particularly noteworthy, and Prince won the case. Such stories as Belinda's and Lucy Terry Prince's constitute early markers of African American women's resistance before the law and demonstrate a commitment to public protest that continued into the nineteenth, twentieth, and now the twenty-first centuries.

The Right to Life, Liberty, and the Pursuit of Happiness

Historians such as John Hope Franklin (1980), Vincent Harding (1981), Benjamin Quarles (1987), and Adele Logan Alexander (1991) have documented many layers in the larger scope of activism in African American communities. They chronicle incidents large and small that have formed the fabric of resistance. From their first moments in captivity, people of African descent found both passive and active techniques for resisting dehumanizing conditions, including participation in conspiracies to revolt, which gave rise to story after story of individuals and groups who worked consistently to take advantage of opportunities to secure rights, to agitate for freedom, justice, and empowerment. During the latter half of the eighteenth century, when Belinda and Lucy Prince were coming of age, the social and political environment was particularly conducive to the nurturing of resistance. This was the era of colonial discontent in America, a time when future leaders were emerging to lead the revolt against the English domination of the American colonies, and thoughts for the formation of a new nation were beginning to take shape. The founding fathers of our nation were embracing the notion of a natural right to life, liberty, and the pursuit of happiness—ideas which drew attention to the troublesome inconsistency of white people claiming individual rights and natural rights for themselves while simultaneously suppressing the rights of people of African descent.

The founding of the United States occurred during an era that was profoundly influenced by ideas associated with the Age of Enlightenment, a major intellectual movement in Europe during the seventeenth and eighteenth centuries. Its proponents varied in their viewpoints but were all generally concerned with the celebration of reason, the quest for knowledge, and an understanding of the nature of man and his relationship to God, reason, and nature. This movement gave rise to reformations across many areas of human endeavor: religion, art, literature, science, economics, government, social and political philosophy, and so on, all of which formed the backdrop to the founding of the new nation.

The intellectual enterprise of the Enlightenment was to understand the universe; to understand man as a rational and creative being; to challenge the authority of religion as the dominant pathway to truth; to establish reasoning as a God-given method of inquiry; to shift the hopes, possibilities, and obligations of mankind away from authoritarian models of social order toward models that embraced a natural order, in which rights were based on being *human,* rather than on being rich or poor, royal or common, even inherently good or evil. Embracing the idea of *human rights* set in motion the articulation of the rights of individuals to self-governance, as well as rights to the pursuit of knowledge, freedom, property, and happiness. In their engagement with such issues, Enlightenment thinkers were eloquent and persuasive.

In England, such thinkers included John Locke, Jeremy Bentham, and Adam Smith. In France, they included Jean Jacques Rousseau, Charles Louis de Montesquieu, and Voltaire. In the United States, a leading voice was Thomas Jefferson, the primary crafter of the central documents that would form the nation: the Declaration of Independence, the Ordinance of 1787, the Constitution of the United States. Ideologically, Jefferson was influenced particularly by Locke and the theory of natural rights, a point of view infused in each of the documents listed above, as each in its own way ignores, confronts, or seeks ultimately to ameliorate the peculiar American institution of slavery. What is more important, however, is that the use of these arguments so persuasively in the move to nationhood served to enliven the discourses around issues of race and freedom in both African American and white communities.

In dominant discourses, incompatibilities between Jefferson's political ideology and his daily practices as a slaveholder illustrated the inherent nature of the new nation's flaws. The conflicts also revealed the political, economic, and social circumstances that served to entrench these ideological flaws for generations to come. Moreover, they established in interesting ways basic terms of engagement for American nationhood and set in motion an embracing of values that would ultimately both inspire and divide the nation.

Jefferson was consistent in his embrace of individual rights. He was equally consistent, however, as a slaveholding owner of a large plantation in Virginia. Upon his death he willed many of his slaves, counted among his possessions, to relatives. Further, in *Notes on Virginia* (first printed privately in Paris in 1785), Jefferson articulated his reluctance to view people of African descent as being equal to whites, particularly in the chapter entitled "Query XIV." In this chapter, he raised many doubts about the physical attributes of Africans, their mental capabilities, and ultimately their capacity to coexist with whites. Even so, as indicated by a letter written in 1809, Jefferson was not ambivalent, at least not theoretically, about human rights. He wrote the letter to Henri Gregoire, a bishop in the Roman Catholic Church in France who was elected to the French Senate in 1801 and who was an abolitionist. Gregoire had read *Notes* and disagreed with Jefferson's characterizations of African Americans. In response, Jefferson stated:

My doubts were the result of personal observation on the limited sphere of my own state, when the opportunities for development of their genius were not favorable, and those of exercising it still less so. I expressed them, therefore, with great hesitation; but whatever be their degree of talent, it is no measure of their rights. (Mellon 1969:109)

With this statement, Jefferson suggests three points: (1) that his view of African Americans was shaped by the region in which he lived, that is, "the limited sphere" of his own southern slaveholding state; (2) that the circumstances within which slaves existed (that is, the oppressive conditions of slavery) limited their ability to actuate or to exhibit their potential; and (3) that regardless of their abilities, or even what he thought of them, that African Americans still held rights as human beings that should, therefore, be respected. Although Jefferson did not go the full length of this view and release all of his own slaves, he did consistently attempt through his proposals of legislation, with both success and failure, to inscribe the solution to these problems in law and to keep the nation true to its stated principles.

Jefferson's distaste for slavery was shared by others whose opposition was in some cases like his own, that is, against the system of slavery but not necessarily in support of the equality of people of African descent. In other cases, there were statesmen who were against slavery, for the emancipation of slaves, and also for the amelioration of their conditions as people who should be fully incorporated into the society. Still other statesmen were against slavery in principle but not inspired by their beliefs to act. Northerner John Adams, who served as the second president of the United States, is an example of this last category. He stated:

I have through my whole life, held the practice of slavery in such abhorence, that I have never owned a Negro or any other slave; though I have lived for many years in times when the practice was not disgraceful; when the best men in my vicinity thought it not inconsistent with their other character; and when it cost me thousands of dollars for the labor and subsistence of free men, which I might have saved by the purchase of Negroes at times when they were very cheap. (Mellon 1969:84)

Adams disliked slavery, but unlike Jefferson he made no attempt during his presidency to bring about any change to the system.

Another example of attitudes during this time was George Mason from Virginia, who drafted the declaration of rights in the state constitution of Virginia, a text that influenced Jefferson's drafting of the Declaration of Independence. Mason denounced slavery as "diabolical in itself and disgraceful to mankind" (Mellon 1969:ix), and he opposed the provision in the U.S. Constitution that permitted the slave trade to continue until 1808. In the northern states, an example was John Jay, a statesman from New York who later served as president of the New York Society for Promoting the Manumission of Slaves. In a letter to Reverend Richard Price (a radical minister who, in England in 1776, published a pamphlet entitled *Observation on Civil Liberty and the Justice and Policy of the War in America*), Jay captured well the basic incompatibility of slavery in a "free" nation. He stated: "That Men should pray and fight for their own Freedom and yet keep others in Slavery is certainly acting a very inconsistent as well as unjust and perhaps impious part, but the History of Mankind is filled with Instances of human Improprieties" (Mellon 1969:ix).

Prominent among the early leaders who both opposed slavery and acted against it was elder statesman Benjamin Franklin. As a northerner, Franklin did not experience the slave system as did his southern counterparts. He was a printer, a working man rather than a member of the educated and economically privileged elite such as Jefferson, George Washington, James Madison, and others. In his early years he had actually encountered few people of African descent. His sense of them, however, to the extent that he considered them at all in his youth, was negative. At the age of forty-five his views were still negative, as indicated below in a paper written in Philadelphia in 1751, "Observations concerning the Increase of Mankind and the Peopling of Countries":

> It is an ill-grounded opinion that, by the labor of slaves, America may possibly vie in cheapness of manufactures with Britain. The labor of slaves can never be so cheap here as the labor of workingmen is in Britain. Any one may compute it. . . . Reckon then the interest of the first purchase of a slave, the insurance or risk on his life, his clothing and diet, expenses in his sickness and loss of time, loss by his neglect of business (neglect is natural to the man who is not to be benefited by his own care or diligence), expense of a driver to keep him at work, and his pilfering from time to time, almost every slave being by nature a thief. (Sparks 1840 2:314–15)

Franklin during these years saw no profit in slavery but was not an advocate for the emancipation of African Americans.

Over the next three decades, Franklin's views changed substantially. This shift in perspective is evident in a letter written on November 4, 1789, to John Wright, a member of the British Abolitionist Society. In this letter Franklin is responding to a point made in the society's annual report, which referred to abolitionist activities as beginning in England in 1758. Franklin corrected this point by asserting that George Keith, a member of the Society of Friends, had written a paper against slavery in 1693, in Philadelphia, and that there were many other instances of protest after that date—including three publications in 1728, 1729, and 1736 that he had himself printed, the first two for Ralph Sandyford and the third for Benjamin Lay. Franklin then stated:

By these instances it appears, that the seed was indeed sown in the good ground of your profession [abolition], though much earlier than the time you mention, and its springing up to effect at last, though so late, is some confirmation of Lord Bacon's observation, that a good motion never dies; and it may encourage us in making such, though hopeless of their taking immediate effect. (Sparks 1840 10:403)

With this statement Franklin recognized the importance of standing up for principles, whether the effort results in immediate success or not. In his own life, the seeds of abolition had by 1787 been well planted. During that year he became president of the Pennsylvania Abolition Society, the oldest society of its kind, demonstrating his beliefs in human rights and in the Declaration of Independence. Franklin's last public act before his death, in fact, was as president of the society. On February 3, 1790, he sent a memorial to Congress from the society in which he appealed for the nation to live up to its principles:

That mankind are all formed by the same Almighty Being, alike objects of his care, and equally designed for the enjoyment of happiness, the Christian religion teaches us to believe, and the political creed of Americans fully coincides with the position. . . . Your memorialists, particularly engaged in attending to the distress arising from slavery, believe it their indispensable duty to present this subject to your notice. . . . [T]hey earnestly entreat your serious attention to the subject to slavery; that you will be pleased to countenance the restoration of liberty to those unhappy men, who alone in this land of freedom, are graded to perpetual bondage, and who amidst the general joy of surrounding freemen, are groaning in servile subjection; that you will devise means for removing this inconsistency from the character of the American people; that you will promote mercy and justice toward this distressed race; and that you will step to the very verge of power vested in you for discouraging every species of traffic in the person of your fellow men. (Mellon 1969:21–22)

According to Matthew T. Mellon (1969), the timing for this appeal to Congress was not the best, coming soon after a similar request from the Society of Friends. The debate was contentious and foreshadowed the issues that would divide the nation during the Civil War. Congress ended discussion of the appeal on March 23, 1790, sent the memorial to committee, and determined that the government would not interfere with the slave trade until the year 1808, as decided in the Constitutional Convention. President Washington chose not to push an issue that threatened to divide the newly formed nation. Congress decided not to act on subsequent memorials of this nature but to set them aside. Franklin's response to this defeat was to send a letter to the *Federal Gazette* parodying the arguments that had been used against the memorial. A few days later, on April 17, 1790, Franklin died.

In the context of the revolutionary discourses around them, African Americans during this era were also engaged with provocative notions concerning individual rights and human rights, and particularly with the inconsistencies of slavery in a "free" society. With the formation of a nation based on natural rights and freedom, their desires for freedom for the enslaved and better living conditions for the free-born could be sparked in a different way than they were when the colonies existed under British rule. While white Americans were arguing about race, rights, and property, so too were African Americans. They were encouraged to wage a passionate struggle for liberation, political empowerment, and access to education.[7]

One example is a petition presented on December 30, 1799, by Absalom Jones (a minister and cofounder, with Richard Allen, of the African Church) and seventy-three others from Philadelphia to the President of the United States, the Senate, and the House of Representatives. The petition called for the Declaration of Independence to be honored for African Americans as well and for their rights to be protected in the face of new—and they felt unjust—laws, such as the Fugitive Slave law that had been recently enacted (Porter 1971:330–32). The petition was unsuccessful. After its failure, James Forten, a successful African American businessman who had signed the petition, sent a letter of appreciation for the advocacy of this cause to Congressman George Thatcher.[8] Forten states:

Though our faces are black, yet we are men; and though many among us cannot write, yet we all have the feelings and passions of men, and are as anxious to enjoy the birth-right of the human race as those who from our ignorance draw an argument against our Petition, when that Petition has in view the diffusion of knowledge among the African race, by unfettering their thoughts, and giving full scope to the energy of their minds. . . . While some, sir, consider us as [so] much property, as a house, or a ship, and would seem to insinuate that it is as lawful to hew down the one as to dismantle the other, you, sir, more humane, consider us part of the human race. . . . This address cannot increase the satisfaction you must derive from your laudable exertions in the cause of suffering humanity, but it serves to show the gratitude and respect of those whose cause you espoused. (Porter 1971:333–34)

In the eighteenth century, Forten and his co-petitioners understood the Enlightenment call to dignify humanity, all humanity, and to give "full scope to the energy of the mind." More important, this collective of eighteenth-century activists were representative of others of this era, including African American women, who clearly understood the obvious incompatibility of maintaining slaves in a "free" society, and who were thereby inspired during this revolutionary moment to dedicate themselves to freedom, justice, and equality.[9] They set a pace that was carried on into the nineteenth century by the next generations of men and women, constituting by their ongoing commitments to activism and advocacy a habit of resistance and a tradition of sociopolitical action.

Literacy as a Mandate for Action

A constant theme in the call for an enactment of human rights was a call for literacy. In *Soldiers of Light and Love: Northern Teachers and Georgia Blacks, 1865–1873,* Jacqueline Jones reports that African Americans recognized

the symbolic and practical significance of literacy. After emancipation, going to school became a political act as well as a means of personal edification. Black people joined together to establish schools and hire teachers for old and young alike, and their collective efforts represented both defiance to white authority and an expression of community self-interest. (1980:3)

African Americans understood the implications of literacy and learning in political, economic, and social progress. They could see clearly—from the extent to which they were denied access to it—that education could make a difference for individuals and for whole communities. At this point, however, for a view of post-Emancipation literacy acquisition to have texture and substance, we need a clearer sense of the shifting paradigms of what constituted literacy during the seventeenth, eighteenth, and nineteenth centuries and a clearer sense of the material conditions for learning in both the North and the South.

In "The History of Literacy and the History of Readers" (1988), Carl F. Kaestle reports that literacy rates in precolonial English-speaking America, as compared with European rates, were high and that rates in New England were higher than in other parts of the country.[10] He reports that the literacy rates for males in 1650 were at approximately 60 percent and for females approximately 30 percent with both rates rising steadily as opportunities for schooling increased, so that by the turn of the twentieth century claims of universal literacy could be made—especially among white males. Kaestle cautions that these rates are "crude" measures of literacy and keyed to a recognition of the variable ways over the centuries that lines have been drawn and measures have been administered in determining the difference between literates and illiterates. He points out, for example, that these figures do not account for people who happened not to be signers of public documents, the primary sources of the data, and that these rates were also not discriminating in terms of "native" whites, foreign-born whites, and nonwhites; or regions and income levels; or rural versus urban settings (Kaestle 1988:109–13), not to mention the systemic social practices that would exclude women altogether.

Harvey Graff in "The Legacies of Literacy" (1988) also lists measures of literacy in North America, focusing as Kaestle does on English-speaking areas. He begins in the seventeenth century with signatures and book ownership and expands the list as we get closer to the twentieth century to include the borrowing of books from libraries and other institutions and the ability to read, to fill out applications, to write notes, diaries, letters, and so on. Graff makes two points that I find especially significant for the history of literacy among African American women. One is that the primary users of literacy have been the state, the church, and commerce, institutions that by his reckoning have held cultural and political hegemony over the functions of literacy. His second point is that reading was spread to many "illiterates" and "semiliterates" via oral activities, which indicates that reading was then a collective process, as opposed to the private, silent reading process we now think it to be (Graff 1988:82–91).

On the first point, whatever African American women wanted to do with literacy would at the very essence be perceived by hegemonic structures as going against the grain. Obviously none of those institutions were set up with African American women in mind. On the second point,

the oral dimensions of literacy development deserve much more attention than research and scholarship have typically given them, especially
for groups such as African Americans for whom oral traditions are richly
constructed. The basic point for incorporating both Kaestle and Graff
into this analysis, however, is that they affirm what we know anecdotally,
that from the seventeenth century through the turn of the twentieth century:

1. Literate practices were diversifying, in the sense that reading and
writing were increasingly important to the conduct of business and government, and reading and writing activities were being used by more and
more people for expressive, social, and transactional purposes.

2. Schooling opportunities were rising for both men and women.

3. Boundaries between readers and writers, and speakers and listeners
around texts were fluid, with literacy for most of the time that we have
been measuring it not signaling the negative sociopolitical divide that
currently exists between "literates" and "illiterates."

4. Literate practices are constrained, if not defined, within the hegemonic order, and for those who are not members of that order (women,
nonwhites, members of lower socioeconomic classes), using literacy to
accomplish their own purposes creates adversarial relationships and conditions. The effect, of course, is that people without social position, or
political power, or economic power typically experienced problems in
accomplishing their sociopolitical goals through literacy.

Such factors indicate the changing contours of literate practices during
the period of mass acquisition by African American women, that is, during the nineteenth century. The reminder, then, is to look beyond formal
schooling toward the general fabric of literacy transmission and literate
practices more broadly defined both before Emancipation and after. In
examining literate practices before the Civil War, the inclination is to
make critical distinctions between the North and the South and between
opportunities among enslaved Blacks and opportunities among free,
freed, and fugitive Blacks. Highlighting the distinctions, however, sometimes obscures the fact that there were similarities and that distinctions
are most evident at particular moments in time rather than constantly.

With regard to literate opportunities among the enslaved in the South, unmistakably the institution of slavery depended on hard work and un-questioning obedience to white authority, and those who benefited from this institution were persistent in their efforts to keep it functioning well, such that any practices were tied to whatever was to the advantage of the slaveholders. In order to maintain the levels of obedience many slaveholders felt necessary, several states established laws that prohibited the teaching of slaves to read and to write, skills which these lawmakers thought would contribute to discontent, disorder, and insurrection. For example, South Carolina had such laws as early as 1740, and Georgia by 1755. Worth noting, however, is that history never seems to show evidence of just one single line of interest. In this case, concurrent with those who believed in squashing the literate development of African Americans, there were others who believed differently and who acted on those beliefs. Adherence to laws that sought to make literacy illegal for the enslaved, therefore, were not consistently monitored until the convergence of two sets of circumstances at the end of the eighteenth century.

The first circumstance was the rise of the Industrial Age, with the de-velopment of technologies for the picking, packing, spinning, and weav-ing of cotton. These technologies permitted the plantation system to ac-quire new economic viability. Cotton became King, and the cheaply maintained and unpaid labor force of the slavery system became key to a profitable economic enterprise. In terms of the institution of slavery and the possibility of literacy development among the enslaved, what the emergence of cotton signals is the extent to which slavery was a system that evolved rather than being fully formed from the beginning. Slavery did not begin with a consensus. It grew insidiously based on economic and political expediency, such that over the course of its growth there were quite literally peaks and valleys in terms of what was controlled in the lives of African Americans and with regard to the extent to which such controls were inhumanely applied. When cotton became king, there was an increasingly debilitating effect experienced in the lives of the en-slaved, including a diminishing access to educational opportunity.

The second set of circumstances was the rise in insurrections among the enslaved. At the beginning of the nineteenth century, the revolution-ary spirit was alive and well, in France, in the United States, in Haiti, in Santo Domingo. In the United States, this revolutionary spirit energized a

rising abolitionist movement. Amid this spirit of freedom, slave insurrections were particularly noticeable. They fed a rising concern about the
imbalances in the South in numbers (in some areas African Americans
equaled or even outnumbered the whites), but they also fed a rising concern about literacy and the access to information among the oppressed,
with the sentiment that keeping slaves ignorant of insurrections especially was much preferred. The early 1800s were witness to some of the
most well-known insurrections: Gabriel in Virginia (1800), Denmark
Vesey in South Carolina (1822), Nat Turner in Virginia (1831). These revolts struck fear in many a white southern heart, with a significant degree
of that fear coming from knowledge of the role of literacy in the events
and of the "'sinister' influences of enlightened Negroes" (Woodson 1991:
157; see also Jones 1980; Vaughn 1974). In effect, slaveholders recognized
the likelihood of an occasional call to freedom from the hearts of enslaved men and women. This fact alone was manageable. What was not so
predictable was the potential effects of insurrectionist leaders who were
able to read books about revolutions and revolutionary heroes and heroines, newspaper reports of whatever insurrections were occurring or had
occurred, and abolitionist pamphlets that encouraged the quest for freedom and proclaimed a growing support for the ending of slavery. Literacy in this context was deemed dangerous and intolerable such that, after
the particularly violent Turner revolt, southern sentiments changed. Significant to understanding this shift in sentiment between the North and
the South, and thereby the history of literacy among African Americans
(women included), is the need for a general understanding of a surpris-
ing range of opportunities for education that existed for African Americans from the seventeenth century through the 1830s and the tightening
of proscriptions.

A 1919 historical study by the renowned historian Carter G. Woodson,
The Education of the Negro Prior to 1861, is an excellent account of the
multiple pathways to literacy that were available and the competing attitudes that gave rise to them from the seventeenth century forward.[11] First
of all, Woodson reports that the early advocates of education for African
Americans fell generally into three categories: slaveholders who believed
that education increased economic efficiency; individual social reformers
who operated from a sense of compassion for the oppressed; Christians

of various denominations who believed that education was appropriate for all, including the enslaved for whom slavery brought the advantage of the civilizing elements of Christian principles and the word of God. Consider, for example, these instructions in 1693 from Cotton Mather to masters about their servants:

> 1st. I would always remember, that servants are in some sense my children, and by taking care that they want nothing which may be good for them, I would make them as my children. . . . Nor will I leave them ignorant of anything, wherein I may instruct them to be useful to their generation.
>
> 2d. I will see that my servants be furnished with bibles and be able and careful to read the lively oracles. I will put bibles and other good and proper books into their hands; will allow them time to read and assure myself that they do not misspend this time. (Woodson 1991:337)

Likewise, Bishop Gibson of London addressed letters to the masters and mistresses of English plantations abroad in the 1720s to promote the teaching of slaves:

> But, if I am rightly informed, many of the Negroes, who are grown Persons when they come over, do of themselves obtain so much of our Language, as enables them to understand, and to be understood, in Things which concern the ordinary Business of Life, and they who can go so far of their own Accord, might doubtless be carried much farther, if proper Methods and Endeavors were used to bring them to a competent Knowledge of our Language, with a pious view to instructing them in the Doctrines of Religion. At least, some of them, who are more capable and more serious than the rest, might be easily instructed both in our Language and Religion, and then be made use of to convey Instruction to the rest in their own language. (343)

In 1750 Reverend Thomas Bacon, rector of the parish church in Talbot County, Maryland, made a similar appeal to the women of plantation households, "who by your stations are more confined at home, and have the care of the younger sort more particularly under your management, may do a great deal of good in this way" (350).

Moreover, with the liberation of the American colonies from the British after the Revolutionary War, there was a renewed and more impassioned interest to educate the African Americans, especially if they were not going to be freed right away. Jonathan Boucher, rector of the Church of England in Maryland, raised one such voice. According to Woodson, Boucher belonged to a group of revolutionary leaders who were interested in suppressing the slave trade, liberating the African Americans already in bondage, and educating them for a life in freedom (53). In 1763, Boucher stated:

I do you no more than justice in bearing witness, that in no part of the world were slaves better treated than, in general, they are in the colonies. . . . In one essential point, I fear, we are all deficient; they are nowhere sufficiently instructed. I am far from recommending it to you, at once to set them free; because to do so would be an heavy loss to you, and probably no gain to them; but I do entreat you to make them some amends for the drudgery of their bodies by cultivating their minds. (359)

These attitudes during the founding years of the nation set in motion an array of educational activities and philanthropic commitments that provided the floor from which literacy acquisition in African American communities in the North and in the South developed over the first two centuries of the nation's history.

In the seventeenth century, we can begin accounting for the first literacy workers by means of a narrative that envisioned slavery as a civilizing process. One view in slaveholding nations was that slavery was an advantage to Africans because it brought them from their barbaric and heathen conditions into civilization and introduced them to the word of God. This narrative mediated the sense that by Christian doctrine enslaving others is a sin. Government policies and church policies dictated, therefore, that the slaves (and the Indians) should receive instruction. In Mexico, controlled by Spain, government regulations required that slaveholders instruct their slaves and permitted the free-born children of slaves (that is, mixed-race children) to attend public school or other places where instruction was available. In Canada, controlled by the French, Jesuit priests were identified with literacy development. A typical practice was that they would sometimes call together white settlers, Indians, and slaves and instruct them, either together or separately, often depending on the size of the groups. These practices were continued by French Catholics in the settlement of Louisiana in the eighteenth century. The French Catholics added to these opportunities the chance for some slaves to be sent to France for more religious training and to learn other arts or skills that would be useful to the French colonies. These practices show evidence of an adherence to the Code Noir, which spelled out policies that supported respect for the talents and abilities of slaves and offered protection from maltreatment by masters. In other words, literacy development in both Spanish-held and French-held colonies was quite liberal in its sentiment, although certainly there was significant variation in its implementation. Nevertheless, these practices gave rise to levels of literacy in North America that were, in all likelihood, not equalled in English-held colonies.

While the English held the same narrative of slavery as a civilizing process, the competing value of economic profits seemed to dominate. Teachers and missionaries in English-speaking colonies faced a greater challenge in literacy-development efforts, evidenced by the zeal and consistency with which appeals for literacy were rendered. In English-speaking colonies, the Quakers were particularly active as leaders in reform and literacy activism, with the record of their reform activities stretching well into the twentieth century. There were other efforts, however, that are lesser known. For example, in 1701 the Church of England organized the Society for the Propagation of the Gospel in Foreign Parts. Their mission was to work among Indians and African Americans, and they implemented this mission by sending to the American colonies both ministers and schoolmasters to carry out the work.

Three examples of these literacy activists were Reverend Samuel Thomas, who went to Goose Creek Parish in South Carolina in 1695; the Reverend Doctor Thomas Bray, who went to Maryland in 1696; and Elias Neau, who went to New York City in 1704. In South Carolina, after ten years Reverend Thomas counted among his successes twenty African Americans who could read and write and who knew the English language well; at least one thousand who could read the Bible; and a cadre of white plantation women who were enlisted in the educational cause and who worked with him. Similarly, Bray was engaged in the conversion of adult slaves in Maryland and in the education of their children. Although Bray did not remain in the colonies, in 1701 he helped establish the Society for the Propagation of the Gospel in Foreign Parts. He was involved in sending missionaries to Maryland, and he received funding from M. D'Allone, a Dutchman who was the private secretary of King William, to support the Thomas Bray Mission.[12] After Reverend Bray's death, his followers— known as the Associates of Doctor Bray—extended his work to Philadelphia, where they set up two schools in 1760 and enabled abolitionists to establish a school, which continued in that city for almost one hundred years. This school came to the attention of Deborah Franklin, wife of Benjamin Franklin, whose activities drew her husband into this cause. In 1760, while Franklin served as an ambassador for American colonial interests in London, he became a member of the Associates of Doctor Bray and served as their chairman (Sparks 1840 2:201–02).

In New York, Elias Neau opened a school in his home for African Americans, who came to be taught after their daily chores were completed. By 1708 he had as many as two hundred students and continued his school until his death in 1722 when his work was taken over by others. These efforts and others laid the groundwork for the training of African Americans who would then be encouraged or specifically trained to teach others. In 1744, for example, two African American men, Harry and Andrew, set up a school in Charleston, South Carolina, that was probably attended mostly by free African Americans in the area. The school remained open until 1764 and had as its mission religious instruction and reading so that students could share their knowledge of the Bible with others. Such stories were repeated throughout the English colonies in the eighteenth century, but not without a rising backlash from those who felt that economic imperatives should prevail. The backlash is indicated by the institution of laws, cited earlier, prohibiting the teaching of slaves to read and write. By this era, as evidence of the shifting nature of slavery over time, the images of African Americans were being inscribed in the aristocratic South and elsewhere in nonhuman terms as property, justifying the treatment of them as animals unfit for either mental or moral development. With this shift in attitude and practice, there was a growing disinterest in providing slaves with educational opportunity.

With the existence in the society of activists who remained committed to educational opportunity, however, efforts to prepare African Americans for lives in freedom continued. Some of these advocates contributed land for schools and left in their wills money to support the education of both African Americans and Indians. Anthony Benezet was a French-born resident of Philadelphia who taught African Americans until he died in 1784. Very active in the work of the Society of Friends, Benezet also took part in the 1775 founding of the Pennsylvania Abolition Society, which made it a priority to establish schools for African Americans. Benjamin Franklin became president of this society, from 1787 until his death in 1790. When Benezet died, he left a will that provided a substantial core of funds from which a school was erected in 1787 in Philadelphia where African Americans studied reading, writing, arithmetic, plain accounts, and sewing—which suggests that women and girls attended the school.

Another example of philanthropy during this era was Thaddeus Kosciuszko, a Polish general who fought with the United States during the revolutionary war. During his time in the United States Kosciuszko acquired valuable property, which he left in the care of Thomas Jefferson, his executor, to use to purchase African Americans from slavery and to educate them. Cases such as Kosciuszko and Benezet offer evidence of the precarious balances being struck that permitted African Americans to learn, in spite of a rising tide of disinterest in both the North and the South. A third example was Richard Humphreys, a Quaker silversmith from Philadelphia who left ten thousand dollars (a substantial sum for the day) for "instructing the descendants of the African Race in school learning, in the various branches of mechanical arts and trades and in agriculture: in order to prepare them to act as teacher" (Harrison 1997:45). Through this bequest, a school was established in 1837 and a series of educational activities were supported and coordinated by a Quaker board of managers. In 1852 these efforts were focused toward establishing the Institute for Colored Youth, for the training of teachers for the public schools. In 1922 the institute was purchased by the Commonwealth of Pennsylvania and exists today as Cheyney University of Pennsylvania.

The American Revolutionary War and the founding principles of the nation (such as the establishing of religious rights and individual rights) were instrumental in sustaining an educational commitment among African Americans themselves and among others who supported them. These factors contributed to an escalating movement to end the slave trade and slavery. The principles of revolution institutionalized religious freedom and secured the rights of religious groups to engage in their church-sanctioned activities (including those in the interest of the racially oppressed) without fear of legal persecution. Abolitionist groups drew members whose concerns were rooted in religious beliefs and a commitment against oppression (indicated, for example, by the participation of Quakers, Presbyterians, Baptists, and Methodists). The abolitionist societies also drew members from those inspired by the political discourses on individual rights, discourses which broadened interests in literacy to include religious concerns and political ones. Thus, by the turn of the eighteenth century, education was considered a necessity for good citizenship, not just for the knowledge of God's word. With the merging of religious and political interests, the abolitionist movement added strength to the argument for literacy development among African Americans, such that at the American Convention of Abolition Societies in 1794 and in 1795, there was a call to support educational opportunity. These activities raised the question of what, then, constituted appropriate educational preparation for African Americans, a question that has resounded through the decades to the contemporary era.

From the seventeenth century through the turn of the eighteenth century until 1830, African Americans had variable, though modest, access to educational opportunity in both the North and the South. Certainly, the North offered more formal mechanisms for access, with the existence there of African American schools and white school systems that could be petitioned by free African Americans (who were in a clearer position than their enslaved counterparts to agitate for change in their own interests). By the turn of the nineteenth century, therefore, given the definitions of literacy at the time, there was a substantial core of literate African Americans, which included both free and enslaved men and women in both the North and the South. Quite probably, given typical markers of literacy during this era, their skills weighed more generally toward the ability to read rather than to write, especially among those who lived in the South. Nevertheless, by the standards of the day, literacy was indeed in evidence.

At the turn of the nineteenth century, however, as indicated by the petition from Absalom Jones and the letter to Congressman Thatcher from James Forten, we see a clear shift toward negative fortunes. Congress had already decided, as indicated by their response to the memorial submitted by Benjamin Franklin in 1790, that they would not engage abolitionist petitions but would ignore them until the constitutionally designated year of 1808, when the slave trade was legislated to end. Although many

among Forten's generation of activists commanded a range of literate resources and although they were dedicated to social change, their activities
were nevertheless becoming encircled by a spirit of retrenchment and by
a resurgence of oppressive forces that signaled competing interests, danger, and alarm. Literacy laws across the slaveholding states were being
reinscribed (for example, in Georgia in 1770), and the number of states
with these laws was increasing. Within this context of alarm, slave insurrections, which had been periodic throughout the existence of slavery, became occasions to bolster the backlash and, in effect, to set in motion a
decline in literacy levels, rather than what might have been anticipated as
an amelioration. By the 1830s, despite the considerable evidence of educational progress, educational opportunities for African Americans were
closing, not opening. Efforts to break the spirit of freedom among
African Americans and to short-circuit the momentum for literacy development, however, did not succeed.

Literacy Opportunities after 1800

Setting aside the many instances in which slaves used their literacy to
escape the South (as in the case of Frederick Douglass), some African
Americans engaged in the practice of teaching their fellow bondsmen. An
African American woman in Savannah, known as Miss Deveaux, ran a
school in her home from 1835 through the 1860s; in Charleston another
woman, known as Miss L., used a sewing class as the cover for a school for
slave children; Milla Granson, a house slave in Natchez, Mississippi, ran a
school every night in her cabin between 11 P.M. and 2 A.M. (Holt 93).
Some slaves learned from their masters, who continued to assert their authority to act as they wished with their own slaves and continued to operate on the belief that rudimentary literacy made the slaves better property, more productive, more efficient. Others learned from eavesdropping
at the school doors as they waited to escort the master's children; or
through contact and observation of whites; or from the children of masters who saw no harm in teaching their slave friends; or from the wives or
sisters of masters who sometimes chose to teach their favorites.

One factor during this era of restrictions that has not been fully examined is the nature of many plantation households as elite households; the
literate practices that probably occurred within; and how those practices

might have provided an environment, intentional or not, for the development of literacy. In *Within the Plantation Household: Black and White Women of the Old South* (1988), Elizabeth Fox-Genovese explains that southern society permitted and even fostered women's religious and intellectual development as long as it unfolded within circumscribed social roles (256). Young elite white women were systematically educated to their stations in life as southern ladies, including their developing reading skills and, to some extent, writing skills. While their access to schooling did not equal that of the men of their class, southern women could attend Sabbath schools and local academies, and sometimes they were taught by literate mothers in their own homes. The slave household was, in fact, the domain of the mistress. She was responsible for the early education of her children; she also held dominion over all others in the household (with the notable exception of her husband, of course).

As Fox-Genovese points out, being "the lady" was the central identity of elite white women, an identity they assumed as daughters, wives, mothers, and mistresses of slaves. She says also:

They became themselves through membership in a literate culture—through reading and writing. Whether through light fiction, religious literature, or the prose, fiction, and poetry of their own region and general Western culture, reading helped them to define moral, political, and personal issues. Through reading they extended the implications of their everyday lives and sought models of personal excellence, sources of personal consolation, and standards of social and political good. (1988:242)

My intent here is not to moralize about the participation of slaveholding women in the oppression of people of African descent, but to suggest that in participating in this process they also engaged in other activities that have essentially gone underexamined, such as the formal and informal development of literacy. Fox-Genovese indicates that elite white women became themselves through reading. In doing so, a typical literate practice was that slave mistresses read to their own children, and quite probably, they taught them their letters and other rudimentary reading skills before these boys and girls went on to whatever other education was available to them. In addition, some slave mistresses who felt particularly committed to religious training also read to their slaves and sometimes involved them in family prayers (156).

In terms of the difference that these household habits made to the African American women and girls who shared this space, one thing is certain. There was no systematic literacy education for the enslaved. Although there are many stories of slave mistresses or white children who taught their favorite slaves to read and write, these practices were by all calculations random and quite arbitrary. Most slaves remained illiterate. What seems more systematically useful as the groundwork for the development of literacy among African American women is the incidence of their ability to move about the "big house," a site defineable by the definition of the day as a literate environment.

Because slaves had no personal presence in the eyes of white masters or acknowledgment in their own right, they were actually able to move relatively unnoticed among people who engaged from time to time in literate activities. The slaves could see reading taking place. They could hear it. They could see notes, letters, diaries, newspapers, books, business records and documents. Periodically, if not consistently, they were surrounded by the artifacts of literacy, and at minimum, it did not take very long for them to understand the significance of this material culture. Because the condition of slavery did not automatically determine that the enslaved would be idiots, it is possible to understand how an enslaved child or adult might actually learn in this environment and be in a position to pass along what he or she came to know. The process might have been very much like what Marcia Farr (1994b) describes as learning literacy "lirico." In ethnographic studies of men of Mexican origin who live in Chicago, Farr reports:

A number of the men in their mid-30s and beyond from the Guanajuato *rancho* became functionally literate essentially without formal schooling. They report that they learned literacy lirico; that is they "picked it up" informally from others who used only spoken language—not printed materials—to pass on knowledge of the writing system. The teaching and learning process, then, proceeded through oral language, from one person to another, in informal arrangements. (1994b:18–19).

Quite probably, as in the case of some contemporary Mexican American men, slaves within literate environments such as elite plantation households might actually have managed to "pick up" more than they were intended to pick up.

Among African Americans who were not slaves, barriers to literacy were as much in evidence as for their enslaved brethren, but some opportunities were available. African Americans in the North, and later in the South, had their own private schools. Marianna Davis chronicles, in *Contributions of Black Women to America* (Vol. 2), the commitment of African American women to this educational cause. They demonstrated, in fact, a passionate determination to reduce ignorance, develop literacy, and encourage intellectual development for males and females alike.

African American women began founding schools as early as 1793, when Catherine Williams Ferguson, a former slave, opened a Sunday school, the Katy Ferguson's School for the Poor, in her home in New York City. In the beginning, Ferguson focused on providing religious education and social services for approximately forty-eight orphaned children, twenty of whom were white. She took the children into her own home, found homes for them, taught them how to care for themselves, and taught them scriptures that she had learned from her enslaved mother (who was sold away from her when she was eight years old). With the support of Reverend John M. Mason, her pastor at the Murray Street Church, Ferguson moved her school to the basement of the church and hired assistants to teach the students courses that she was not prepared to teach. For the next forty years, Ferguson supervised both the educational and the social services of the integrated Murray Street Sabbath School, New York's first Sabbath school, and supported its activities by working as a caterer and washerwoman for delicate fabrics (Hallie Quinn Brown 3; A. Johnson 1993:426).

Ann Marie Becroft was also a pioneer in education. She was born of free parents, William and Sara Becroft, in 1805 in Washington, D.C. As a child trying to acquire an education she faced hostility at the white-operated Potter School. At the age of seven, her parents transferred her to the New Georgetown School where she studied with Mary Billing, the white widow who ran the school, until 1820, when Billing closed her school in the wake of the Denmark Vesey revolt and the move to discourage whites from teaching African Americans. That same year, Becroft founded her own school, the first seminary for African American girls in Georgetown. Becroft's school remained open until 1827 when she was invited by the parish priest, Father J. Van Lommel, of Holy Trinity Catholic Church to open a school under the auspices of the church. Becroft retained the leadership of the school until 1831, when she turned it over to a former student, Ellen Simonds, and left to become the ninth nun of the Oblate Sisters of Providence in Baltimore, a teaching order. As Sister Aloysius, Becroft continued to teach until 1833, when, always sickly, she died on December 16, 1833 (Marrow 1993:106).

Also in 1820, Sarah Mapps Douglass established a school in Philadelphia, where she trained two generations of students. Douglass was freeborn in 1806 to a prominent African American family in Philadelphia. Her mother was a founder of the Philadelphia Female Anti-Slavery Society, which Douglass also joined as a young woman. In 1838 this society assumed financial responsibility for the school Douglass had established. In 1853 Douglass joined the faculty of the Institute for Colored Youth, opened by the Quakers in 1852. She soon became an administrator at this institution and continued to train teachers for the public schools until her retirement in 1877 (Lerner 1993:351–52).

Ultimately, many other African American women followed as founders of schools, both national and international.[13] Among the best-known in the United States since the Civil War are Lucy Craft Laney, who started the Haines Normal and Industrial Institute in Augusta, Georgia, in 1866; Charlotte Hawkins Brown, who opened Palmer Memorial Institute in Sedalia, North Carolina, in 1902; and Mary McLeod Bethune, who founded the Daytona Educational and Industrial School for Negro Girls in Daytona Beach, Florida, in 1904. This last institution exists today as Bethune-Cookman College (M. Davis 1981:267–89).

Adding significantly to the efforts of African American women in their own interests were white women such as Prudence Crandall and Myrtilla Miner. In 1832 Prudence Crandall, a Quaker woman, operated a boarding school for African American girls in Canterbury, Connecticut. She was arrested, tried in the courts, and convicted for teaching "colored people who were not inhabitants of the State of Connecticut . . . without first obtaining, in writing, the consent of a majority of the civil authority and the selectmen of the town" (M. Davis 1981:267). Her indictment was eventually overturned, but she was forced to abandon her school in the face of ensuing violence by local residents.

Myrtilla Miner, from New York, opened the Normal School for Colored Girls in 1851 in Washington, D.C. With the help of Quaker groups and Harriet Beecher Stowe, her school became among the first to provide systematic opportunities for higher education for African American women.[14] Miner modeled her school on seminaries for white women and made every effort to assure that it was a first-class teacher-training institution. She was ridiculed for her efforts, her teachers and students were subjected to abuse from local residents, and the school was set on fire. Despite these difficulties, however, the Miner School continued to function, and today Miner Teachers College, part of the coeducational University of the District of Columbia, stands in tribute to these original efforts and as evidence that Miner's goal of excellence was eventually achieved (M. Davis 1981:270; Ihle 1986 Modules 3 and 4: page 3).

Another means to literacy for African Americans in the North was that they had some degree of access, especially in urban areas, to public schools (mandated by law in this region), or to local academies. At least, they could petition to attend. Consider Maritcha Lyon, for example. Lyon's parents petitioned for her to attend the high school in Providence, Rhode Island. When she enrolled, she obviously faced overt racism, as she reports in her memoirs:

By this time I had become one of the foremost of the leaders [but] the iron had entered my soul. I never forgot that I had to sue for a privilege which any but a colored girl could have without asking. Most of the classmates were more or less friendly. If any girl tried to put "on airs" I simply found a way to inform her of my class record. As I never had less than the highest marks, to flaunt my superiority in scholarship was never hard. (Sterling 1984:189)

From these experiences, Lyon proceeded to fashion an excellent record. She became an assistant principal in Brooklyn, New York, after the Civil War; she participated in the Black Clubwomen's Movement, a critical mechanism for the participation of African American women in public arenas;[15] and she wrote a biography of her friend, Dr. Susan McKinney Steward, the founder of a New York women's club and one of the first African American women to receive a medical degree (Sterling 1984: 441–42, 450).

Further, northern African American women also had two other types of access—to Sabbath schools (Katy Ferguson's school, for example) and to the books and libraries of employers and friends. Maria W. Stewart attended Sabbath schools. In her essay "Religion and the Pure Principles of Morality: The Sure Foundation On Which We Must Build," she stated:

I was born in Hartford, Connecticut, in 1803, was left an orphan at five years of age; was bound out in a clergyman's family; had the seeds of piety and virtue early sown in my mind, but was deprived of the advantages of education, though my soul thirsted for knowledge. Left them at fifteen years of age; attended Sabbath schools until I was twenty; in 1826 was married to James W. Stewart; was left a widow in 1829; was, as I humbly hope and trust, brought to the knowledge of the truth, as it is in Jesus, in 1830; in 1831 made a public profession of my faith in Christ . . . and now possess that spirit of independence that, were I called upon, I would willingly sacrifice my life for the cause of God and my brethren. (28–29)

This quotation illustrates how she hungered for knowledge, took advantage of the learning opportunities available to her (most specifically Sabbath schools), and was inspired by the material circumstances of her life to sacrifice herself for the causes of God, which included justice and empowerment for herself and her people.

With regard to access to the books and libraries of employers and friends, consider the example chronicled by Harriet E. Wilson, author of *Our Nig* (first published in 1859). Wilson wrote:

She learned that in some towns in Massachusetts, girls make straw bonnets— that it was easy and profitable. But how should *she,* black, feeble and poor, find any one to teach her. But God prepares the way, when human agencies see no path. Here was found a plain, poor, simple woman, who could see merit beneath a dark skin; and when the invalid mulatto told her sorrows, she opened her door and her heart, and took the stranger in. Expert with the needle, Frado soon equalled her instructress; and she sought also to teach her the value of useful books; and while one read aloud to the other of deeds historic and names renowned, Frado experienced a new impulse. She felt herself capable of elevation; she felt that this book information supplied an undefined dissatisfaction she had long felt, but could not express. Every leisure moment was carefully applied to self-improvement, and a devout and Christian exterior invited confidence from the villagers. (1983:125–26)

This passage shows evidence of the arbitrary nature of advocacy, of the value assigned to reading even in the lives of ordinary working people, and the inspiration that the opportunity to learn could have, even for those who were "black, feeble, and poor." Frado felt "capable of elevation" and experienced a new impulse for self-improvement.

Literacy for escaped slaves was quite an asset, as illustrated by the auto-biographical narratives of Frederick Douglass. As his story suggests, African Americans in this group who were able to read and write significantly increased their chances of success and survival both in the escape and afterward. Once free, rather than living unprotected in isolation, these ex-slaves typically joined communities of free Blacks in the North, and thereby had the opportunity to take advantage of strategies for enhancing literacy.

In terms of literacy opportunities in the South, obviously there were differences between the North and the South, but several conditions gave rise to the acquisition of literacy—not only among the enslaved but frequently among free and freed African Americans.[16] A primary means to literacy for members of southern free-Black communities was that they were typically skilled workers or craftsmen. As artisans who had acquired the skills of their various crafts, they usually had also managed to acquire some degree of literacy, in order to conduct business. Often in the early stages of their working lives, their literacy skills (to keep records and figures) were typically in the interest of slaveholders who recognized the economic advantages to themselves of having literate workers. However, later, as they were sometimes able to purchase their own freedom and the freedom of their family members, they used literacy in their own interests.

Another means to literacy among free Blacks in the South was via the support of white men who sometimes arranged and paid for the education or training of their Black children, siblings, or other family members. Consider, for example, the striking case of the families chronicled by Adele Logan Alexander in *Ambiguous Lives: Free Women of Color in Rural Georgia, 1789–1879* (1991). Alexander uses her own family in Sparta, Georgia, as the centerpiece of a historical account of free African Americans in middle Georgia, totally surrounded by a slaveholding society. She recounts living conditions and refers to an array of literate practices that help to explain how individual white people supported the literacy and learning of their African American relatives. She states:

In addition to sponsoring them [his children] in his church, a man of Nathan Sayre's achievements might have educated his children, and some of his books such as *Arithmetic, Schoolcraft, Godman's Natural History,* and *The Bridget Bubble Family* clearly focused on a growing family's needs and interests. He must have believed in educating young women, judging by his interest in and financial support of the Female Model School. Nonetheless, the girls' academic attainments were minimal, though they were accomplished musicians and musical evenings were regular events at Pomegranate Hall. (1991:85)

Pomegranate Hall was the home of Judge Nathan Sayre, his "wife" Susan Hunt, who was biracial, and their three children—two females and one male. Alexander reports that Mariah, one of the daughters, was baptized in the Presbyterian Church to which Sayre and the white Hunts belonged. She also reports that the girls apparently studied music at the local Female Model School, and in keeping with the literate practices of the day, they learned to read and to write but did not pursue academic subjects.

After the Civil War, with the opening of Atlanta University for African Americans, African Americans in the South had easier access to higher education. Adella Hunt, the granddaughter of Nathan and Susan, was among the first from her area to benefit. Her mother, Mariah, had followed her mother, Susan, in marrying a white man, Henry Hunt. When opportunities opened at Atlanta University, Adella enrolled with the support of family and influential friends. She graduated in 1881 from the Normal Department, one of the first African American women to receive a degree from this institution. Such stories of support are liberally sprinkled throughout the records of Oberlin College, Wilberforce University, Fisk University, Atlanta University, and many other institutions that offered educational opportunities to African Americans.

Taking into account these types of complexities in literacy acquisition and literate practices among free and enslaved African Americans over time, the literacy rates among early generations of African Americans in the United States grew by all sorts of traditional and nontraditional strategies whereby men, women, and children managed to acquire basic reading skills and sometimes writing skills and to pass them along to others. Vaughn estimates (1974:2) that literacy levels in the adult population of African Americans were at about 5–10 percent in 1860. He posits also that this level actually represented a substantial decline from the period before 1830. The decline after 1830 can be accounted for through the convergence of the rise of the Industrial Age; the backlash against an energetic abolitionist movement in the face of substantial economic interests; the incidence of attention-getting slave revolts; and changing narratives

and justifications for continuing slavery at all costs. These events contributed to shifts in sentiment about educational opportunity for African
Americans, generally. The result of the shifts was a tightening of proscriptions, which would not be relieved in any substantial way until the escala-
tion of tensions between the North and the South as a precursor of the
Civil War and ultimately the acquisition by the Union Army of the first
southern contraband, that is, the freeing of the slaves who occupied the
Sea Islands off the coasts of South Carolina and Georgia.

Charlotte Forten and the Port Royal Commission

The story of Charlotte Forten offers a particularly instructive occasion
for understanding a merging of resources among northern advocates, including African Americans, with the literacy needs of southern African
Americans. From November 7, 1861, to January 1, 1863, three events converged to form the locus of a history-making process.[17] Forten, a member
of the affluent and widely respected Black abolitionist Forten-Purvis
family from Philadelphia, emerged as an African American woman who
wanted to make a difference.

The best-known of the three events occurred on January 1, 1863. As
president and commander in chief of the Army and Navy, Abraham Lincoln issued a proclamation that came to be known as the Emancipation
Proclamation. It was signed on September 22, 1862, and stated:

all persons held as slaves within any state or designated part of a State, the people whereof shall then be in rebellion against the United States, shall be then,
thenceforward, and forever free; and the Executive Government of the United
States, including the military and naval authority thereof, will recognize and
maintain the freedom of such persons, and will do no act or acts to repress such
persons, or any of them in any efforts they may make for their actual freedom.
(The Emancipation Proclamation)

President Lincoln gave all states in rebellion the time between September 22, 1862, and January 1, 1863, to declare their allegiance to the United
States, with the threat that, if they did not, their slaves would be confiscated and freed on the latter date. None of the rebelling states returned to
the Union and the proclamation was issued. The Civil War battles raged
on; several million slaves were "freed." With this stroke of the law, the war
ceased to be only a contest for political control and economic power over

southern agricultural resources. Symbolically and practically, it became a crusade against slavery—with African Americans being compelled in their newly acquired freedom to make their best and clearest case for their potential as human beings with rights.

As significant historically as the Emancipation Proclamation was, this event alone does not adequately reveal the significance of this period in the history of literacy among African American people. Two additional events help make the moment clearer. Chronologically (even before the Emancipation Proclamation), the first important event was the victory of Union troops over Confederate troops on Hilton Head Island. On November 7, 1861, the Union navy launched an assault on Confederate forces on Hilton Head Island in the interest of setting in place a blockade of Port Royal Sound, the access way to several critical southern ports. The Confederates were defeated in six hours. Across the islands that bordered the sound, slaveholding residents immediately abandoned the area, leaving behind fifty plantations and over ten thousand men, women, and children of African descent as "contraband." This "contraband," in the form of both confiscated lands and confiscated slaves, came under the control of the U.S. Treasury Department.

The second event, which grew directly out of this first one, was the Port Royal Experiment, launched by Treasury secretary Salmon P. Chase with the support of others, including abolitionists such as Robert Purvis (Forten's uncle) and Wendell Phillips. Shortly after the battle for control of the Port Royal Sound, Edward L. Pierce, a Boston attorney, was identified as the point person for the experiment. The effort of the experiment was twofold. One part was economic: the thinking of the day was that the freed people on the Sea Islands needed to be managed in order to expedite the claiming of the land that they occupied by the U.S. government and also to expedite the development of the critical resources on the islands, including an especially valuable variety of cotton, which could be grown only on the islands and was the highest-yielding variety of cotton in the Americas.

The second part of the experiment focused on the "contraband" people. Pierce proposed that the government send teachers, ministers, and superintendents to provide assistance to the freed people. He suggested that the salaries of these workers should be paid by private agencies, with the government agreeing to provide an allowance for transportation, housing, and subsistence. Several groups responded to the call for private support, including the New England Educational Commission, the Freedmen's Relief Association of New York, and the Port Royal Relief Association of Philadelphia. This collective of associations formed the core resources around which the Port Royal Experiment was conducted.

On September 16, 1863, six days before the signing of the Emancipation Proclamation, President Lincoln sent instructions to the Board of Tax Commissioners for the District of South Carolina, which by this time was under the control of a federally appointed governor. Lincoln's letter gave instructions for the sale of confiscated lands, including the selling of land to the freed slaves, but it also stated:

You will set apart for school purposes in a convenient form for use as a farm or farms, one or more tracts . . . not exceeding 160 acres . . . you will receive and collect such rents and issues as appropriate and apply the same to the education of colored youths, and of such poor white persons, being minors, as may by themselves, parents, guardians, or next friends, apply for the benefit thereof, and you are authorized to establish such schools, and to direct the tuition of such branches of learning as you in your judgment shall deem most eligible, subject nevertheless to the general direction and control of the Secretary of the Treasury. (Basler 1953:455–56)

This letter underscored the twofold nature of the experiment, in its identifying both economic and educational interests. This support of education marked the very first federal funding for educational opportunity for African Americans. The imperative of the participants in this project was "ultimately to prove to a skeptical public that Negroes were worthy of their freedom" (Jacoway 1980:xiii), a freedom that was clearly forthcoming as set forth by the signing of the Emancipation Proclamation a few days later. In truth, because of the battle on November 7, 1861, thousands of slaves—the "contraband"—were already free on the islands, with their fate precariously in the balance. Their cause, in the interest of the totality, was the first hurdle to be crossed.

In the eyes of the northern missionaries who came south, the Port Royal Experiment needed to convince white America—and, they felt, the freed slaves as well—that "blacks could be uplifted and thereby rendered non-threatening—and that in the meantime, blacks could find a place in the American system that would allow them a measure of dignity" (Jacoway 1980:254). There is much evidence to indicate that the missionaries were passionately committed to this cause. In coming south, however, they were immersed in cultural traditions that were not their own. Typically, while the missionaries were often impressed by the energy and passion brought by their African American charges to the opportunities to learn and improve themselves, the missionaries nonetheless enacted culturally biased notions they had brought with them concerning what they would find in the South and the people they would "cultivate." In effect, they thought of African Americans as deserving freedom and educational opportunity, but they still found it difficult to think of African Americans as being equal or to treat them as such (as illustrated by Forten's experiences with her white colleagues).

The journals that she kept during these years show that Charlotte Forten did not view freed slaves as either contraband or unequals. She viewed them as downtrodden members of her own race, as her own people, and she felt obligated, as a person who had benefited from greater opportunity, to lend a helping hand. On a trip from St. Helena across the sound to Buford, she observed:

On the Bay—as they call it. Saw the building which was once the Public Library. It is now a shelter for "contrabands" from Ferandino [Florida]. How disgusted the rebels w'ld be. I suppose they w'ld upturn their aristocratic noses and say "To what base uses etc." It does *me* good to see how the tables are turned. . . . Few persons are to be seen in the streets, some soldiers and "contrabands." I believe we saw only three ladies. But already Northern improvements have reached this southern town. One of them is a fine new wharf which is a convenience that one wonders how the "Secesh" c'ld have done without. They were an uncivilized people. I noticed more mulattoes there than we have on St. Hel.[ena]. Some were very good-looking. Little colored children—of every hue were playing about the streets looking as merry and happy as children ought to look—now that the dark shadow of slavery hangs over them no more. (Forten 443)

In this passage, her use of quotation marks clearly shows that Forten questioned the label "contraband"; she also considered the slaveholding South to be "uncivilized." Equally interesting, she noticed "three ladies" (white women, presumably) and "mulattoes" and "children—of every hue," who were not so much in evidence among the dark-skinned people of St. Helena. She called these multi-hued children "very good-looking." These references suggest some ambivalence in terms of her valuing of "race" in our contemporary terms, but the passage indicates, nevertheless, a radical attitude for the day. She refers to "the dark shadow of slavery" being no more and to her special delight that the "tables were turned" by the freed people from Ferandino who were being sheltered in a building they would never before have been allowed even to enter—the public library.

Forten's noticing of the change in use for the library is particularly significant. Having been raised in a remarkably active family, in which both the women and the men provided her with models of political activism and models of excellence in cultural achievements, Forten held a passion both to achieve and to serve. She wrote often in her diary about her hopes. At nineteen, for example, after her father, Robert Forten, had granted her permission to continue her education, she wrote:

At last I have received the long expected letter, which to my great joy, contains the early desired permission to remain. I thank father very much for his kindness, and am determined that so far as I am concerned, he shall never have cause to regret it. I will spare no effort to become what he desires that I should be; to prepare myself well for the responsible duties of a teacher, and to live for the good that I can do my oppressed and suffering fellow creatures. (1988:105)

Throughout this period, Forten demonstrated her love of learning, keeping an amazing account of the books she read (more than one hundred are referred to) and other literary activities. She found, as she stated in her diary, that books were a special blessing:

And how blessed it is that the wealth of the ages can be ours, if we choose to grasp it! That we can live, not in this century, this corner of the world alone, but in every century, every age, and every clime! That we can listen to the words of orators, poets and sages; that we can enter into every conflict, share every joy, thrill with every noble deed, known since the world began. And hence are books to us a treasure and a blessing unspeakable. (Forten 1988:361)

An assessment of Forten's activities shows that she did indeed prepare herself well for teaching, and that the opportunity for her to fulfill the companion goal, to serve, came with the Battle for Port Royal Sound and the launching of the Port Royal Experiment.

With the encouragement of John Greenleaf Whittier, renowned poet and family friend, Forten applied to be a teacher in South Carolina through both the New England Commission, which did not agree to support her request, and the Port Royal Relief Association, which did accept her—the only African American woman to be included on the initial teams. These pioneers would be stationed across the network of islands, with Forten being sent to St. Helena Island to work with Laura Towne and Ellen Murray, two white women. In September 1862, Towne and Murray had set up the Penn School, named in honor of William Penn and the state from which Towne, Murray, and Forten came.

On Tuesday, October 28, 1862, at the age of twenty-five Forten arrived on St. Helena and sailed into history as the first African American woman to participate in the very first federal-tax-supported effort to educate African Americans.[18] Her training for this moment had been thorough. Her education had begun in the Lombard Street Primary School in Philadelphia, a school operated at that time by her aunt, Margaretta Forten. When Forten was ready for additional education, her father arranged for her to live in Salem, Massachusetts, with a family friend and fellow abolitionist, Charles Lenox Remond, his wife Amy Remond, and their children.[19] In Salem, Forten became the first African American to attend the Higginson Grammar School. At graduation, her poem, "A Parting Hymn," was selected as the best in the class, and it was honored at the graduation ceremony. After the Higginson School, Forten enrolled in the second class of the newly founded Salem Normal School (now Salem State College), where again at graduation her valedictory poem was honored. This poem was published a month later in William Lloyd Garrison's newspaper, the *Liberator,* marking the beginning of Forten's long and illustrious career as a highly respected writer.

After graduation from the Salem Normal School, Forten became the first African American to teach at the Epes Grammar School in Salem, where she gained support and recognition from her students, their families, and the town in general for the excellence of her teaching. Three years later, she accepted a position at the Higginson School where she had been a student earlier. During these years, Forten continued to write, publishing a short story in the *Ladies' Home Journal,* poetry in the *Christian Recorder,* and poetry and an essay in the *National Anti-Slavery Standard.*

Throughout this period, in addition to her academic preparation, Forten was also an active member of the Salem Female Anti-Slavery Society. She tirelessly attended speeches and other abolitionist activities in Salem and in nearby Boston. Further, as she had in her own home in Philadelphia, as a tenant in the home of Charles Remond, the most renowned Black abolitionist of the day, she had the opportunity to meet and interact in a sustained manner with national and international leaders—writers, political activists, intellectuals. In addition to her own family members, the list included Harriet Tubman, John Greenleaf Whittier, Wendell Phillips, Harriet Martineau, William Lloyd Garrison, William Wells Brown, Lydia Marie Child, and many, many others.

When Forten joined the Port Royal Association and traveled to St. Helena Island, she took with her a sense of ethos that had been defined by a history of academic success, a history of success as a writer, and training in the curriculum of northeastern schools and academies. Moreover, Forten evidenced a social consciousness that had been hewn within the richness of her family's political commitments; their circle of equally dedicated friends and acquaintances; and the politically and culturally active communities in Philadelphia and Salem in which she had lived. Forten was well positioned, then, to participate in the operation of a school on St. Helena Island as a twenty-five-year-old woman ready to teach and to "live for the good that she could do."

At the Penn School, Forten worked assiduously to form meaningful relationships with the community despite their being suspicious of her elite bearing. Fundamentally, the great majority of enslaved people, especially ones who had been isolated as this community had been on the coastal islands, had neither seen nor imagined before even the possibility of a Black person of Forten's achievements—well-educated, well-dressed, so much the genteel lady. They had to adjust to Forten, and Forten, being of a different class and personal history, also had to adjust to them. In the meantime, she taught them reading, writing, oral recitation, numbers, music, and whatever else seemed handy to share. She sought to instill pride, self-respect, and self-sufficiency. She tended to her students, their families, and the wounded soldiers who still occupied the island and who from their island camp were frequently engaged in the war that raged around them.

Forten, however, had never been particularly strong physically. She suffered bouts of illness throughout her life that she described in her diary most often as "lung fever." Physically, therefore, she found the Sea Island environment harsh. The heat was intense. The fleas, mosquitos, and other insects were unbearable in summer. The sparsely furnished housing was drafty in winter. There were few comforts or luxuries and much disease, but Forten was committed to the task and remained steadfastly at her post until May 1864.[20] In her committing herself to this project, one additional circumstance, however, added to the general framing of her historical contribution. I hypothesize that surrounding Forten's achievements was an atmosphere of a basic lack of regard, created by the ways that Forten's white coworkers viewed her. By all evidence, she was generally well considered by Towne and Murray, but not quite as a co-equal.

Laura Towne, in her diary entries at the beginning of her work on St. Helena, described the freed people she met in bestial terms. She considered them strange, ignorant, barbaric, and unrefined: "it certainly takes great nerve to walk here among the soldiers and negroes and not be disgusted or shocked or pained so much as to give it all up" (Holland 1855:7). To her credit, Towne did not give up, however. She later seemed proud of the "naturalness" with which she and her household (with no mention of Forten being a member of this household) could sit down with "two colored people," Miss Lynch and Mr. Freeman who were "educated and talked well"—when, in fact, one might assume that she sat down with an educated African American woman every day and also worked with her and interacted with her constantly. She wrote, "I actually forget these people are black, and it is only when I see them at a distance and cannot recognize their features that I remember it. The conversation at dinner flowed just as naturally as if we were Northern whites" (Holland 1855:146).

It is clear from Towne's record of service at the Penn School that her personal experiences among African Americans mediated the sense of racial strangeness that she felt existed between the African Americans and herself. The years of personal interactions in all likelihood shifted her attitudes away from a viewpoint that African Americans are "beasts" toward a more positive view and greater expectations. What also becomes evident in Towne's diary, however, is that the need for such mediation in the early days of the school affected how Forten would be treated as an African American woman in Towne's household. Towne provided considerable detail about daily life on St. Helena; she allowed Forten only a minimal presence in her story, however. For example, she does not ac-knowledge Forten's arrival to the school as a new faculty member. She does not mention their professional or personal relationship as members of the same household mutually committed to a task they both perceived to be noble. She did not acknowledge Forten's departure from the island. In fact, Towne mentioned Forten only three times during the full two years that Forten shared her living and working space.

More to the point of this analysis, Towne gives no indication that Forten was an experienced and respected teacher (unlike herself, who had medical training but no teaching experience); or that Forten was a recog-nized poet; or that she was the person responsible for John Greenleaf Whitter writing "Whittier's Hymn" for the school's 1863 Christmas pro-gram. Towne reports this event in her diary but with no indication of Forten's role as anything other than the person who decorated the room for the program. In fact, given the account of Penn School life in Towne's diary, without the juxtaposition of the account in Forten's diary, a reader would be hard-pressed to think of "Lottie" as anything other than a ser-vant. Forten exists in Towne's world and imagination very much in the way that Toni Morrison describes in *Playing in the Dark* (1992).[21] Forten is part of the unarticulated backdrop against which Towne's story is writ-ten and acquires meaning.

Despite this tableau of dispropriation, however, Forten did not ac-knowledge in her diaries that relationships with Towne or Murray were at all problematic. In all likelihood, she was not privy to Towne's diary and the lack of presence awarded her in it, and Towne apparently offered no direct barrier to her day-to-day work. Instead, Forten concentrated, not on a general atmosphere of non-regard, but on doing the good that she could do. Her entries demonstrated that she was less concerned about her personal trials and tribulations than she was about using her experiences, her expertise, and her network of resources in the interest of helping the most downtrodden of her community, of her race. With this focus, Forten set quite a standard of excellence and left a lasting impression on the St. Helena community.

During her years on St. Helena, Forten published two letters in the *Liberator* and two essays in the *Atlantic Monthly.* She shared with her reading public perceptions of life in the Sea Islands. After her Port Royal experiences, she continued to write poetry and to contribute frequently to the periodical press, becoming nationally known for her achievements as a writer. Later, she married Reverend Francis K. Grimké, a noted clergyman and spokesperson for African American people. At his side, she continued a life of advocacy and community activism, primarily in Florida and Washington, D.C., and in 1896, after decades of service, she joined forces with hundreds of other African American women across the United States and became a founding member of the National Association of Colored Women (NACW).

After Charlotte Forten resigned from the Penn School, it continued to thrive and to make a critical difference in the educational lives of the people of this area. Laura Towne continued to operate the school until her death in 1901. In 1900, during the era of industrial education, the name of the school was changed to the Penn Normal, Industrial, and Agricultural School. The curriculum, however, was broad and included vocational, agricultural, and academic offerings, with the primary mission of the school being the production of teachers who could serve their community's educational needs.

In 1948, Beaufort County began offering public education to St. Helena Island, which then shifted the mission of the Penn School from providing schooling to providing community development services in the ongoing interest of supporting the full participation of the people of St. Helena in political, economic, and cultural life. With this change in mission, the institution had yet another name change. It became The Penn Center, Inc., as it is today. In the 1960s The Penn Center served as a retreat and training center for the civil rights movement, and it began securing a new place nationally and internationally as a site for meetings, informal educational training, leadership training, business training, and other community development activities. In 1974, this fifty acre site was designated a National Historic Landmark, and it remains today an invaluable resource to the residents of St. Helena, as well as to others around the world.

The Opening Doors of Opportunity

Throughout the pre–Civil War era, African Americans helped themselves to literacy in provocative and creative ways (M. Davis 1981:266), but after the Civil War they were energized to take supreme advantage of what had previously been denied them. This energy was cycled in three ways: the Sabbath school movement; the missionary school movement; and the common or public school movement. In discussing the Sabbath school movement, James D. Anderson (1988) explains that we actually know very little about this system. We do know that, before the rise of "free" or "public" schools, these church-sponsored, community-run schools provided basic literacy instruction—in the North before the Civil War (Katy Ferguson's school in New York, for example), and especially after the Civil War in communities of ex-slaves across the South. This system was run predominantly by African Americans themselves and operated in the evenings and on weekends, reaching thousands of students who did not have the option of attending week-day schools. In this way, the African American community itself was largely responsible for laying the fertile foundation for universal literacy in African American communities.

Anderson reports that conservative estimates prepared by the Freedmen's Bureau in 1869 indicate there were 1,512 Sabbath schools with 6,146 teachers and 107,109 students (1988:13). Anderson goes on to state:

> Sabbath schools continued to grow in the black community long after Reconstruction. In 1868 the African Methodist Episcopal church (AME), for example, enrolled 40,000 pupils in its Sabbath schools. By 1885, the AME church reported having "200,000 children in Sunday schools" for "intellectual and moral" instruction. These Sunday schools were not devoted entirely to Bible study. . . . Universal education was certain to become a reality in black society, not because ex-slaves were motivated by childlike, irrational, and primitive drives, but because they were a responsible and politically self-conscious social class. (13–15)

Anderson emphasizes that the energy with which free Blacks and ex-slaves pursued efforts to universalize education in African American communities helped to spur general efforts across the South to take control of educational opportunity and to institute mass education for whites (poor and elite) and also for African Americans (26–27).

A second effort toward literacy development was the missionary school movement. During the Civil War, various northern community and church organizations intensified their "home" mission activities, as compared with their "foreign" mission activities. These efforts became a

primary mechanism for the advocacy of freedom, justice, and empowerment. These types of activities began in 1862 when the Port Royal Commission sent a corps of teachers to South Carolina, with the white missionaries often bringing with them (as Laura Towne did) a desire to
work—but also patronizing attitudes and opinions of African American
people that were based on racial stereotypes rather than on significant
personal experience. Despite such attitudes, missionary activities escalated through the end of the Civil War and afterward. In the years immediately following emancipation, northern missionary groups joined
hands with many communities of African American men and women in
their educational enterprises, and they remained for almost three decades
a primary means for educational advocacy across the South. Both groups
(missionaries who were northern whites and African Americans, and the
southern African Americans) worked together tirelessly to eradicate illit-
eracy, even though confronted by the dangers of racism and sexism, as
well as by the devastation of extreme poverty.

As indicated by the research of Jones (1985), the largest of the missionary organizations was the American Missionary Association (AMA),
which supported more than 5,000 teachers in the South between 1861 and
1876. In Georgia from 1865 to 1873, these groups sent approximately 368
teachers, 7 of whom were known to be African American women, and
this story repeats itself throughout the southern states. Records preserve
some names of African American women—Mary S. Peake, Emma V.
Brown, Sara G. Stanley, Ellen Garrison Jackson, and Blanche V. Harris—
but many others remain nameless in the background (Sterling 1984:261–
305).

The volunteers of the home mission societies formed a significant part
of the literacy workforce in urban areas and in rural ones until the early
1870s when the third effort emerged, the common school movement.
During the 1870s, southern leaders rose to regain their authority by supporting the education of African Americans through the establishing of
public schools. In large part, southern gentlemen sought to reduce the influence of northern liberals, who came with humanitarian ideals to educate and uplift the deprived and downtrodden to a fuller participation as
American citizens. Many of these southern gentlemen saw the political
and economic advantage of a literate African American population, but

they also abhorred the apparent desires of northerners to re-create a northeastern culture and to denigrate southern social order and habits. Southern leaders were aided in this quest by many industrial philanthropists, who sought to maintain the status quo, to push industrial models of education, and to discourage liberal arts education.

No matter the form of its coming, however, the rise in educational opportunity for African Americans in general—and, by extension, to African American women—was greeted as manna from heaven. A case in point is the development of public schools in the city of Atlanta, Georgia.[22] In 1871 Atlanta opened its first public school for African Americans, the Gate City School or the Fourth Ward School, referred to locally as the Houston Street School. It was operated by African Americans, many of whom had been trained at Atlanta University, established in 1865 by the AMA. Shortly thereafter, the Atlanta school board also opened the Roach Street, Pittsburg, and Summer Hill schools. Many African American parents saw this opportunity for advancement and took it. They welcomed the chance for free education for their children and for themselves, and they were eager to learn. The schools literally overflowed with students, giving rise in short order to overcrowding, inadequate resources, and of course underpaid teachers.

Schools of Their Own

Some African American parents, ones with the resources to take advantage of other options, typically did not favor public schools. They did not want to subject their children to the abuse of white southerners or to a southern-designed system of "Black" education, which they knew to be inferior. They preferred private schools such as the Morris Brown Grade School in Atlanta that were still being run by philanthropic support, with a significant percentage of that support coming from the freed men and women themselves.

Such is the history of Spelman College, which began as a seminary on April 11, 1881, with the support of the Women's Baptist Home Mission Society along with the African American men and women who supported the Black Baptist churches in the Atlanta community and throughout the state of Georgia. The founders were Sophia B. Packard and Harriet E. Giles (two white women from Salem, Massachusetts) who came to At-

lanta at the invitation of Father Frank Quarles, the pastor of Friendship
Baptist Church. This triad had the goal of starting a school for recently
freed African American women and girls. After seeing in their travels in
the South the devastating conditions for African American women in the
aftermath of slavery and the Civil War, these two women, who had been
trained and had taught in seminaries in New England, determined that
the need for schooling among African American women was especially
critical. Their perception fitted perfectly with the desire of Father Quarles
and his church membership to educate the girls of their community, especially since a school for the boys—the Atlanta Baptist Seminary, later to
become Morehouse College, had been established in 1867.

Such efforts were repeated across the South as a network of private
schools was established that would ultimately form the core of what today is the collective of historically African American private colleges and
universities. This collective started with Wilberforce University in Ohio
and Lincoln University in Pennsylvania, both of which were established
in 1854. The core group was expanded during the era of the Morrill Act,
passed in 1862 and renewed in 1890. This act gave rise to land grant institutions and the establishing of the contemporary network of historically
African American public colleges and universities. This network of public
and private institutions continues today, at the beginning of the twenty-
first century, having forged a remarkable historical record for the education of African American people.

As the history of these institutions suggests, during the post–Civil War
era, seminary education became a welcome resource to the African
American community and gave rise to stories of learning and achievement that continue (as in the case of Spelman), over a century later. Clara
Howard is one such story (Royster 1993a:586–87; Guy-Sheftall and Stewart 1981:98; Read 1961:116,350). Howard was born in Greenville, Georgia,
on January 23, 1866, one of nine siblings. She was taught the basic skills by
her father, a literate skilled worker and local business man, who after the
Civil War moved from Greenville to Atlanta to increase economic and educational opportunities for his family. He refused to send Howard to
public school, choosing instead Spelman Seminary, whose leaders and
teachers he respected and whose brand of liberal arts education he felt to
be worthy. These teachers were known for holding steadfastly to stan-

dards of excellence that replicated to some extent the New England experience they themselves had known as students and teachers in the seminaries there.

Howard was a member of the first graduating class of Spelman in 1887, and she was one of the first Spelman graduates to teach as a missionary in Africa, serving in the French Congo (1890–1895) and Panama (1896–1897). She was a devout Christian in her beliefs, as her family had been, and committed herself in these early years to serving the communities she felt were in the most dire need. In choosing foreign missions as an arena for contribution, Howard faced many dangers. First, as one of the few women of her generation to be awarded her own missionary assignments (instead of an assignment issued to a husband), Howard faced the perils of an African American woman traveling alone with no protection from either systemic or random acts of racism or sexism. She faced peril also from physical dangers in what were at that time uncharted geographical regions filled, in the case of Africa, with wild animals, with people potentially hostile to imperialist encroachment, and with high probabilities for devastating and deadly diseases.

By 1897 Howard was forced to end her service as a missionary because of recurring bouts of malaria, but not before demonstrating that her desire was to educate and uplift in the same way that Sophia Packard and Harriet Giles (the principals at Spelman) had done in her own case. Howard was joined in this endeavor by other Spelman alumnae such as Nora Gordon, Emma Delaney, Margaret Rattray, Ora Milner Horton, Flora Zeto Malekebu, many of whom were African-born, and a line of Spelman women even today who continue to choose Africa as their vineyard. Most of these women were teachers and established schools that still exist all of these decades later.

When her missionary service was over, Howard returned to Spelman to become a long-term staff member and an active member of the Atlanta community, ministering to and advising generation after generation of students whose lives she was able to touch and to inspire. She left behind a legacy of service, as well as evidence of her commitment to "humanity," and to "the race," broadly defined. On November 23, 1969, Spelman College dedicated a dormitory, Howard-Harreld, in honor of Clara A. Howard, its first seminary graduate, and Claudia White Harreld, its first college graduate, both of whom had distinguished careers as educators and humanitarians. Howard and her contemporaries led lives of commitment, inspiring many and providing a type of nurturing support that also required those in their charge to think well of themselves, expect much of themselves, and work steadfastly to do good works in the service of others.

Another early Spelman Seminary graduate was Selena Sloan Butler, Class of 1888. Butler was born in Thomasville, Georgia, on January 4, 1872. She was educated by missionaries who encouraged her to continue her education. She was sponsored at Spelman by her minister and received a diploma in Spelman's second graduating class in 1888. For the next five years, Butler taught English and elocution in the Atlanta public schools and later at the state normal school in Tallahassee, Florida (later to become Florida A & M University). In 1893 she married Henry Rutherford Butler, a graduate of Lincoln University and the Meharry Medical College. Butler's husband continued his studies at Harvard Medical School and she attended the Emerson School of Oratory. Elocution and oratorical training were common interests practiced among African American women during this era, in support of their obvious desires to develop public-speaking abilities. In 1895 Butler and her husband returned to Atlanta—her husband to practice medicine, and Butler to teach.

In the years that followed, Butler built a distinctive record as a public speaker, locally and nationally, and as a community activist. Among her many accomplishments:

She was a delegate, representing the Atlanta women's Club at the founding convention of the National Association of Colored Women in 1896.

She organized, in her home, the first kindergarten for African American children in Atlanta, for twenty neighborhood children, since, even by the turn of the century, she could not find a preschool for her son.

She established, edited, and printed the *Woman's Advocate* from 1906 to 1907, a four-page newspaper devoted to news and problems of particular interest to African American women.

She was active in World War I with an entertainment group associated with Camp Gordon, near Atlanta, and in charge of the Auburn Avenue branch for the sales and distribution of War Savings Stamps and Certificates.

She was founder and first president of the Georgia Congress of Colored Parents and Teachers, in 1920 (African American parents were not allowed member-

ship in the already established white parent-teacher organizations); and with Alice McLelland Birney was cofounder of the National Congress of Parents and
Teachers Associations, in 1926.

She was appointed by President Herbert Hoover in 1934 to serve on the White
House Conference of Child Health and Protection, after having served as chair
of the Colored Division of the Georgia State Committee on Race Relations and
as a member of the Georgia Commission on Interracial Cooperation.

She was asked by the American Red Cross in World War II to head a corps of
Gray Ladies (the only known African American group in the United States at
that time) for service to soldiers in the hospital at Fort Huachuca, Arizona,
where she was living at the time with her son, Henry R. Butler Jr., the assistant
chief of Medical Services and the chief of the Cardiovascular Section.[23]

There are other stories also. Mary Ann Brooks, for example, was a student in Spelman's primary department in the morning and taught children in her neighborhood in the afternoon. Victoria Maddox Simmons, a
classmate of Selena Sloan Butler, while still a student taught in the Model
School at Spelman and came back after graduation to teach again in the
Model School. She was one of the first in a long line of Spelman women
who would return to the college as faculty. Eventually, Simmons went on
to fashion a noteworthy career in the public schools, after having given
birth to eight children of her own. In 1956 a public elementary school in
Atlanta was named in her honor.

Another critical point to be made about literacy levels until the turn of
the twentieth century can be illustrated by the research of Elizabeth Ihle
(1986). She reports from her study of Black women's education in the
South that, until relatively recently in our country's history, the most
widespread schooling for any group was elementary schooling. In fact, as
Ihle points out, "for the first four decades after the Civil War, a black person with just three or four years of formal schooling was considered educated by the standards of the day" (Ihle 1986 Modules 3 and 4: page 4).
This situation did not change significantly, especially in the South where
most African Americans lived, until the 1870s and the rise of free public
high schools. Discriminatory practices around race, class, and urban
(versus rural) sites continued to operate, however, well into the twentieth
century. "Between 1900 and 1915, the South established over 600 four-year
public high schools for whites and nearly 600 three-year ones, but only 64
public ones existed for blacks" (Modules 3 and 4: page 5).

These data become instructive in light of the infamous Washington-DuBois debates, as they encoded concern for what should constitute appropriate education for African Americans. Washington made a case for industrial training; whereas DuBois argued for an academic education, especially for the "talented tenth" who could then return to their communities to provide much-needed leadership. Typically, we have viewed this dialogue in terms of post-secondary education, but it was also a critical dimension in debates around post-elementary education as well. By the Washingtonian model, industrial education really began after the acquisition of basic skills such as reading, writing, and arithmetic. There was little or no purpose in this curriculum for including courses in the sciences, languages, literature, or other areas that today we would consider the academic disciplines.

For African American women, then, and especially for those who wished to go beyond basic literacy, there was a litany of obstacles. Opportunities were obviously limited because of race; they were also limited because of class. Poor people, regardless of racial group, were often denied access or were unable to take advantage of opportunities because of the constancy of the struggle simply to provide themselves and their families with food, clothing, and shelter, especially in a context such as the South, which did not particularly value literacy for any non-elites. This class bias indicates also an obstruction based on region. The South, with its elite preferences, was slow in providing educational opportunity, generally, and certainly in providing equal opportunity. Yet another obstruction was population density, in terms of the disparities between opportunities in cities versus the rural areas where most African Americans lived at the time. The obvious point is that African Americans in cities found more opportunities for literacy development than those in rural areas.

Last, but certainly not least, there was the obstruction of gender. Debates were raging concerning the appropriate education of women, especially by the last quarter of the nineteenth century. More insidious, negative stereotypes of African American women grew out of "blame the victim" explanations of their moral character and out of the class- and race-bound images of the "cult of true womanhood" (Du Bois and Gordon 1984; J. Hall 1993; Royster 1997). The dominant group placed African American women at the bottom of an evolutionary scale that privileged white men by a process of "natural" selectivity. This scale defined African American women in the natural order not only as intellectually and socially inferior to others but also as amoral, licentious, and lascivious. After the Civil War, African American women lived in a nation that discounted them at every turn, and it was their job to turn the tide, to acquire literacy in large numbers, and to make this resource count. They faced these challenges as women alone—and as women who came together in a whole collective of community organizations that converged in the 1890s as the Black Clubwomen's Movement (see chapter 5).

Coming to Voice: Maria W. Stewart, a Case in Point

As the story of African American women's literacy gained momentum during the nineteenth century, and especially after the Civil War, what stands out clearly is that during this era they hungered for knowledge in the interest of sustaining both themselves and "the race." They were helped in their struggles by many; they helped themselves; they also helped others. What becomes much clearer, as the contours of specific activities come into view, is that these early generations of women were literally pioneers, who chiseled out for themselves and for others a place that had not been envisioned before. They incorporated into a reconstituted sense of self-in-society traditional patterns of belief and action that remained useful to them throughout the transition from African contexts to American contexts. These pioneers forged new traditions that propelled forward waves of African American women who would use language and literacy to meet expressive and transactional needs, and who would do so significantly in the interest of the community. The pioneers succeeded in going against the grain of cultural expectations by developing what Paulo Freire (1988) calls a "critical consciousness." They reenvisioned their context, reshaped their sense of reality, charted courses of action, including rhetorical actions, that would lay the foundations from which a tradition of literacy and social action would emerge. Such is the case with Maria W. Stewart.

From the testimony of Stewart's first essay (cited earlier), we learn that Stewart's opportunities for formal schooling were minimal and that she was able to acquire literacy mainly through the instruction she received in Sabbath schools. We also learn about the material conditions of her life.

Early in the essay she shares many biographical details, which have now been fleshed out by the research of Marilyn Richardson (1987), who edited and introduced a volume of Stewart's writings.[24] Maria Miller was born in Hartford, Connecticut, in 1803, where she was "bound out" (hired out to work) at the age of five in the home of a clergyman. At fifteen, she had completed her indenture and left this household, and (by M. Richardson's reckoning) she supported herself as a domestic servant. At the age of twenty-three in Boston, Massachusetts, she married forty-seven-year-old James W. Stewart, a financially successful shipping agent who outfitted whaling and fishing vessels. With this marriage, Maria W. (from her husband's middle initial) Stewart moved into the African American "middle class" society in Boston, a small but politically active group who managed to acquire some level of financial security amid discriminatory employment and housing practices and who were very successful in achieving a status of respect within their own racial group.

As members of this small group of elites, the Stewarts witnessed a time of lively social and political activities and the emergence of men, both locally and nationally, who continued the struggle for change and who revitalized long-standing commitments to abolition. Two examples of this leadership illustrate this point. The first example, the minister who married the Stewarts, is Reverend Thomas Paul (1773–1831), the founding minister of Boston's African Baptist Church. This church was the site of both educational and political activity in Boston during this era. Under Reverend Paul's leadership, not only was the church the site of a school for African American children, it was also the place where the first meetings of the New England Abolitionist Society were held, illustrating the close ties between literacy activities and political activism in the African American church, as a central community institution.

The second example is David Walker (1785–1830), a person whom Stewart in her first essay called "noble, fearless, and undaunted" (30) and who was clearly an influence on her thinking. Walker was the prosperous owner of a clothing exchange shop, which was used to outfit sailors. This enterprise probably made authorities suspicious that Walker was a conduit for abolitionist materials getting into the South—along with James Stewart, another person in the shipping business and a friend of Walker. Walker was considered questionable for reasons other than the nature of his business, however. He was an outspoken person and an active member of the newly founded Massachusetts General Colored Association (formed in 1826, the year of the Stewarts' marriage). This organization was dedicated to bettering the local conditions of African Americans and to agitating for the abolition of slavery.

Walker was also an agent for and a contributor to *Freedom's Journal,* the first newspaper issued in the United States by African Americans. It was begun in 1827 by John B. Russworm and Samuel B. Cornish with the intent of keeping African Americans abreast of political concerns of the day—including, for example, international liberation struggles (such as in Greece, Poland, and Haiti) and slave uprisings in the South. The perception of Walker as a militant radical, however, resulted in large part from the publication in October 1829 of his appeal, "To the Coloured Citizens of the World." This manifesto was an incendiary declaration that unequivocally denounced American slavery as vicious and that, just as unequivocally, encouraged slave uprisings (see Walker 1993).

In addition to the political activism within its African American community, Boston was also the city where white abolitionists William Lloyd Garrison and Isaac Knapp published the *Liberator,* an anti-slavery newspaper, from January 1, 1831, to December 29, 1865. The printer for the paper was Stephen Foster, who was assisted in this responsibility by his African American apprentice Thomas Paul (Cain 1995:5), presumably the same Thomas Paul who was the pastor of the African Baptist Church. To be noted is that the readership of the *Liberator* was overwhelmingly African American. According to William E. Cain (1995):

the bulk of the support—three-quarters of the subscription list—derived from the free black population in the North. By the close of the first year, there were only fifty white subscribers; after two years the number was still less than four hundred. Nearly half of the mailings were to New York, Philadelphia, and Boston, where significant numbers of blacks resided . . . its maximum number of subscribers never exceeded 2,500–3,000 range. (5)

The 1820s and 1830s, therefore, were a time of intense political activity in the African American community, as these decades most certainly were also a time of massive ill-treatment of African Americans. As a slaveholding nation, the United States was a place where racism and white supremacy reigned unchecked, such that despite their free status, African Americans in Boston and other cities were continually subjected to job discrimination, inferior housing, insult, and injury at the will of those who oppressed them (Quarles 1969). Maria and James Stewart were very much a part of this scene.

On December 17, 1829, three years after their marriage, James Stewart died after a sudden illness, and Maria Stewart's financial status experienced a downward spiral. Although her husband was a relatively wealthy man and she should have received, therefore, a substantial inheritance (according to his will, one-third of his estate), the reality for Stewart was quite different. Her husband's white business colleagues were determined to get everything, and they had the power, privilege, and authority to do so. Stewart took them to court, but after two years of legal battling in which she experienced blatant displays of discrimination for both her race and her gender, she found herself stripped almost totally of all that he had owned. She was incensed by the discrimination and the injustice. Exacerbating this indignation was another event that occurred only six months after her husband's death. On June 18, 1830, David Walker, Stewart's hero, was found dead near the doorway of his clothing shop.

By all these events and more, Stewart was made keenly aware of the oppressions that encircled her and her race, from the harsh working conditions she had endured as a child to the discriminatory treatment she had received in court. In 1831, after two years of loss and debilitating circumstances, Stewart's response to this situation was twofold. On one hand, she chose to cling to her spiritual beliefs, finding a strength and solace that compelled her to confess publicly her faith in Christ. Her second response was more unusual. Stewart had the desire to speak out publicly about discrimination and injustice and about the need for political and economic activism. In this era, women were not granted this privilege. The woman's role in society dictated that such actions were unseemly, a violation of "woman's place." Women were not public speakers; men were. Women's domain was not politics or public discourse; it was in the home. Despite the many ways that African American women's working lives were not spent in their own homes, this view of woman's sphere still constrained how they were permitted to participate in their worlds. Regardless of whether women held complementary interests, or sustained parallel circles of activity among their own gender, the public political scene in the African American community—as it was in the nation at large—was dominated by men. Maria Stewart's desires to speak, therefore, went against the prevailing tide of her times. Consequently, it was remarkable that she permitted herself the desire to speak; it was much more remarkable that she was assertive enough to find a means to do it.

Against the backdrop of this era and the challenging circumstances of her own personal history, Maria Miller Stewart constitutes a distinctive case among African American women, and especially for an analysis of the convergence of literacy with the desire to be an agent for change. Stewart lived in the actively political context of Boston. She lived among men who worked energetically and aggressively to claim their rights to life, liberty, and the pursuit of happiness as equals among men. She lived among women who seconded this claim and worked just as energetically and aggressively to support their families and to sustain their communities. These women contributed financially to the stability of their homes through the jobs they held. They worked actively in their churches and their clubs to educate themselves and their children, to keep informed about the community's needs, to find ways to lend a helping hand in addressing these needs. Stewart lived among people who valued education highly and who used literacy, especially during this era of the rise of the African American press, to facilitate their activities and to proclaim justice and empowerment for all. Stewart was situated, therefore, in a context in which reform was not just interesting but deemed critical to survival.

Not only was the context around her instructive, Stewart gained wisdom also from her own experiences. She knew—concretely and personally—hard work, racial slurs and insults, discrimination, and domination. She did not have to be told about racism, or white supremacy, or poverty and injustice. Her own life offered clear and present testimony to their existence and to the need for drastic social and political change. Moreover, she had experienced life in a community that was committed to resisting oppression; she had seen firsthand examples of activist leadership and models for lives dedicated to political struggle. Between her husband's death in 1829 and the end of her lawsuit in 1931, however, Stewart had also reflected on her life and conditions. Both widowhood and the need to sue for her inheritance provided lenses (terministic screens) through which she could reconsider her options, or lack of options, as a free woman of color. She had the opportunity to think about how community leaders were responding to such problems, and, given her own frustrations, she was primed to look for remedies. Moreover, Stewart could see from all around her that the African American cause, as mirrored by her own circumstances, was an urgent one.

By these processes, Stewart envisioned a world in which the lives of African American people—and thereby African American women—should be better. She saw specific solutions for the multitude of problems that existed, and she was inspired to use writing to take a political stand, to fashion her own authority to speak, and to articulate mandates for community action. In keeping with Gadamer's view (see chapter 2), Stewart experienced a fusion of horizons. She had a buildup of frustrations in her life at a time when the spirit of reform in her community was intense. This fusion created a space in which she—as a linguistic being, a person capable of voice—was enabled to come to hermeneutic consciousness, that is, to a more substantive sense of herself in the world and to a more critical sense of what is questionable. She could ask with a clearer view of her own authority: Why is there no justice for African Americans? What are these wrongs about? How can we turn this world toward a better path? When shall we see justice? With such questioning, Stewart could also raise for herself the most consistent questions in the struggle among African Americans for change: If not now, when? If not me, who?

Adding to this transformative moment, however, was something extra. As an African American woman, Stewart had an opportunity for the expression of her thoughts in public. She came to voice; selected the essay as her genre of choice; and recognized the existence of a brand new forum for the participation of African Americans in public discourse—the periodical press. In the fall of 1831, she decided to enter the newly opened offices of the *Liberator* to see if Garrison and Knapp would publish her essay, "Religion and the Pure Principles of Morality: The Sure Foundation on Which We Must Build." They did just that, on October 8, 1831.

From this base, Stewart began a three-year stint as a public figure in Boston. During these years she published a pamphlet (1831) and a collection of religious meditations (1832), and she delivered four public lectures (from 1832 to 1834) that were printed in the *Liberator* (xiv). At this point, Stewart ended her public career amid much controversy. She was a woman raising a strident voice and carving a brand new "woman's space" at the podium in a world that did not believe in a public presence for women. To some extent, Stewart was tolerated momentarily, given the status that her husband had held in the community and given the "liberty" that she could demand as his widow. However, Stewart was still, ultimately, a woman (and a young woman at that), and what she did during those three years on the public page and at the podium was deemed inappropriate. She was derided for these actions, and doors in Boston soon closed to her.

Stewart left Boston in 1834 and moved to New York. In 1835, Friends of Freedom and Virtue (as inscribed on the title page) published a collection of her writings entitled *Productions of Mrs. Maria W. Stewart, Presented to the First African Baptist Church & Society, Of The City Of Boston*. This publication was used as part of a collection of abolitionist materials that served to shape and define the reenergized abolitionist activities of this era. Even more significant for African American women, perhaps, is that it also served as inspiration for women coming after Stewart to continue what she had begun. With the growth of the abolitionist movement, there was a rising stream of women speakers—including Sarah Remond, Frances Watkins Harper, Sojourner Truth, Charlotte Forten, Harriet Tubman, and so many others, who would make their voices heard on the page and at the podium.

Much later in her life, in 1879, Stewart published another edition of this collection, adding letters from friends and colleagues and a biographical sketch. Between these two moments of public expression, however, Stewart's commitment to self-improvement, community service, and political activism did not end. In New York, she began a career as a teacher at the Williamsburg colored school. She joined a female literary society. She attended the Anti-Slavery Convention of American Women in New York in May 1837. She also continued to lecture. According to the biographical sketch included in the 1879 collection, Stewart left New York in 1852 but continued her teaching career in Baltimore and Washington, D.C. During these years, her account indicates she was constantly in dire financial straits, teaching as she found the opportunity to do so. Ultimately, Stewart took a position as matron of the Freedmen's Hospital (now the Howard University Hospital), where she lived, managed housekeeping needs, and continued to teach. In December 1879, Stewart died in this hospital, but not before she had submitted and won a claim to receive a pension as the widow of a war veteran, based on federal legislation passed in 1878 permitting such claims. She was able to document that her husband had served in the U.S. Navy during the War of 1812. With this last public act, Stewart demonstrated once again two of the moral principles that fired her soul: (1) the law should bring justice for all; and (2) African Americans, even a seventy-six-year-old African American woman, should insist on claiming their legal rights and should work tirelessly to make the system work for everyone.

The Formation of Ethos

One of the first tasks a writer faces is the need to form an ethos, a way of being in the world, that permits the writer to create and present to the world a dynamic speaking and writing self. An analysis of ethos formation among African American women benefits from the use of two terms used by Sharon Crowley (1994). *Situated ethos* acknowledges the existence of power relationships within the communicative environment, and the need, in this case, for African American women to define themselves against stereotypes and cultural expectations. *Invented ethos* acknowledges the need of these writers, therefore, to invent themselves in writing space and to create their own sense of authority, agency, and power within the text.

Coming to voice for Maria W. Stewart was a multilayered act of defiance, but the very defiance of it serves to reaffirm the sense of mission she consistently articulates. In her first essay, "Religion and the Pure Principles of Morality," Stewart says:

Feeling a deep solemnity of soul, in view of our wretched and degraded situation, and sensible of the gross ignorance that prevails among us, I have thought proper thus publicly to express my sentiments before you. . . . [I] have merely written the meditations of my heart as far as my imagination led; and have presented them before you in order to arouse you to exertion, and to enforce upon your minds the great necessity of turning your attention to knowledge and improvement. (28)

First of all, clearly Stewart is not just meditating. She intends to have a public audience; she clearly wants to "arouse [them] to exertion," to action, with the specific action including "attention to knowledge and improvement." Her ethical move, however, is to use a typical apologetic strategy in the classical rhetorical tradition, that is, to assume a stance of modesty and to appeal for the generosity of her audience's judgment. In assuming this stance, Stewart acknowledges how unusual it was for a woman to speak, but she justifies this breach of proper behavior on two counts. One is the claim of extreme circumstances. From her point of view, the "wretched and degraded situation" of African American people—both enslaved and free—signaled crisis and demanded voice, even her voice.

A second claim, however, is that her authority to speak comes not from her own desire but from God:

> I am sensible of my ignorance; but such knowledge as God has given me, I impart to you. I am sensible of former prejudices; but it is high time for prejudices and animosities to cease from among us. I am sensible of exposing myself to calumny and reproach; but shall I, for fear of feeble man who shall die, hold my peace? Shall I for fear of scoffs and frowns, refrain my tongue? Ah, no! I speak as one that must give an account at the awful bar of God; I speak as a dying mortal to dying mortals. O, ye daughters of Africa, awake! Awake! Arise! No longer sleep nor slumber, but distinguish yourselves. (30)

Stewart acknowledges the distance between what she is doing as a woman in public space and what social mores dictate is more appropriate behavior. She claims authority, though, based on both the urgency of the need and her intention to do what God wills her to do. In centering this authority in God, she claims for herself and all "daughters of Africa" an equal right and responsibility to develop God-given talents and abilities and to use them for righteousness:

> From the moment I experienced the change [that is, the change brought on by her public profession of faith], I felt a strong desire, with the help and assistance of God, to devote the remainder of my days to piety and virtue, and now possess that spirit of independence that, were I called upon, I would willingly sacrifice my life for the cause of God and my brethren. (29)

With this essay, Stewart is indeed proclaiming that she has obviously been "called upon" to speak or she would not, out of respect for modesty and propriety, be speaking. Her very first words recognize the power structures surrounding her and the distribution, or lack thereof, of privileges. Stewart presents herself as a "true follower of Christ," a woman made free of "former prejudices" and worldly concerns (such as female propriety, life and death) by her belief in the will of God and by her devotion to righteousness. In creating a speaking self, Stewart recognizes the social practices but situates herself outside these traditional expectations—and righteously so.

In a different essay, "Mrs. Stewart's Farewell Address" (65–74), Stewart continues to work on establishing her entitlement to speak, or rather (in this essay), her right to have spoken. In saying goodbye, she does not simply set herself outside social expectations. What she does instead is to subvert what constitutes these expectations by extending the boundaries to include her biblical and historical forebears, other women who responded to their worlds in the way she was responding to hers: Deborah, Esther, and Mary Magdalene from the Bible; the Greek Oracles; the Roman Sibyls. She claims them as models we should not forget, and she underscores by their example the notion that women have indeed always spoken out. Stewart contextualizes her behavior within the historical fabric of women's lives over time, demonstrating that she is neither the first nor the only one, and that she should not be the last. With both claims, being entitled by God and situating herself within the history of women's public discourse, Stewart defines herself as an instrument of God, seeking to bring His word in Jeremiad fashion, to bear in order to "promote the good of souls" (41) and to appeal for righteous behavior.[25]

Stewart conveys a view of herself as a politically conscious evangelist. She sees evils in the world that could be addressed through the goodwill, hard work, and the good sense of men and women, all in the service of the Spirit. In reflecting on the atypical nature of her actions at the end of her first essay, she says:

what I have done, has been done with an eye single to the glory of God, and to promote the good of souls. I have neither kindred nor friends. *I stand alone in your midst* [my emphasis], exposed to the fiery darts of the devil, and to the assaults of wicked men. But though all the powers of earth and hell were to combine against me, though all nature should sink into decay, still I would trust in the Lord, and joy in the God of my salvation. For I am full persuaded that he will bring me off conqueror, yea, more than conqueror, through him who hath loved me and given himself for me. (41)

Stewart invents herself in the text as a warrior for righteousness, whose voice becomes a mighty sword in the defense of good against evil. When she says she stands "alone in your midst," she implies she has assumed a place previously unknown in her community, and that assuming this place has come with considerable cost in exposure and vulnerability. She emphasizes, though, that as one who "trusts in the Lord" she is made strong enough to endure whatever comes her way. Stewart also says that from this place, where she has chosen to stand because of her principles, she has become much more attuned to herself in the world, and through this awareness, able to see what is questionable, to put her mind to the task of finding solutions, and to speak about her viewpoints in public. In the quotation above, Stewart indicates that the process of finding this space was for her a clarifying one. She was able to do what she felt she had to do despite "the fiery darts of the devil, and the assaults of wicked men." She found strength in God—a strength that has helped her, and she believes will help others, in the face of complex tasks. She presents herself as a person well fortified by her beliefs, dedicated to using her talents and abilities for good, and, more clearly perhaps than all else, free to speak and to act for righteousness.

The Writer's Choice

In analyzing Stewart's rhetorical choices, there is much to notice. First of all her creation of a speaking self who trusts in the Lord and follows His will serves as a primary mechanism for simultaneously making a space in which her audiences would be willing to interact with her.[26] In a sense, she creates a spot at which they can suspend judgment against her as a woman in public by focusing instead on the urgency of the subject matter. Centralizing the subject matter, then, makes it possible for her to return to the woman speaking and to suggest that credible sources, such as the Bible, Greek literature, Roman literature, and so on, all chronicle examples of other women who because of similar moments of urgency have spoken out in public about important subjects. The critical difference that Stewart underscores, again, is the urgency, the lack of desire for personal gain, and the need to use all of the community's resources, including the intellectual powers of its women. Stewart's essays put emphasis on the message, not the messenger.

Stewart directs her essay toward "people of color," as Garrison's editorial remarks point out at the beginning of the text. She "calls out," however, a broad range of readers by direct or indirect address. Daughters of Africa, brethren, and friends constitute the primary audience to whom she speaks, but she also speaks to different configurations within this group, and to others who are more likely to constitute "overhearers," people that she wished to have listen but who are probably not paying attention. Beyond the three groups (daughters of Africa, brethren, and friends), her audience categories include Africa's sons, parents, children, maidens, youths (males), those more powerful and eloquent, virtuous women, "the church" (that is, spiritually minded men and mothers in Israel), backsliding children, mothers. In the category of "overhearers," Stewart speaks expressively, as indicated by the exclamatory form of the sentences, to "America" and to "great and mighty men of America." With each of these groups, Stewart would like God to "Raise up sons and daughters unto Abraham, and grant that there might come a mighty shaking of dry bones among us, and a great ingathering of souls" (34). She wants action. She states her purpose in short order, in the very first paragraph: "to arouse you to exertion" and "to enforce upon your minds the great necessity of turning your attention to knowledge and improvement."

If we accept Stewart's construction of her authority to speak as emanating from her dedication to serving the will of God, then the message that she proclaims in support of these purposes is brought *by* her but *from* God, rather than from herself. She states these messages in several variations, but in the main she uses this essay to name (that is, to restate) a three-part problem: specifying, from her point of view, not just that the conditions for African Americans are wretched and degraded but to contextualize this fact in a way that permits her audience to see and understand what could and should be going on in the face of this situation. Stewart says: "It is not the color of the skin that makes the man, but it is the principles formed within the soul" (29).

In other words, she asserts that African Americans need to get clearer about the principles that "form their 'souls,' to see that their souls are equal in value and possibility to other men's souls," and to claim, therefore, their rights. "We need never to think that anybody is going to feel interested for us, if we do not feel interested for ourselves. That day we, as a people, hearken unto the voice of the Lord, our God, and walk in his ways and ordinances . . . that day the Lord will raise us up, and enough to aid and befriend us, and we shall begin to flourish" (38). She clearly presents the view that African Americans should not wait for others to do for them what they could do now for themselves. "Oh then, turn your attention to knowledge and improvement; for knowledge is power. . . . Let nothing be lacking on your part; and in God's own time, and his time is certainly the best, he will surely deliver you with a mighty hand and with an outstretched arm" (41). She reminds the groups that if African Americans do what they can do for themselves, then they can be quite confident the Lord will bring down his wrath—that is, vengeance—on those who continue to commit wrongs against them.

In addition to the delivery of these messages in all their variations, Stewart offers specific strategies in their support, strategies that can be categorized generally in four ways: religious arguments, invoking passages from the Bible that support the notion that all are created equal in the eyes of God; legal arguments, invoking the Constitution of the United States as a document that has inscribed this view into the law of the land; economic arguments, outlining in specific terms actions that can be taken by women and men in order to achieve financial stability for the community and to strengthen its institutions (schools, businesses, churches); and self-improvement arguments, asserting that the African American community needs to take responsibility for moving itself forward and not wait for the kindnesses of others. Stewart takes her readers on a winding view of specific, concrete choices for making their world better. She draws together the heart, the mind, and the soul in suggesting across logical, ethical, and pathetic arguments that there really are many, many things that can be done if, as Freire suggests in his context, "there might be a thorough reformation among us" (1988:36). Freire's term for reformation was the development of a "critical consciousness." Stewart, in a similar way, is talking about "religion" (listening to God rather than man) and the "pure principles of morality" (doing what we know to be right and good). Stewart's reformation calls for the uniting of a compassionate heart, a principled soul, and an active mind under the rubric of living by the word of God. It is no surprise, therefore, that although many of her arguments are rooted in logos and strongly rational, what shines through most distinctly are those rooted in pathos. One example of this latter strength is her exclamation to America:

Oh, America, America, foul and indelible is thy stain! Dark and dismal is the cloud that hangs over thee, for thy cruel wrongs and injuries to the fallen sons of Africa. The blood of her murdered ones cries to heaven for vengeance against thee. Thou art almost become drunken with the blood of her slain; thou hast enriched thyself through her toils and labors; and now thou refuseth to make even a small return. And thou hast caused the daughters of Africa to commit whore-doms and fornications; but upon thee be their curse. (39)

This passage especially, in its prophecy of retributions to come, illustrates that Stewart's essays can be comfortably placed within the Black Jeremiad tradition (Howard-Pitney 1990), as she situates her meaning against prevailing cultural myths about the glory of the nation.

One last point to be made about Stewart's rhetorical choices is her use of the rhetorical question (or erotema) or an implied rhetorical question. Stewart was a passionate speaker, taking her cues in all likelihood from the evangelical practices of her day. As a woman speaking, this trope was particularly useful since it permitted her to raise and voice various questions that she thought might be emerging in the minds of her audience. Her later essays take even greater advantage of this subtle way of influencing response, but the strategy is evident even in this first essay. Two examples illustrate the point. Stewart says, "I suppose many of my friends will say, 'Religion is all your theme'" (32); she then proceeds to discuss in greater detail the importance of spiritual strength and a commitment to moral principles. A few pages later, she says in rapid sequence, "Do you ask, what can we do? . . . Do you ask where is the money? . . . Do you ask the disposition I would have you possess?" (38). Stewart builds persuasive momentum as she answers precisely and specifically each of these questions in turn, ending with this statement:

Possess the spirit of independence. The Americans do, and why should not you? Possess the spirit of men, bold and enterprising, fearless and undaunted. Sue for your rights and privileges. Know the reason that you cannot attain them. Weary them with your importunities. You can but die if you make the attempt; and we shall certainly die if you do not. (38)

Stewart's interest, in resonance with a critically conscious viewpoint, was to reclaim the "souls" of her people, to focus their actions toward positive change, and to inspire them as she had been inspired to be bold, courageous, and tireless in the struggle for a better world. As a writer, Stewart was a woman with a mission. Although it may not be appropriate to label her a master stylist as an essayist, it is totally appropriate to acknowledge her intellectual power and her ability to display consistently moments of both clarity and eloquence. She set a pace in essay writing that provided a noteworthy beginning for the use of this genre by African

American women for sociopolitical purposes. Stewart found herself at a moment of opportunity and she used it well.

Stewart's most active participation in public discourse was short-lived. She was successful, however, in demonstrating a potential and a possibility that had not been recognized or permitted before. Across the collective of her essays, she envisioned a different world and laid out a manifesto for belief and action. She fashioned a new space for herself as an unauthorized speaker, making a point of entry into a conversation that had previously been closed. She stepped into the fray and extended an invitation for others to follow, to make their own room, and to leave behind legacies of work well and righteously done. As one of the first African American women to take the public podium, to raise her voice, and to leave a written text behind, she (along with Lucy Terry, Phyllis Wheatley, Ann Plato, and others) signaled the coming of a new technology in a distinctive set of hands.

As we look now from a twenty-first-century vantage point at these early generations of women, we understand that they were separated from their original homelands by space, time, and cultural context. We understand that they had adjustments to make in new contexts. What we also know, however, is that those very first women did not leave behind their potential for growth and learning. We can see that over the centuries, on the continent of North America, they created legacies for those who would follow. As eighteenth- and particularly nineteenth-century women acquired literacy, they began to raise their voices via a new technology, the written word. This technology, and especially the essay as a frequently chosen genre, enabled them to show to the world, as Maria Stewart advocated, distinctive intellectual powers. In using this new technology, they remained true to imperatives that were in the interest of the community. Today, after so many generations of literate women have written in public for whatever causes and purposes they have identified as meaningful, African American women have built a tradition of literacy and action and have established a place for themselves as users of the word, as "dark spinners of word magic."

Chapter 5

From This Fertile Ground

Formal Training in the Development of Rhetorical Prowess

The ultimate outcome of education as it touches upon the individual's life is to strengthen her freedom to become what she is willing and able to become. It would include a daring to dream as well as to labor, a daring to pursue as well as to conform, a daring above all else to be true to herself, or to strive to realize what trueness to self could mean, what it will involve and what it will cost. It would seek opportunities to help students develop the courage to face their limits and capacities, their feelings and thoughts, with understanding, as each one strives to realize her own destiny. This is the key to human growth—to strive, to seek, to struggle toward self-fulfillment.

Jeanne L. Noble, *The Negro Woman's College Education*

In 1956 Jeanne L. Noble became the first researcher to publish a scholarly work on African American women and higher education for a mainstream market.[1] Her book, *The Negro Woman's College Education*, published by the Teachers College of Columbia University, received the 1955 Pi Lambda Theta Award from the National Association for Women in Education. It was a landmark publication that examined the goals and aspirations of contemporary African American college-educated women and analyzed the types of curricula available to them, the opportunities that were encouraged and not encouraged for them as college-educated women, their attitudes about their training, as well as their views on professional and community leadership. Noble discussed what it meant during this time to be Black and female in American culture and what, therefore, the education of African American women should take into account. In the very last chapter of the book, after acknowledging the need to prepare African American women to participate in the world of work, Noble makes the statement above and succeeds in articulating imperatives for education that resound through the decades and still ring true, not only for the women of the 1950s but also for the first generations of college-educated women as well.

If we consider that higher education is defined ideally as a way of maximizing one's talents and abilities and of expanding one's horizon, then two basic questions arise for the African American women of the nineteenth century who were privileged to set the pace for educational achievement and for rhetorical performance:

1. How might the enhancing of their rhetorical abilities through educational opportunity have become a part of their agenda for using their talents well?

2. How might they have conceived of their new, expanding horizons as a newly forming educated elite who would become leaders of the nation, or the race, or their gendered group?

Chapter 4 makes a case for the high levels of motivation that African American women exhibited in acquiring literacy and learning, and it chronicles the many ways they found to use their knowledge in acts with social and political consequence. In this chapter my goal is to look beyond basic literacy to higher education and the major resource it became as it extended both formal and informal means by which African American women could develop rhetorical expertise and use that expertise in accomplishing what remained a primary task—making the world a better place.

The nineteenth-century women who became the first generations of college-educated women established a pattern of engagement. First of all, they demonstrated their strong desires to become all they might be. They wanted the freedom to learn, and to do whatever their talents and abilities permitted. Anna Julia Cooper, a prominent member of this group, was an eloquent spokesperson. She presented a poignant case for women's educational opportunity in a collection of essays entitled *A Voice from the South: By a Black Woman of the South* (first published, 1892), using her own experiences to suggest a pattern for others like herself who hungered for knowledge and for the opportunity to achieve. Cooper says, "I constantly felt (as I suppose many an ambitious girl has felt) a thumping from within unanswered by any beckoning from without" (1998:76).

For African American women, the privilege of claiming space for their own intellectual development, of asserting an entitlement to pay attention to their own dreams and the nourishment of their own spirits rather than to their capacity simply to serve others, was indeed new and unusual.

Second, African American women of this era wanted to participate in the economy, in support of themselves and their families, with options beyond farm work, domestic service, or personal service (as seamstresses, for example), the typical choices for African American women to generate income until well into the twentieth century. These women wanted to enter the professions. After the Civil War, there was a tremendous need for teachers for both free-born and freed African American men, women, and children whose opportunities to learn had been denied by law in the South for well over a century and severely constrained by predominant practice throughout the nation. Fortunately, even before the Civil War, teaching was a type of work that was sanctioned as being appropriate for women, so African American women were able with this new opportunity to rise to the occasion and begin preparing themselves to fulfill the need. In particular, as evidenced for example by the enrollment records of Atlanta and Fisk Universities, they entered colleges and universities that offered normal school training, which would equip them well to teach.

Third, this generation of African American women recognized the burdens they carried in the interest of the race. As the first of their group to have educational opportunity, they were charged, not only with making use of those opportunities but also with extending them. They understood they were the keepers of a sacred trust, and they wanted to make the most of it. Their participation in public discourse concerning sociopolitical issues (such as the publication of Cooper's *A Voice from the South*) offers evidence of the central ways in which these women used their rhetorical abilities to make these issues (that is, their issues) the subject of concern in public space. They engaged in oratorical events; they wrote in the public arenas available to them (such as the African American periodical press) about their desires and aspirations, and about the forces and systems that constrained them and thereby stood in the way of the progress and achievement of the community. As Cooper states: "Only the Black Woman can say 'when and where I enter, in the quiet, undisputed dignity of my womanhood, without violence and without suing or special patronage, then and there the whole Negro race enters with me'" (1988:31).

The barriers to success for African American women in this quest, however, were multiple, including those related to their being of African descent, female, and quite often also of low socioeconomic status. Racial oppression, of course, and the limits it placed on educational opportunity were consistent across all educational levels. Consequently, the problems in higher education circles mirrored those related to the acquisition of basic literacy as well. People of African descent were deemed inferior and unworthy, generally, so it comes as no surprise that the acquisition of higher learning carried with it the ongoing struggles against these prevailing sentiments: to gain admission; to have talents and abilities recognized and nurtured; to create spaces—particularly within the often cold, unaccommodating environs of white institutions—that permitted at least a modicum of solace, affirmation, and reward.

A second set of barriers is related to gender. In making a case for the higher education of women, again, Cooper's was a particularly eloquent voice. She cites a book by Silvain Marechal that appeared in 1801, entitled *Shall Woman Learn the Alphabet.* This book proposes a law forbidding women to learn the alphabet and cites authorities who suggest that women who are educated lose their "womanliness." Cooper quotes Marechal as saying, "if women were once permitted to read Sophocles and logarithms, or to nibble at any side of the apple of knowledge, there would be an end forever to their sewing on buttons and embroidering slippers" (1988:49). As this essay, "The Higher Education of Women," continues, Cooper uses Oberlin College, her own alma mater, as an example of how unfounded such fears were at the turn of the nineteenth century; she acknowledges the growth of women's education, generally, and discusses ways in which educated women have been a positive and powerful force in society. At this point in the essay, however, Cooper notes that "my pen is devoted to a special cause" (73), the cause of African American women, and she proceeds to make a case for higher education for this group. At the end of the essay, she states:

I ask the men and women who are teachers and co-workers for the highest interests of the race, that they give the girls a chance! We might as well expect to grow trees from leaves as hope to build up a civilization or a manhood without taking into consideration our women and the home life made by them, which must be the root and ground of the whole matter. Let us insist then on special encouragement for the education of our women and special care in their training. Let our girls feel that we expect something more of them than that they merely look pretty and appear well in society. Teach them that there is a race with special needs which they and only they can help; that the world needs and is already asking for their trained, efficient forces. Finally, if there is an ambitious girl with pluck and brain to take the higher education, encourage her to make the most of it. . . . Let her know that your heart is following her, that your hand, though she sees it not, is ready to support her. . . . Let us then, here and now, recognize this force and resolve to make the most of it—not the boys less, but the girls more. (78–79)

On one hand, this passage illustrates the extent to which Cooper was influenced by the cult of true womanhood and its construction of women's place as domestic.[2] These values are clearly implicated as Cooper shapes and directs her arguments. Nevertheless, even as she acknowledges the prevailing view of domesticity as the right and true place for women, Cooper also succeeds in speaking eloquently for educational opportunity and for the freedom of women, even African American women, to become whatever they are willing and able to become.

Still, in the last quarter of the nineteenth century when Cooper was writing, the place of women in higher education was contentious. Women's sphere was considered to be in the home. It was not in the workforce, or in college, or in any other public place, and it did not matter ideologically that the cult of true womanhood simply had never held true for the overwhelming majority of poor and immigrant white women or African American women whose experiences throughout their time in the United States had included, unquestionably, work outside the home. All women were held to this standard.

One example of the problem is illustrated by Mary Church Terrell's experience. Terrell belonged to an affluent family and had the option, unlike most African American women, of actually living according to the codes of true womanhood. She was not compelled to work; she had the privilege of a comfortable, leisure-filled life. She, however, wanted to go to college and to use her abilities in an active way. Noble quotes Terrell as saying:

It was held by most people that women were unfitted to do their work in the home if they studied Latin, Greek, and higher mathematics. Many of my friends tried to dissuade me from studying for an A.B. degree. After I had finished college my father did not want me to get a job teaching. He felt that he was able to support me. He disinherited me, refused to write to me for a year because I went to Wilberforce to teach. Further, I was ridiculed and told that no man would want to marry a woman who studied higher mathematics. I said I'd take a chance and run the risk. (23)

Terrell did take a chance. She taught at Wilberforce University and at the well-respected M Street School in Washington, D.C. In 1895 she became the first African American to serve as a member of the Washington, D.C., Board of Education. And she did marry—Robert Terrell, the first African American to serve as judge of the municipal court in the District of Columbia; it was a marriage that continued to support her status as an affluent woman.

In addition, Terrell built a reputation as a person of considerable rhetorical ability, through her contributions to the periodical press and through her work as a community activist. She was a founder in 1892 of the Washington-based Colored Woman's League, which joined in 1896 with the Boston-based National Federation of Afro-American Women to form the National Association of Colored Women. Terrell was elected the first president of the new organization; served two consecutive terms in this position; gave the organization its motto, "Lifting As We Climb," in her first presidential address; and remained extremely active in local, national, and international causes as a social activist until her death in 1954 at the age of 91.[3]

Further complicating women's place in higher education for African American women were the stereotypes about character that continued to plague them because of their roles as "breeders" and rape victims during slavery and because of the images of them as being licentious, amoral, animalistic. After the Civil War, as well as before, African American women were not just restricted in terms of sphere, as in the case of white women, they also remained degraded and devalued. The results were twofold. Like women in general, African American women struggled to be permitted to learn and to use their learning potential, as intellectuals. They also experienced a unique struggle—for respect and goodwill. A light was cast on them as people positioned sociopolitically as being in need of redemption. In order to have even a chance of respectful treatment, behavior needed always to be beyond reproach.

From the point of view of the social order, African American women were not women whose virtue was mandated to be respected and protected, whether they wanted it so or not, as in the case of "respectable" white women. Instead, they were women whose morality, if indeed they were perceived to exhibit moral behavior, was a surprise, and by implication therefore suspect. Education for African American women by this reckoning was not simply a matter of the development of the mind and guidance toward appropriate womanly activities. It was also a matter of emphasizing the importance of the development of moral character. In other words, if African American women students happened to come to college with good habits of morality (which these stereotypes suggest was doubtful), the sentiment was that their habits might not be really stable. The assumption was that their virtue, even more so than women generally, was always in need of management.[4]

The goal seemed not to be necessarily to treat them as ladies, but to repress in them other inclinations and to make them ladies. In interpreting the difference by degree in attitudes toward white women and African American women, one might surmise that for white women, lady-ness, especially with a flattening of class distinctions, was an unmarked category, that is, a natural expectation. For African American women, however, regardless of class, it was a marked category. The term "African American woman" (or Black, Negro, or Colored woman) did not automatically inscribe the assumption of "morality." By stereotype, "moral" as an identity marker for African American women was acquired, not ascribed, and thereby typically marked by descriptive language, that is, in language that pointed out or brought direct attention to the presence, rather than the assumed absence, of lady-ness. The focus, therefore, on "making ladies" was considerable—as illustrated by the curriculum of the Normal Course at Atlanta University, which included a course in good morals and gentle manners; by the existence of the White Shield Society, an organization designed to encourage virtuous and pious behavior among women students, at colleges such as Spelman and Hartshorn; or by a variety of rules and regulations throughout the network of African American colleges and universities to monitor women's behavior.[5]

Issues of class presented obvious barriers as well. A few students were from more affluent circumstances (such as Frances Josephine Norris and

Mary Church Terrell at Oberlin, or Adella Hunt at Atlanta University) or had parents or patrons who could put forth the extra effort to support them (such as Selena Sloan Butler or Clara Howard at Spelman). Many, such as Cooper and Ida B. Wells, were in need of financial assistance. More often than not, they were compelled to work and to disrupt their education periodically because of a lack of funding. As in Charlotte Forten's case (despite her being from an affluent extended family, as a student Forten was always needy), the women who experienced financial need had to contend consistently with an absence of the resources required to make learning easier—from adequate food, clothing, and shelter to money to pay tuition and buy books.

Consider the appeal that Cooper makes in *A Voice from the South* for financial support from the community and not just from the family or even individual benefactors:[6]

One mind in a family or in a town may show a penchant for art, for literature, for the learned professions, or more bookish lore. You will know it when it is there. No need to probe for it. It is a light that cannot be hid under a bushel— and I would try to enable that mind to go the full length of its desires. Let it follow its bent and develop its talent as far as possible: and the whole community might well be glad to contribute its labor and money for the sustenance and cultivation of this brain. Just as earth gives its raw material, its carbons, hydrogen, and oxygen, for the tree which is to elaborate them into foliage, flower and fruit, so the baser elements, bread and money furnished the true brain worker come back to us with compound interest in the rich thought, the invention, the poem, the painting, the statue. (1988:262–63)

Cooper understood intellectual work and the place of respect it should command in the community. She understood the role it fills in the interest of the nation. She was clear that people—even women—who are capable of engaging in this work should be appreciated, respected, unencumbered, allowed to flourish intellectually in whatever directions their talents might take them. She had the insight and the skill to articulate for anyone who would listen just what the injustices and the impact of the injustices were. In speaking out so clearly and so well, she opened a space for possibility that had not existed before, again making a case for the higher education, not just of women in general, but of African American women.

All of these factors and more combined to form the material contexts and conditions under which rhetorical training took place and rhetorical actions were carried out during the last quarter of the nineteenth century, when the first cadre of college-educated African American women was assembling. What seems evident in the means and mechanisms of the assembly process is that the women had clear and specific relationships to the material world and these relationships were constant reminders of critical mandates for sociopolitical action. These women were beset by their own needs; but their needs reflected also the problems and concerns of the group at large and its collective interests in progress and productivity. The constant presence of such materiality conveyed to them, therefore, a visceral sense of urgency, the need for barriers to be dismantled and for encumbrances to be removed so that both they and the community could benefit from productivity and achievement. The women's response was to enter colleges and universities in ever increasing numbers, and the general pattern of their engagement while in these environments was to work hard and to take advantage of whatever opportunities and resources were available.

Pathways to Opportunity Before the Civil War

According to Carter G. Woodson (Woodson 1991:256–64), the first organized efforts in the United States to provide higher education for African Americans were instituted because of the colonization movement. In 1817, for example, the colonizationists opened a school in Pasippany, New Jersey, and in 1829 they opened another in Newark. Both ventures failed, in significant part because of opposition from many white abolitionists and free African Americans who disagreed with the basic premise of preparing African Americans for relocation to Africa. The position of those opposed to colonization was that African Americans should be educated for living in the United States. In addition, there was the sense among this opposition group that, given the apparent immobility of white institutions in refusing to admit African Americans, there was a dire need to establish colleges especially for African Americans, but with a curriculum that suited the making of a life at "home."

This strategy gained momentum in 1849 with the founding of the Allegheny Institute and Mission Church, a mission later renamed Avery Memorial African Methodist Episcopal Church (the college part of the mission was renamed Avery College). This renaming was a tribute to Reverend Charles Avery who was the primary philanthropic supporter. Avery was a member of the Pennsylvania Abolition Society, a minister, and a generous contributor to projects that promoted the intellectual equality of African Americans. Avery's wealth resulted from cotton mills and the pharmaceutical industry, and upon his death in 1858, he left an estate of three hundred thousand dollars to be applied to the education and Christianization of Africans and African Americans (Blockson 1994:136–37). Although this college/church no longer exists today, in its own time it held the distinction of being operated primarily by educators who were African American (with the exception of its first principal), and after the Civil War it continued to build a reputation of excellence under the leadership of the highly respected Reverend Henry Highland Garnett, who became its president (Woodson 1991:256–72).

In 1851 Myrtilla Miner opened a school for the higher education of African American women in Washington, D.C. With the help of the Quakers (including Harriet Beecher Stowe) and other contributors, she was able to offer signal opportunities to young women until her death in 1866, even in the face of hostile reactions from the white community. By 1856 the doors of Wilberforce University in Xenia, Ohio, were open, making this institution the first to be controlled by African Americans, with responsibility for the university being assumed by the African Methodist Episcopal Church in 1862. Also in 1856, Lincoln University in Chester County, Pennsylvania, opened after having been incorporated in 1854.

With regard to the American Colonization Society, their repeated failures to establish institutions served to shift the focus of their efforts. Instead of confronting resistance from white abolitionists and free African Americans, they began to arrange more quietly for the education of individuals at existing institutions. Moreover, instead of trying to educate those who were relocating to Africa before they left the United States, the society shifted its strategy to educating these folk after they reached Liberia, a primary site for relocation. To accommodate this policy, the College of West Africa was founded in Liberia in 1839, and Liberia College was incorporated in 1851 with doors opening to students in 1862.

In the meantime, Oberlin College became the first white institution of higher education in the United States to offer women and people of color entry into higher education without their having to petition on an individual basis. Needless to say, the path of petitioning had not been an easy one, as evidenced by the small numbers of African American men and women who were successful in this venture, at any level, not just the college level. Woodson reports that, before 1840, less than fifteen African Americans were able to enroll and successfully matriculate in an American college, with Alexander Twilight becoming the first college graduate when he completed studies at Middlebury College in 1823, followed shortly thereafter by John B. Russwurm at Bowdoin in 1828 (Bain 1999).

Oberlin Collegiate Institute, which became Oberlin College in 1850, was founded in 1833 and chartered in 1834.[7] The mission of the institution was based on five ideas: the establishment and maintenance of a Christian college by a Christian colony; the coeducation of the sexes; the establishment of a school where work was considered honorable and where it was possible for industrious students with limited means to meet expenses; the development of high scholarly achievements with the expectation that students would go out into the world ready to do whatever the world needs; opposition to slavery, which by 1835 manifested itself in the opening of institutional doors to people of color. These ideas offered a compelling invitation to both women and African Americans, who at the time basically had nowhere else to go, and both groups enrolled immediately—first in the preparatory program and then (in the case of the men) in the regular college course, which became known as the "gentlemen's course," or (in the case of the women) in the literary course, which became known as the "ladies' course."

With regard to women, in the college's first public announcement John J. Shipherd, one of the founders of the colony and the college, stated among its objectives: "The elevation of female character by bringing within the reach of the misjudged and neglected sex all the instructive privileges which hitherto have unreasonably distinguished the leading sex from theirs" (Hosford 1937:5). This statement came to be known as the Oberlin Magna Charta for womankind, a statement, according to Frances Juliette Hosford (1937), that did not serve to prescribe how women's opportunities might be manifested at the college but that did open the way for women students to blossom and make their own possibilities, as was the case for African American students as well.

In 1860, in response to the accusation that Oberlin was a "colored" school, President James H. Fairchild asserted that Oberlin was never designed to be a "colored" school but, rather,

> to offer to the colored student one advantage, as pressing as any other—that is, to the extent of its influence, to break down the barrier of caste, and to elevate him to a common platform of intellectual, social, and religious life. This result it aims to secure, by admitting him, without any reservation or distinction, to all the advantages of a school, having a fair standing among the colleges of the land. Such a work, a distinctively colored school could not effect. However high its literary character, it must lie on the other side of that barrier of caste, which a false system has reared between the races. (Fairchild 1871, 32)

As was the case with women's education, what Oberlin offered to African Americans was opportunity rather than plan. In both cases students came and were inspired to achieve, but at no time did the percentage of African American students, men and women combined, exceed 8 percent, which was the high point during the decade immediately after the Civil War. In "Oberlin College and the Negro Student, 1865–1940," W. E. Bigglestone reports:

> In reality the college never enrolled many Negroes. They made up four or five percent of the student body between 1840 and 1860, rose to seven percent or eight percent during the decade after the Civil War, and then declined to five or six percent. In the period 1900–1940 the number of black students rarely exceeded four percent of the total student body. (1971:198)

Bigglestone also reports that the educational environment was not without problems. There were incidents of insult, inequity, and mistreatment. Nonetheless, Bigglestone states, "What was expected of Oberlin was not even asked of most schools. The fact it was expected left Oberlin much richer for it" (219), and so too the African American students who were educated there, especially during an era when they had very few other places to go.

African American women, in this scenario, constituted a group that merged Oberlin's interests in two targeted constituencies. They were both women and African American, and, like the white women and the African American men, they too enrolled enthusiastically in Oberlin.[8] One of the first women of African descent to enroll was actually an African-born woman who at about seven years old had been captured, sold, and enslaved.[9] She ended up on the *Amistad,* a small ship that became famous for the insurrection that occurred on it, and for the legal case that ensued. The insurrectionist group, including the child Margru (one of three girls on board with fifty men), were defended before the U.S. Supreme Court by former president John Quincy Adams. The group was educated during the long process of the trials, freed, and eventually resettled in Africa. Margru continued her education at a mission school under the tutelage of Reverend William Raymond, the leader of the missionaries who traveled with the *Amistad* group on their return to Africa. In 1846 Margru came back to the United States under the sponsorship of abolitionist Lewis Tappan, a New York merchant, to attend Oberlin where she remained until 1849. At Oberlin, she was known by her Anglicized name, Sarah Margru Kinson, the name she preferred. In a letter to Tappan, Kinson wrote, "I am studying very diligently so as to be qualified to do good in the world as this was my object in coming to Oberlin" (Lawson 1984:14).

Kinson returned to the mission station at Kaw Mendi in Sierra Leone where she worked as a missionary and teacher through the American Missionary Association (AMA), one of only a few Black women and one of even fewer unmarried women.[10] A few years later, Kinson married fellow missionary Edward Henry Green, and they both continued in their commitment to missionary work. In terms of her own work, Kinson and her fellow missionary, Hanah More (a white woman who conveyed to the AMA a preference to work with white women instead of with Kinson), set up an African women's sewing society called the Modest Dress Society. The thirty-six women who formed the group were required to wear western clothes to attend.[11]

As president of the group, Kinson told stories and delivered informal sermons. These acts of public speaking were not foreign to her since she had occasionally recited biblical passages in public as a child; spoken about Christianity at various churches in the town of Oberlin when she was in college; and participated without hesitation in formal and informal learning experiences at Oberlin. In Africa, however, Kinson was at first reluctant to engage in public speaking in support of what she perceived to be the place of women. She soon became more assertive, however, and as Ellen NicKenzie Lawson reports, she wrote to Lewis Tappan,

"I am not ashamed to tell you that I am preaching to my country people" (1984:22). In 1855, in support of her new role as preacher, the Greens set up their own mission, believing (unlike the AMA) that Africans should be converted by Africans. At this point, their support from the AMA was soon withdrawn amid controversy surrounding Kinson's husband, at which point Kinson faded from AMA records.

As Robert Samuel Fletcher (1943) reports, the first African American woman student to graduate from Oberlin was Lucy Stanton in 1850. Stanton completed the nondegree literary course, the program deemed most appropriate for women. The curriculum for women offered its own challenges and an interesting array of courses that complemented the classically defined regular degree program (the gentlemen's course). The ladies' course prepared women to be good wives for professional men—and to teach before marriage.[12] It did not, however, prepare them to engage in the world of public discourse as ministers, lawyers, scientists, or other professionals, as the men's curriculum was preparing the male students. Nevertheless, the ladies' course was indeed a four-year college-level course, and the fact that it was not a degreed program does not minimize Stanton's achievement (or the achievement of the other women who completed this course). Her level of preparation was far beyond the typical educational preparation for women of her day (or for most men as well), and it placed her solidly among the highly educated intellectual elite. By 1860 President Fairchild reported that seventeen African American women had completed the ladies' course (Fairchild 1871:32). These graduates included, among others, Ann Maria Hazle, who became a teacher in Ohio; Sarah J. Woodson, who became the first African American woman to become a college professor (at Wilberforce University); Blanche V. Harris, who worked with the AMA and who (along with other women such as Charlotte Forten) became one of the first African American teachers to be sent to the South, in her case to teach the freed men, women, and children in Mississippi.

In terms of formal training, in the preparatory course (where women students typically began), the focus of the curriculum was on reading, spelling, writing, arithmetic, ancient and modern geography, Latin, Greek, and English grammar, composition, world and U.S. history, and religion. In the ladies' course, Oberlin offered philosophy and religion,

Greek grammar and literature, English literature, mathematics, sciences (including chemistry and astronomy), geography, archaeology, and world and U.S. history, as well as grammar and composition. In composition, writing essays was considered more appropriate for women than engaging in oratory or public debate, deemed the territory of men. Notable, however, is that the ladies' course did include some direct training in logic and rhetoric as evidenced by the use of various textbooks of the day: Whately's *Logic and Rhetoric*, Paley's *Evidences*, and Butler's *Analogy*.

During the nineteenth century, emphasis was on disciplining the thinking, paying systematic attention, especially by the end of the century, to rhetorical concerns related to both the art of speaking and the art of good writing. Instruction included class work related to invention, arrangement, the use of appeals, qualities of style that combined epistemological and belletristic principles, and the management of voice, gesture, and expressiveness in oral delivery.[13] To be reemphasized, however, is that women were encouraged to write, not to speak publicly.

In 1837, four white women who had completed the preparatory program requested and obtained permission to enter the gentlemen's course. Three of them graduated in 1841, the first women in the United States to receive the bachelor of arts degree. The gentlemen's course was a classical curriculum, modeled on that of Yale University. As was typical of such a curriculum, the training included attention to and practice in public speaking, since the professions into which the men would be entering demanded these abilities. The women enrolled in the gentlemen's course in the early years, however, did not find these opportunities available to them, given the view that women simply would have no need for such skills. Nevertheless, the women were able to participate indirectly or vicariously. They were privileged, as all students at Oberlin, to a lively community of oratory from speakers on the campus and in the community. The women were able to listen and observe, to read and write, but not to speak in public before a mixed audience (that is, before men and women). For their first few years in the gentlemen's course, for example, since it was inappropriate by the codes of the day for women to speak, even their graduation essays, a major ritual of the graduation ceremony, were read by a male teacher (until they petitioned to read their own).

Further, and perhaps most instructive of all for the rhetorical development of the women, were the literary clubs (Hosford 1937; Fletcher 1943). The men of Oberlin organized the Oberlin Lyceum in 1834, and a second club shortly thereafter, but the men were quickly followed in these types of activities by the women, who organized the Oberlin Ladies' Literary Society in July 1835. In 1839 in a formal statement concerning their purposes and activities, a committee from the group wrote:

We have connected with our Seminary, a Literary & Religious association, in which capacity we meet frequently and each one in turn, according to appointment, writes and communicates to us her thoughts on some important and interesting subject. We hold correspondence with many distinguished & pious ladies of our own and other lands and with some who have left for pagan shores, by this means we collect much valuable information and often have our spirits refreshed. (Fletcher 1943:761–62)

In the early 1850s a second society, the Young Ladies' Lyceum (renamed the Aelioian Society in 1861), was organized to rival these activities. Both groups read various works (as the club titles indicate), wrote essays and poetry, and spent their meetings reading essays and poems aloud, listening to musical performances, discussing the issues of the day, and occasionally even debating the issues of the day. Discussion and debate topics varied: from the frivolous, "Resolved that a cow is better than a dog"; to the literary, "That the influence of the writer is greater than that of the orator"; to the domestic, "That domestic happiness is enhanced by housekeeping"; to women's rights, "That women should enter the medical profession"; to contemporary issues, "That a slaveholder can be a Christian"; to current events, "That the extension of [U.S.] territory is beneficial to this nation." The lists of topics for both women's and men's clubs were long and provocative.

By 1858 the two women's clubs and the two men's clubs had joined together to produce a monthly magazine, entitled *Oberlin Students' Monthly,* modeled after the *Atlantic Monthly,* in which they systematically presented thirty-five or forty pages of essays, stories, poetry, editorial comments, Oberlin news, book reviews, and musical compositions. During this same period, Oberlin clubs joined with other colleges and universities, both national and abroad, to publish an intercollegiate magazine, the *University Quarterly,* housed at Yale University. This publication presented news and essays from students in over thirty colleges in the United

States, England, and Germany. Both these enterprises were disrupted by the outbreak of the Civil War, but they had laid the groundwork, along with other curricular and extracurricular activities on the campus, for a continuing commitment (after the country was again at peace) to both oratory and written expression.

Into this vibrant intellectual environment, with its various and sundry opportunities for learning, generally, and the development of rhetorical expertise, in particular, African American women entered. They were enrolled in courses across the preparatory, gentlemen's, and ladies curricula. They were privy to a consciously constructed atmosphere of academic achievement and public concern that gave rise to a richly endowed discourse community. They were also active in the extracurricular opportunities provided by the literary clubs. Lucy Stanton, for example, was very active with Lucy Stone (a well-known white student activist who went on to establish a national reputation as a social activist) in bringing debate to the agenda of the Ladies' Literary Society, even though debating was not sanctioned as an acceptable activity for women students. In 1850, the year of Stanton's graduation, she was elected president of the society and presided, according to archival records, "with dignity and honor" at the society's annual celebration. A few days later at her graduation, Stanton delivered her graduation essay, "A Plea for the Oppressed," which was published in the *Oberlin Evangelist* and also in *Condition of the Colored People,* a collection published in 1852 by Martin Delaney, a nationally recognized African American abolitionist.

After graduation, Stanton continued to exhibit skills as a writer, orator, and leader. In 1866, after the Civil War, she went south to teach in Georgia, then in Mississippi, and later in Tennessee, before retiring in the city of Los Angeles. She became an officer in the Women's Relief Corps, an auxiliary to the Civil War veterans' organization, a grand matron of the Order of Eastern Star (the sister organization of a Black Masonic Order), and president of a local chapter of the Women's Christian Temperance Union. In 1909, one year before she died, the *Los Angeles Daily Times* paid tribute to her as a person who had been a pioneer of change.

Twelve years after Stanton's graduation from Oberlin, at the commencement of 1862, the historical record shows that Mary Jane Patterson became the first African American woman to receive a bachelor's degree from an accredited American institution. Mary Georgianna Mitchem, however, was the first African American woman to enroll in the gentlemen's course in 1855. Mitchem completed three years of the program, leaving before graduation to get married and to follow a career as a teacher in Illinois and Wisconsin before dying from tuberculosis in Minnesota in 1868. While at Oberlin, Mitchem (like Lucy Stanton) served as president of the Young Women's Literary Society, debated issues, and delivered essays. Stanton and Mitchem set a pattern of leadership by African American women students in the literary clubs, making way for others (Fanny Jackson Coppin, Anna Julia Cooper, Mary Church Terrell, and so on) to continue in the garnering of rhetorical experience and expertise.

Mary Jane Patterson, the first to receive the bachelor of arts degree, entered Oberlin in 1858. Born in Raleigh, North Carolina, Patterson was brought to Oberlin by her parents, who left Raleigh during the 1850s when persecution of free African Americans in the South intensified. Like many parents of the first group of African American women college students, the Pattersons were impassioned to provide the best opportunities possible for their children and willing, therefore, to move bag and baggage to wherever those opportunities were available. From Oberlin, Patterson went on to teach for seven years at the Institute for Colored Youth in Philadelphia and then at the M Street School in Washington, D.C., where she became the first African American principal, a position she held until 1884, when she went back to full-time teaching until her death in 1894. In Washington, Patterson became active in organized social reform activities, joining other women in these enterprises, including women who had graduated from Oberlin after her (Anna Julia Cooper, Mary Church Terrell, Ida Gibbs Hunt, all from the Class of 1884) as well as other college-educated women in the Washington, D.C., area who formed by the 1890s a significant core of educated elite.

I do not wish to distinguish during this era between the women who graduated from college, still a very small number by 1900, and those who completed non–bachelor of arts programs, such as the normal course (that is, teacher-training sequences), or those who took courses of various sorts but did not graduate. Given the levels of literacy and academic achievement of their day all these women, graduates or not, belonged to an educated elite. The very fact of their enrolling in a college class was not typical of the general population. It was emblematic of special opportunity and special success. Measuring success by matriculation in college environments rather than completion of the bachelor's degree permits us to credit one pattern in particular. Several women, including Ida B. Wells at LeMoyne-Owen College and Fisk University and Selena Sloan Butler at the Emerson School of Oratory enrolled in college courses to receive elocution training rather than a college degree, a pattern that supports paying more attention to African American women's clubwork, and to the occasions that arose in this work to participate in public discourse.

To illustrate, the activities of the Washington-based women mirrored the activities of African American women across the nation. They formed a growing collective of women, active in their local communities, working collaboratively to support social and political causes, including education, social welfare, political and economic participation, and so on. These were the groups to whom a clarion call for action would be directed in 1895—at the first national gathering of African American women, in Boston, Massachusetts.[14] This meeting gave rise, a year later, to the founding of the highly active national network of African American women's clubs that was organized in 1896 as the National Association of Colored Women (NACW). The NACW was committed to social reform at the local, regional, and national levels. In the context of this history of reform, Patterson's status as the first African American woman to be awarded the B.A. in the United States meant quite literally that she led a vanguard that signaled the beginning of a new era of possibility, the opening of a brand new door. By the last two decades of the nineteenth century, there existed across the United States a critical mass of African American women who were highly educated professional women primed to make a difference in the communities in which they lived and worked.

According to Ellen NicKenzie Lawson (1984), by 1865 Oberlin had opened its door to at least 152 women who can be identified as African American. They were enrolled in the preparatory school and in the college. Those enrolled in the college programs (approximately 61) constituted a significant portion of the first wave of college-educated women. They entered Oberlin, were formally trained as intellectuals, and were privileged to exist as budding rhetors amid a general spirit of social activism. They went forward, especially after the Civil War, to form a core of

African American women who saw themselves as agents of change, as people who could and should get things done. With this type of ethos, nurtured both formally and informally by a spirit of both intellectual engagement and social activism, these women made changes—at both local and regional levels—in the lives of individuals and whole communities through the professional and community services they provided and through the insights and leadership they offered.

The Oberlin story, therefore, is a clear marker of a shift in educational opportunity. Mary Jane Patterson was followed in the completion of the B.A. at Oberlin by Fannie Jackson Coppin and Frances Josephine Norris, both of the Class of 1865; by Mary Church Terrell, Anna Julia Cooper, and Ida Gibbs Hunt, all of the Class of 1884; and by at least 150 other women who saw at Oberlin a bright and guiding star. These women were leaders while they were students at Oberlin, using the resources of the institution to enhance their talents and abilities through the array of opportunities available to them. After Oberlin, they were inspired by their opportunities to achieve. They demonstrated leadership abilities that were unparalleled in terms of power and influence, and they set the pace for how leadership among African American women would be shaped for generations to come.

Pathways to Opportunity After the Civil War

In 1856 Wilberforce University and Lincoln University became two of the first institutions in the United States to be established for African Americans. After the Civil War, however, there was an increased interest in establishing additional institutions to meet the special needs of the newly configured free communities of African Americans. Atlanta University was one such institution. Educational activities that were its precursor began in 1865; the university was officially chartered as an institution on October 16, 1867.[15] It was established with the support of the AMA and a combination of both southern and northern clergy and businessmen. This collective set up a curriculum, consisting of a preparatory department, a normal course, a scientific curriculum, a theological curriculum, and a college curriculum. In planning these areas, institutional leaders recognized the critical needs of the African American community to develop professional expertise, and to take care of itself rather than be dependent on the kindness and support of the white community. Teacher training, therefore, was a top priority, as indicated by an appeal on the last page of the 1869–1870 university catalog:

There should be a School in every community in the State, but there are no teachers. In every community, however, there is at least one young man or woman who, if educated, would make an excellent teacher. Let, then, the members of the community each contribute a small sum monthly for the support of some one whom they may choose to send here to school, and let that person agree to teach for them a certain time in return for this aid. In this way a large number of competent teachers might soon be raised up. Why will not many communities and churches act on this suggestion?

As in the case of Oberlin, African American women heard this call for teachers and found the invitation compelling.

In the first class enrolled at Atlanta University there were 178 students, 27 of whom were women—one of whom, Lucy Craft Laney, was also listed in the 1871–1872 catalog as a member of the first college class, along with Adella Cleveland and Elizabeth Outlaw. Laney was born in Macon, Georgia, in 1854, the daughter of Louisa Laney and David Laney, a Presbyterian minister and a well-respected religious and community leader.[16] After graduating from Atlanta University, Laney began a teaching career in Milledgeville, Georgia, but she taught also in Macon and Savannah before moving to Augusta, where she was an active participant in the struggle for the first public high school for African American students in Georgia. These events helped establish her reputation as a charismatic speaker and an educational leader and signaled a growing pattern of activity for her as a social activist. In subsequent years, Laney participated actively in the NACW, the Southeastern Federation of Women's Clubs, the Georgia State Teachers' Association, the National Young Women's Christian Association, and other community development activities.

In 1886 Laney founded the Haines Normal and Industrial Institute in Augusta. As the leader of this institution, she was the only African American woman to serve as head of an institution affiliated with the Presbyterian Church. She also served as mentor and friend to Mary McLeod Bethune, who apprenticed with her at the Haines Institute before Bethune founded her own school, the Daytona Educational and Industrial School for Negro Girls, in 1904. Bethune would be recognized for this work and would become advisor to leaders of the nation, including President Franklin Delano Roosevelt. The Daytona Educational and Industrial School survives today as Bethune-Cookman College.

At Atlanta University, the curriculum of the Preparatory Department (in which Laney first enrolled) and that of the College Department both followed a classical model, very much like the Oberlin curriculum, using basically the same textbooks as was typical of the day. By 1874, also typical of the day, there were clearly gender-defined separations in the curriculum. Women enrolled overwhelmingly in the Normal Course, instead of the college preparatory, the scientific, the theological, or the college course, all of which were more academically rigorous than the Normal Course.

The Normal Course was the teacher-training curriculum, which accounts in large part for the numbers of women enrolled. The first-year offerings included instruction in English composition; in mathematics, history, and science; in good morals and gentle manners; in reading, writing, and spelling. During the second year, added to the list were the science of government, and the theory and practice of teaching. In the third year, the sciences were expanded and political economy was added to the list. Then, in the fourth year, rhetoric (the Art of Discourse) was added, along with mental and moral philosophy, logic, a course called Evidences of Christianity, and an expanded mathematics sequence that included algebra and geometry. Despite the gender distinctions, however, all students enrolled in the university were required to have rhetorical exercises and weekly Bible lessons.

The women students at Atlanta University found themselves in an environment where learning was taken seriously, whether they, as African American females with intellectual potential, were taken seriously or not. They read broadly and had the opportunity to engage with varieties of text under the guidance of their teachers and in the company of their fellow students. They were privy to sermons, lectures, and other presentations on campus and in the general community and were privy to the discussions generated in response to these events. They received formal training in composition, logic, rhetoric, and elocution and had, therefore, the opportunity to think of themselves as readers, writers, speakers, and thinkers. In other words, these women were able to hone skills that

African American women before them had very few opportunities either to think about or to develop.

In addition to classroom-related activities, there were also extracurricular opportunities. As an institution that had articulated one of its purposes to be Christian education, Atlanta University soon established the Young Women's Christian Temperance Union (YWCTU), an organization that offered opportunities for both leadership and rhetorical development. Through their membership in the YWCTU, the women heard prominent temperance leaders, including Atlanta University alumna Georgia Swift King (Normal Class of 1874), and they competed in oratorical contests themselves, with the Demorest Prohibition Prize Medal being the most prestigious prize.

Debating at the university was another popular extracurricular activity. The male students organized their first club, the Howard Normal Debating Club, in 1869–1870, and activities gained momentum in 1905 with the emergence of the public debates of the Triangle Debating Union. This union involved an annual series of public debates that pitted Atlanta University teams against the teams of two other African American universities, Fisk and Howard. Records indicate that women were not members of these organizations and did not participate actively in the debates, but they were able to attend and enjoy the public events. In 1884, amid controversy about whether women of the Normal Course should be allowed to continue enjoying the activities, the women students decided to form their own organization and thus began the Phyllis Wheatley Literary Club.

At the public meetings of the Wheatley club, the women recited quotations from African American authors, featured debates, presented instrumental and vocal musical performances, and gave readings—presumably most, if not all, of which were their own writing. By 1903 two additional literary organizations were founded, the Athene Debating Society and the Douglass Literary Society, which was open to the first- and second-year high school students enrolled in the university.[17] The purpose of this latter organization was to train its members in English composition and parliamentary procedures and to offer entertainment.

Perhaps the most striking extracurricular experiences for the students, though, were the campus lectures. Even though segregationist policies excluded African Americans from many public lectures and concerts in the city of Atlanta, the university was consistent in making arrangements for national figures to speak on campus. Students were able to hear political figures such as former President Rutherford B. Hayes; social activists such as Frederick Douglass; Julia Ward Howe, the writer of the "Battle Hymn of the Republic"; woman suffragist Susan B. Anthony; renowned educators, such as the presidents of Harvard University, Johns Hopkins, and the University of Minnesota; and many, many others of equal renown. These visitors helped create for all students, including the women, a world of ideas and rhetorical engagement from which they could identify models of thought and action.

The programs at Atlanta University and Oberlin were typical of the type of formal and informal training that the first generations of college-educated African American women were able to receive. Many of the women were interested in more, however. They recognized the nobility of teaching as a profession, but some of them were more interested in becoming medical doctors or other health practitioners, or lawyers, journalists, businesswomen, or community development specialists. In the nineteenth century the doors to these professions existed still with substantial barriers before them, barriers that remained for African American women until well into the second half of the twentieth century and the time of Jeanne L. Noble's study.

Blazing New Trails to Professional Identity

In *Woman's Legacy: Essays on Race, Sex, and Class in American History* (1982), Bettina Aptheker pays tribute to the early generations of African American women in their "Quest for Dignity" in professions other than teaching. She confirms that the numbers across professional arenas were extremely small, offering even stronger evidence that these early pioneers were unique and courageous. Based on her research, we can generate a list of "firsts" that underscores the remarkable ways in which African American women were learning and achieving:

Sarah Winifred Brown was the first African American woman to receive the B.S. degree (from Cornell University in 1897).[18]

Sarah Mapps Douglass, a founding member of the Philadelphia Female Anti-Slavery Society and director of the girls' department of the Institute for Colored

Youth in Philadelphia, was the first to complete a medical course at a university in the United States (the Ladies' Institute of the Pennsylvania Medical University) in 1858.

Sarah Parker Remond, member of the Boston Female Anti-Slavery Society and abolitionist orator, was the first to receive a medical degree from the Santa Maria Nuova Hospital, a medical school in Florence, Italy, in 1871.

Rebecca Lee was the first to receive a medical degree from an institution in the United States (from the New England Female Medical College in 1864) and to practice medicine.

Dr. Halle Tanner Dillon was the first woman (white or African American) licensed to practice medicine in Alabama; Dr. Verina Morton-Jones was the first in Mississippi; Dr. Matilda A. Evans the first in South Carolina; Dr. Sara G. Jones the first in Virginia.

Mary Eliza Mahoney was the first to receive a diploma in nursing (from the New England Hospital for Women and Children in Boston) in 1879.

Ida Gray was the first to receive a degree in dentistry (from the University of Michigan in 1890).

Matilda Lloyd, Margaret A. Miller, Bella B. Coleman were the first women to receive degrees in pharmacy (from Meharry Medical College in 1894).

Charlotte E. Ray was the first to receive a law degree (from Howard University in 1872).

Sadie Tanner Mossell Alexander was one of the first three women to receive a Ph.D. (in economics from the University of Pennsylvania) in 1921.

In addition to their achievements in the professional arena, these women were remarkable in terms of their social advocacy and activism and the consistency with which they wrote and spoke in public arenas in the interest of social change. Two examples from this early generation of achievers are Susan Smith McKinney Steward and Mary Ann Shadd Cary.[19]

Susan Smith McKinney Steward, born in 1847, was the seventh child of Sylvanus and Ann S. Smith, members of the African American elite in Brooklyn, New York. In 1867 Steward entered the New York Medical College for Women,[20] and she graduated in 1870 as class valedictorian (which entitled her to present the valedictory address) and also as the third African American woman to receive a medical degree in the United States. Steward was the first African American woman to practice medicine in New York, specializing in obstetrics and gynecology but building a practice, despite race and gender barriers, that served both men and women from both the African American community and the white community. She was the only woman on staff at the Long Island College Hospital, where she did postgraduate work. She was also on the staffs of the New York Hospital for Women, the Brooklyn Women's Homeopathic Hospital, and the Brooklyn Home for Aged Colored People, and she had offices in both Brooklyn and Manhattan.

Steward was an active participant in the Kings County Homeopathic Medical Society and in the Homeopathic Medical Society of the State of New York. As William Seraile reports (Hine 1993:1109–12), Steward presented two papers before the state society, one in 1883 and another in 1886, demonstrating her concern not only for her patients but for the knowledge-making enterprises of her professional community. Steward practiced medicine in New York for twenty-six years, and when she retired, she joined the faculty of Wilberforce University where she served as resident physician.

Despite her active medical career, Steward was married twice (to William G. McKinney, an itinerant preacher, and Theophilus Gould Steward, chaplain of the Twenty-Fifth U.S. Colored Infantry), had two children, and led an active life as a community organizer. Her accomplishments suggest she made little distinction between her commitments to professional service and her commitments to community service more generally. She was active in missionary work in her own church, the Bridge Street African Methodist Episcopal Church, where she was also church organist and choirmaster. She was a passionate supporter of woman suffrage and along with her sister, renowned educator Sarah Smith Garnett (who was married to Reverend Henry Highland Garnett, the president of the Avery Memorial African Methodist Episcopal Church mentioned earlier), was a founder of the Equal Suffrage League. She was an organizer of the testimonial dinner honoring anti-lynching activist Ida B. Wells and subsequently a founder of the Woman's Loyal Union, one of two leading women's clubs in the New York area that would participate in the founding of the NACW in 1896. She was president of the Women's Christian Temperance Union of Brooklyn and active throughout the latter part of her life in women's club work, including NACW activities at the national level.

Amid this slate of activities, Steward was a prolific writer and a frequent public speaker. Two events offer evidence of the ultimate range of her potential impact on audiences. One occasion was the delivery of a paper, "Colored American Women," in London at the First Universal Race Congress in 1911, and a second was the delivery of another paper, "Women in Medicine," before an NACW meeting in Wilberforce, Ohio. Steward was obviously recognized for her talents, experiences, and achievements, as evidenced by the publication of the latter paper in pamphlet form and its receiving wide circulation throughout the United States.

Mary Ann Shadd Cary is another example of a professional woman who sustained a lively record as a social activist, not just in her professional role as a journalist but in public arenas more generally. Similar to the better-known Ida B. Wells-Barnett, Cary began her professional work as a teacher who became a journalist. Cary later became the second African American woman to receive a law degree (from Howard University in Washington, D.C.). She was born in Wilmington, Delaware, in 1823, the first of thirteen children of politically active parents, Harriet and Abraham Shadd. Her father, a local businessman, was a delegate to the annual Conventions of Free People of Color and served as convention president in 1833. He was also a subscription agent for William Lloyd Garrison's *Liberator,* and the Shadd home was a stop on the Underground Railroad. Cary was educated for six years in a Quaker school in West Chester, Pennsylvania, where her family moved when she was ten years old. With this preparation, she opened her own school at the age of sixteen, in Wilmington in 1840, and later taught in New York City and Norristown, Pennsylvania.

After the passage of the 1850 Fugitive Slave Law, which permitted slaveholders to come North to recover their property and which cast abolitionists as criminals for helping fugitive slaves, Cary joined the exodus of free and fugitive African Americans to Canada.[21] In Windsor, Canada, where she went first, Cary established an integrated school, supported by the AMA, and simultaneously became involved in a campaign against unscrupulous anti-slavery agents who were more concerned with filling their own coffers than helping immigrants resettle in Canada. Only six months after her arrival, Cary had published a pamphlet, *A Plea for Emigration, or, Notes of Canada West, in its Moral, Social and Political Aspect.* This document was detailed in its data about Canada's climate, geography, job opportunities, and so on, and it remained in print for several years as a primary recruiting tool for immigration to Canada. While the pamphlet is evidence of her support of Canadian immigration and particularly the opportunities that it offered for African Americans to be autonomous and self-reliant, Cary vehemently opposed the Refugee Home Society and its agents (such as Mary and Henry Bibb) of whom she deeply disapproved.[22]

Cary waged her first political campaign against this group and lost—an experience that helped her realize the importance of having a forum from which to speak. The Refugee Home Society had a weekly newspaper, the *Voice of the Fugitive,* in which they attacked Cary and set up public sentiment against her. Cary had no such forum from which to defend herself. Her insight about space to speak led to her joining Samuel Ringgold Ward, a traveling agent for the Anti-Slavery Society of Canada, and to her establishing her own newspaper, the *Provincial Freeman,* in Toronto and Chatham in 1853.[23] This act established her as the first African American woman to own, write for, and edit her own newspaper.

Cary's work in this campaign for the independence of African Americans shifted her life away from teaching and placed her on a path of activism that was extraordinary for women of her day. Much of her time was spent traveling, writing, and lecturing frequently on Canadian immigration. In 1855, for example, after much controversy she succeeded in speaking in Philadelphia before the all-male, eleventh annual Colored National Convention, something no woman had ever been allowed to do. During this same trip, she also lectured at a benefit given in her honor and participated in a formal debate on the question, "Shall the Free Colored People of the United States Emigrate to Canada?" Her male opposition, a noted debater, was surprised when the judges awarded the win to Cary.

Cary's husband died in 1860, leaving her and their children without funds at a time when her newspaper, always in need of financial support, was floundering. Cary returned to teaching to earn an income, but her writing activities also continued. She compiled a biography for Osborne Anderson, the printer of the *Provincial Freeman,* a man who was the only African American leader of John Brown's raid on Harper's Ferry to survive. In addition, Cary was a regular contributor to the weekly *Anglo-*

African, a newspaper founded in New York in 1859 by Thomas Hamilton and supported after 1860 by the African Methodist Episcopal Zion Church. However, Cary's most extraordinary activities during this period of the Civil War were connected with her serving as a Union Army recruiting officer at the recommendation of Martin R. Delany (medical doctor, Black nationalist, first African American to be commissioned as a major in the U.S. Army, and highest-ranking African American man in the Freedmen's Bureau).

After the Civil War, Cary moved to Washington, D.C., where she opened another school, attended the Howard University Law School, and, after graduating, opened a law office. One of her first political battles was to challenge the House of Representatives Judiciary Committee for the right to vote. She won. She became one of the few women to vote in a federal election during the era of Reconstruction. At this time, Cary was also involved in women's rights issues generally. On February 9, 1880, she organized the Colored Women's Progressive Franchise Association. The purpose of the organization was to assert the equal rights of women through a twenty-point program. The program included gaining the right to vote; it also included a commitment to expanding women's work opportunities, establishing and supporting newspapers under the control of African American women, establishing African American banks, and developing African American businesses within the community, all of which offer considerable evidence that Cary's vision as a community leader included the general well-being of the community, not simply the interests of women alone.

By all accounts, as a pioneering journalist, Cary used her literate abilities well with regard to professional mandates in communicating the issues of her day to the reading and listening public. The range of her participation as a public voice was not confined within the pages of the newspapers for which she wrote. Her activities indicate she held a passionate regard for women's concerns and for the well-being and autonomous interests of the community at large. She campaigned on the page, at the podium, and also before the bar of justice, and she served as a model of literacy in action for the women in journalism who would follow her, such as Ida B. Wells and Pauline Hopkins.

An easy conclusion to draw from Cary's work (and Steward's as well) is that her concerns for the blossoming of African American potential wherever it may reside created a particular vision for action. She saw in teaching one opportunity to address needs, in journalism another, and in the legal profession yet another. All fitted well within long-standing African American women's mandates for how one should participate in one's community and fulfill roles significantly defined in the interest of the well-being of both self and society.

After the Civil War, with the rise in numbers of college-educated and professional African American women such as Steward and Cary, there was indeed a blossoming of intellectual potential within this group, and an increase in opportunity for these educated elites to channel their energies with greater impact than ever before. In *A Voice from the South* (1892), Cooper states:

In this last decade of our century, changes of such moment are in progress, such new and alluring vistas are opening out before us, such original and radical suggestions for the adjustment of labor and capital, of government and the governed, of the family, the church, and the state, that to be a possible factor though an infinitesimal one in such a movement is pregnant with hope and weighty with responsibility. To be a woman in such an age carries with it a privilege and an opportunity never implied before. But to be a woman of the Negro race in America, and to be able to grasp the deep significance of the possibilities of the crisis, is to have a heritage, it seems to me unique in the ages. (1988:143–44)

The material world around African American women of this era, the day-to-day texture of their lives across the multiple ways that those lives might be defined, was clear, a clarity that helped them to be well attuned to issues of equality, justice, and empowerment. This generation of women was fired within cauldrons that dictated the need for action. Within an environment of activism, they quickened their understanding of the sociopolitical context and refined their mandates for action. They garnered knowledge and experience in public discourse; they developed skills and expertise as language users through the variety of literate practices in which they engaged. With enhanced abilities, over the years after their college and university training, these women were able to transform the communities in which they lived. They were movers and shakers. They were the "race women," the club women, the managers of programs, deliverers of professional and community services. They interpreted

African American experiences from their various and sundry professional standpoints and were central players in the sustaining of life and culture. They were people who used language well, as writers and speakers. They got many critical jobs done in their communities, and done very well.

This cadre of nineteenth-century pioneers—starting with the trailblazers of the first half of the century and continuing with the standard-bearers of the latter half—created a space for the voices of African American women, which had not existed before. What is noteworthy, given the material circumstances of their historical context, is that they were able to do so, not just with a vision for leadership and a passionate regard, but with specific training, both formal and informal. Their rhetorical acts were inspirited by mandates for resistance and defiance, in response to needs that were ever present around them. They set the agenda for advocacy and action that paved the way into the twentieth century. As Cooper states in the quotation above, this group of women believed they were privileged to a new day, to a new "woman's era." What Cooper did not emphasize was that this belief could be attributed in large part to their own aggressive commitment to making it so.

Cooperative Endeavor and Sociopolitical Mandates

I have concentrated so far in this chapter on the sociopolitical context for literacy and rhetorical development and at the achievements of individual women. However, the story of the development of rhetorical prowess among nineteenth-century African American women would remain lacking without attention to their cooperative reform efforts. In order to tell this story, it is important to draw in, once again, the habits of cooperative activity that are traditional among women of West African descent.

As documented by Sylvia Ardyn Boone in her work on Mende women in Sierra Leone, traditional women's societies in African communities (which typically operated in secrecy) often encompassed dimensions of women's lives other than the primary purposes for which the society might be established or be perceived to operate. For example, in discussing the Sande Society as a powerful patron of the arts in West Africa, Boone suggests that looking at women's lives through this organization brings into focus its influence throughout their lives more generally:

Mende women love Sande: they sing its praises; recite its virtues, dance in its honor. They treasure it, preserve its virtues, and pass it on to the next generation. In return Sande is the guardian of the women: their spokesman, shield, protector, battling to give women life space, power, health, love, fertility, self-expression. And, as it guards and cherishes the women, they in turn rally round it and hold its standards high. (Boone 1986:15)

I do not seek in this analysis to make such a totalizing place for African American women's organizations in their lives, although I do acknowledge the potential for such a placement in the lives of some women. I am suggesting, instead, that looking through an organizational lens at elite nineteenth-century women is productive for us to come to a more generative understanding of how their rhetorical practices operated as a resource in service of long-standing sociopolitical mandates. I am asserting that cooperative activity through the establishing of sociopolitical organizations was a traditional practice, which gained renewed vitality when employed by nineteenth-century African American women (and men also) in response to pressing community needs. I am also asserting that this work shaped how African American women, as they engaged in rhetorical practices, would form ethos and would consistently use language (spoken and written) as a tool for social and political change.

If we accept the notion that African women came to this continent with the habit of working cooperatively to carry out day-to-day responsibilities, to meet their personal needs, and to meet the needs of the community, and that they passed these habits on to subsequent generations, then it should come as no surprise that cooperative practices, including the formation of societies, are much in evidence throughout the history of African American women in the United States. The question is not, then, whether there were such activities, but the extent to which we can document such practices as they were contextually defined. For this study, the inquiry on cooperative reform is bifocal. Attention centers on (1) what the contextualized definitions of cooperative reform by African American women illustrate about the roles of literacy as a newly developed resource for community progress and survival; and (2) elite nineteenth-century women, as a case in point for cooperative endeavor. Highlighting elite nineteenth-century women also has two focal points. On one hand, I interrogate the process whereby African American club women were enabled to reaffirm deep-seated imperatives to use intellectual powers fully in order to sustain both self and community. On the other hand, I interrogate how these women actually exhibited rhetorical prowess in the use of literacy as a specific tool for engagement in public discourse and for social change.

Shifting the analytical gaze away from the fact that African American women worked cooperatively to address daily needs—during pre–Civil War days, for example, to get cotton picked or plantation homes cleaned or young children cared for, or to heal the sick—this analysis pays attention in a more macro- rather than micro-level way. I position organized reform activities as behavior. They are an outward manifestation of a commitment to achievement in the completion of tasks, demonstrating personal ability and expertise. They are also a commitment to social responsibility, to the obligation to use resources, both personal and professional, in the interest of the welfare of the community.

Joining Hands to Lift and Climb

It is ironic that—after the American Revolution, which established the United States as an independent nation and which claimed inalienable rights for all men to life, liberty, and the pursuit of happiness—conditions actually grew more restrictive for the significant numbers of free African Americans across the United States, in both the North and the South. These deteriorating conditions set in motion the formation of societies, a familiar tool among both women and men, in support of political activism and resistance.[24] The emergence of organizations with such agendas suggests that, as a particular type of cooperative practice, African American societies have traditionally reflected and been shaped by the material conditions of the community, not just by a desire for the social engagement of individuals. African American societies have consistently shown evidence of a basic mandate—that is, the need for those forming such alliances to operate in conscious regard of political and economic forces. In the face of such forces, the autonomy of the 319,000 free African Americans living in the United States by 1830 was highly constrained, and it became more difficult for them to live lives of honor and self-respect.

Exacerbating these conditions by the 1830s were the violent slave insurrections, which occurred early in the century (Gabriel in 1800, Denmark Vesey in 1822, Nat Turner in 1831), and also the American Colonization Movement, established as an African resettlement program for free

African Americans. By all accounts, free African Americans were a group curiously "misfitted" in a country that avowed liberty and justice for all but so openly accepted slavery as a "natural" condition for people of African descent. Within such an incommodious environment, the need for African Americans to organize in their own interests was evident.

One of the first of these organizations was the African Society, organized in Boston in 1796. The first item in the bylaws of this group stated:

> We, the African Members, form ourselves into a Society, under the above name, for the mutual benefit of each other, which may from time to time offer; behaving ourselves at the same time as true and faithful citizens of the Commonwealth in which we live; and that we take no one into the Society, who shall commit any injustice or outrage against the laws of their country. (Porter 1971:9)

The first known African American women's societies were also established in the 1790s as auxiliaries to church organizations.[25] The churches themselves had been formed typically in response to discriminatory practices in the white churches. Within the newly formed African American churches, mutual aid societies quickly developed in support of church members who found themselves in distress. The African Methodist Episcopal Church, an organization founded in 1787 by Richard Allen and Absalom Jones, is one case in point; the United Daughters of Allen was the women's auxiliary. According to Dorothy B. Porter, their mission was to take care of the weak and infirm, to feed the hungry, to clothe and shelter those in need, and to provide opportunities to the extent possible for learning and cultural enrichment (Porter 1936:555).

In addition to the mutual aid organizations, however, African American women were active also in other types of organized reform activities. Across the northeastern and midwestern states before the Civil War, they participated in Bible, missionary, and reform societies to develop religious and moral consciousness; in educational and welfare societies in support of socializing values; by the late 1820s in literary societies for educational improvement and for the training of leaders, orators, and writers (political and literary); and by the 1830s in separate anti-slavery societies in response to discriminatory practices in white anti-slavery societies. Included, for example, among the organizations of the northeastern women was the Afric-American Female Intelligence Society, formed in Boston in 1832, the group before which Maria Stewart spoke.

After the Civil War, cooperative activity escalated. A slate of organizations in both the North and the South included groups of women who participated in the woman suffrage movement, in order to gain the vote for women; in temperance reform, which used an anti-drinking springboard to refocus attention on issues of home and family and on community development; and in the literary clubs and benevolent organizations of various sorts in which the women were already experienced. By the post-Reconstruction era, African American women had accumulated a long, rich history of community activism. They were leaders, with skills learned from experience and expertise garnered in running different types of community organizations and engaging in different types of social reform. Most consistent, across these networks of clubs, African American women acquired and refined skills as writers and orators that were unique for their day.

Given this analysis, with its emphasis on rhetorical practices, I am asserting that a critical view of women's participation in this organizational work offers an opportunity to look beyond the work itself to what this pattern of behavior suggests about the formation of ethos in rhetorical decision-making. As this group of women began acquiring professional identities, in addition to their personal identities, I suggest that their participation in organizations reaffirmed traditional social identities (that is, the roles of women as interpreters of life, teachers and transmitters of culture, and preservers of the community and the race) within a context of cooperative political activity. The merging, therefore, of these identities (personal, historical, social, professional, even political) gave rise to a particular type of process for the formation of ethos among these women as writers and speakers in public domains.

In being active members of these various and sundry organizations with their variable range of interests (social, political, religious, cultural), each woman was compelled to take into account (and some more consciously than others) her own intricate relationships to the material conditions around her, given the work of the organizations to which she actually belonged. Each was called upon to participate in the setting of mandates for action, as this process became a central subject of discourse across the networks of cooperative endeavor. Some were often called upon, as organizational leaders, to articulate their own mandates—in order to join in the negotiation of what the group mandates should be and to define courses for both their own individual actions (uniquely expressed) as well as the actions of the group itself or even a network of groups (as in the case of their international work). In such a scenario, although individual expressions of identity, ethos, and action are certain to differ, what becomes constant is the action itself—in this case the obligation to speak up, to write, to engage in rhetorical action. Also constant is the extent to which this obligation is shaped by *work* and by *context*.

From this perspective, the pattern—rather than the specifics—of ethos formation indicates an engagement with rhetorical decision-making that positioned "paid" work (professional activity) and "volunteer" work (community activism) as part and parcel of the same agenda. Along with other organizational activities, the obligation to speak up and to write in support of the sociopolitical agenda were normalized as appropriate work, regardless of the person's other work or professional roles. If a club woman had the opportunity to speak or write, she was obligated—by the norms of her community and the sociopolitical agenda set by that community—to do so.

We can take Susan Smith McKinney Steward as a case in point. As a physician and a community activist, Steward's sociopolitical mandate apparently included the work she was paid to do as well as work she was not paid to do, and rhetorical action (speaking and writing) were appropriate to both arenas. With this combination of paid and volunteer service, Steward created conceptual links that permitted both these commitments to hold a common space in her life, a space in which activities that might be perceived as dualities operated equitably and inextricably and a space in which speaking and writing were perceivable as usable tools. The material conditions of the world around Steward, particularly as she was enabled through her organizational work to see the resonances between her view and the views of others, dictated that her volunteer work had priority, just as her paid work did. The evidence of the linkage is that she worked untiringly in both fields, with each commitment coming within the purview of a commitment to self and community, and with each area offering her opportunities to speak and to write.

The record of her life supports the assessment that Steward perceived herself to be the holder of particular personal and professional resources, including rhetorical abilities, that she was privileged to bring to bear across needs. I am suggesting, therefore, that in her life and work she constitutes not merely the example of a busy, talented, competent woman, but also the example of a woman who saw her work as not limited in concept by either profession or volunteerism, making all the more useful the opportunity to maximize her talents and abilities by working cooperatively with others who were likewise situated. These women, with a multiplicity of personal and professional resources, could do more together than any one of them could or should try to do alone. Cooperative community activity became, for this group, a mechanism of choice in critical intervention. In making this choice, they participated in strategies for sociopolitical activism (including networking with African American men and other groups) that have successfully sustained the African American community through the centuries to the present day.

Taking into account this history of activism, it is a simple step to imagine the relative ease with which two club women in New York—Victoria Earle Matthews and Maritcha Lyon—could, in 1892, spearhead the hosting of a testimonial dinner for Ida B. Wells in support of her anti-lynching campaign that drew over 250 women from New York, Boston, and Philadelphia.[26] It would be equally simple to imagine that a few months later Josephine St. Pierre Ruffin of Boston (who attended the meeting) could send out a call and successfully convene the first *national* convention of African American women. One co-organizer of this occasion for national organization was Victoria Earle Matthews. She wrote for the *New York Age* and for several other newspapers around the country and is perhaps best known as the founding director of the White Rose Mission. This mission provided a home and protection for African American women and girls who had recently migrated from the South. It functioned also as a social center for community women and children, and as a training ground for self-improvement and for Christian living. Maritcha Lyon, the other co-organizer, was a writer and an educator, one of the first African American women to be named an assistant principal, in a public school in Brooklyn. Both women were active in social reform and were experienced in ministering to the sundry needs of their communities. Two months after the testimonial dinner for Wells, they founded a club, the Woman's Loyal Union of New York and Brooklyn, with Matthews serving as the first president.

In hosting the dinner for Wells, Matthews and Lyon wanted to pay tribute to Wells's work, which they deemed admirable and courageous, and also to raise funds to support her continuing to carry on her work. The dinner was successful in accomplishing these goals. The collective of women presented Wells with five hundred dollars and a gold brooch in the shape of a pen. The women attending the dinner considered the gathering to be more than just a tribute to Wells, however. By 1892, after a century of cooperative community action on the local level, these very active women had already begun to establish a nationwide network of African American women and to centralize an agenda for the work they were already doing. Wells and her story of terrorism provided, therefore, a perfect occasion for them to gather, to support her and at the same time energize their own efforts toward establishing a national women's organization. This gathering signaled that the seeds for a national level organization had been firmly planted. As Dorothy Salem states:

The national club movement among black women was the culmination of three factors. First, by 1890 the women had developed local leadership attempting to respond to specific community needs. Second, common interests and/or issues brought women together as a group above denominational or regional rivalries. Finally, several incidents demonstrated the need for a national organization to promote a positive image of black women, to preserve their relatively privileged status, and to provide moral and educational guidance to the less privileged in their communities. (Salem 1990:12)

After the testimonial, Josephine St. Pierre Ruffin and her daughter Florence Ruffin Ridley returned to Boston and played central roles in establishing a few months later the Boston New Era Club.[27] They also began publishing the first monthly magazine to be published by African American women, *Woman's Era*. Ruffin served as editor of the paper and Ridley as assistant editor. Departmental editors were Medora W. Gould, Leslie Wilmot, M. Elizabeth Johnson, Marion Ridley, Irene De Mortie, and Hannah Smith. In the first issue, published on March 24, 1894, in the premier editorial Ruffin skillfully acknowledged that there might seem to be no obvious reason for a group of African American women to start a new publication. She then made just as skillful a case for the void that she and her editorial team perceived to exist despite this sentiment:

The need of such a journal has long been felt as a medium of intercourse and sympathy between the women of all races and conditions; especially true is this, of the educated and refined, among the colored women, members of which class may be found in every state from Maine to Florida, but in nearly all of these places an important factor, and receives little or no recognition, and the one more than all others which prevents her from making the most of herself and taking her legitimate place among the advanced women, is the limitation of her surroundings and the circumscribed sphere in which she must move. (8)

Ruffin made a place in public discourse for elite African American women, and she drew correspondents from women's clubs across the nation in the effort to make good use of the publication. Department heads included Victoria Earle Matthews in New York; Fannie Barrier Williams in Chicago; Josephine Silone-Yates in Kansas City; Mary Church Terrell in Washington, D.C.; Elizabeth Ensley in Denver; and Alice Ruth Moore in New Orleans. *Woman's Era* became a primary vehicle of communication and of community formation, transmitting messages of political and social reform to elite African American women across the land. The publication was a vital source of information about family life and fashion; a place for the discussion of critical issues, such as health care, educational opportunity, and the participation of women in community development; as well as a place to discuss issues such as lynching, the rising number of Jim Crow practices, prison reform, and other issues of importance to the community at large.

As Ruffin, Ridley, and the other members of the Woman's Era Club spread their influence, the equally influential Colored Women's League of Washington, D.C., was engaged in similar operations. The Washington group was led by Helen A. Cook, Mary Church Terrell, Anna Julia Cooper, Charlotte Forten Grimké, Josephine B. Bruce, Mary Jane Patterson, and others. Both groups formed alliances among clubs in the interests of establishing a national organization. Ultimately, the two national organizations—the Washington-based National Colored Women's League and the Boston-based National Federation of Afro-American Women—joined together to form the NACW, an organization that still exists, more than one hundred years later. The consolidation was achieved on July 21, 1896.

One month later, the newly elected president of NACW—Mary Church Terrell from Washington, D.C.—issued a public announcement in *Woman's Era:*

We, the Colored Women of America, stand before the country today a united sisterhood, pledged to promote the welfare of our race, along all the lines that tend to its development and advancement . . . we hope to run the whole gamut of human progress and reform. . . . In myself I am nothing, but with the loyal support of conscientious, capable women, all things are possible to us. . . . The magnitude of the work to which we seem divinely called and are solemnly pledged, far from affrighting and depressing us, inspires to greater effort. (Beverly Washington Jones 1990:131–32)

Their motto was "Lifting As We Climb," and they called for the careful, conscientious study of questions that deeply and directly affected African American people in general, and African American women in particular. The national agenda included providing for the future of the race by changing the conditions (housing, education, health care, and so on) that make a difference in the lives of children; improving the conditions for working women; and maintaining a "healthy" public opinion about the race and its women. The NACW agenda also included paying attention to public policies and social issues, such as Jim Crow laws, prison reform, and lynching.

The momentum created by this groundswell of organized action among African American women at the turn of the nineteenth century carried this group forward into the twentieth century with considerable energy. Consider, for example, the activities of African American club women in support of their advocacy of literacy development. In the 1890s, African American club women led the nation in establishing kindergartens for African American children, and in holding what they called Mothers' Meetings, meetings designed to address everything they could manage to address that could improve the lives and conditions of children by directing attention to women's needs as they reflected and revealed the needs of children and families.

The story of Atlanta's Neighborhood Union, under the leadership of Lugenia Burns Hope (wife of John Hope, president of Morehouse College) illustrates the intensity and impact of these types of efforts over the next three decades. This group was organized in 1908 from a core group of nineteenth-century club women who had been particularly active in establishing daycare centers for children. Its purpose was to be "the moral, social, intellectual, and religious uplift of the community and the neighborhood in which the organization or its branches may be established" (Rouse 1989:65–66). The union was divided into four departments: the Moral and Educational Department, the Literary Department, the Musical Department, the Arts Department. Each department had standing committees on which the members served.

These women became the watchdogs of the African American community in Atlanta, signaling alarm, agitating for change, providing much-needed services. As early as 1908 they conducted surveys to identify urgent needs. They communicated these needs to local government officials; garnered resources to address them; and did not rest until some type of action was taken, while they advocated additional actions. In 1913, for instance, the union began investigating the city's African American public schools. They found unhealthy sanitary conditions, poor lighting and ventilation, overcrowded classrooms, severe understaffing with double sessions being conducted by the same teachers, inequities in teacher salaries, and so on. They interviewed each member of the city council, the mayor, members of the board of education, African American ministers, other African American club women, and members of other African American community organizations. They solicited help from every influential person and group possible, including their husbands (all influential men in the community); they solicited alliances with influential white women. Through this agitation, they managed to get a school built here, or a salary raised there.

One of their most successful campaigns grew from their opposition to efforts to deny African American children access to literature after the sixth grade, a policy supported by the industrial education movement. The union opposed inequities in educational opportunity and resources; they opposed especially a public education that sought to limit African Americans to industrial education, even though they were contributors to the tax base and thereby eligible for access to publicly funded education in all forms. The union waged their campaign for eleven years, and their efforts contributed significantly to the opening in 1924 of the first African American public high school in the city of Atlanta, Booker T. Washington High.

In looking back at the Black Clubwomen's Movement and other movements to follow (including the Black Sorority Movement), what stands out clearly is that this national network for community activism was indeed a multiply defined network, made up of several different types of organizations with varying commitments. While there were striking similarities of interests within this group, and a consensus about general community needs (for example, the need for education and for political and economic power), the club movement actually permitted women with different matrices of identity, different perceptions of needs, and different priorities for sociopolitical mandates (cultural, social, political, economic, religious) to form a shared space—a community. From the shared space of club work these women articulated "a common good," charted courses of action, raised voices in counterdistinction to mainstream disregard, and generated at least the capacity—if not the immediate possibility (consider, for example, the eleven-year commitment of the Neighborhood Union)—to make themselves heard and appropriately responded to. By this process, the club women sustained their roles as critical sources of support for the educational, cultural, social, political, and economic development of the African American community.

Club work functioned as more than a simple community maintenance program. The arenas for club work were also arenas for the negotiation of action, and for constructing alternate access to spheres of power. Club work formed a space where African American women were able to generate and convey messages and to influence public policy. With this sense of club work, African American women can be repositioned in terms of ethos, action, and sociopolitical location. Through their community activism, they served the communities, certainly. Simultaneously, however, they also created for themselves a means by which (1) to develop, enhance, and make manifest their intellectual abilities—for example, in calling for, defining, and carrying out an agenda for community research and action; (2) to carry forth traditions of community leadership that emerged from their own uniquely situated sociopolitical place in society; and (3) to gain an informal training ground that facilitated the use and refinement of their rhetorical abilities in public discourse. Although a group perceived by larger society as peripheral to public negotiations and public policy-making processes, African American women constructed and used persistently their own available means of persuasion for social and political change.

African American Women in Public Space

In "The Public Sphere: An Encyclopedia Article (1964)," Jürgen Habermas chronicles the emergence of a public sphere as an eighteenth-century phenomenon.[28] He points out that public discourse was made possible with the rise of the bourgeoisie and the movement of politics from the private domains of the monarchy to public areas such as republican clubs, cafés, political rebellions, and so forth, and with the emergence of an independent public press, such as newspapers. The periodical press has functioned traditionally as a basic tool for public discussion and deliberation, whereby problems and issues receive attention from diverse viewpoints and whereby opinions of a readership (including readers and listeners) can be shaped and directed toward action. The periodical press has also functioned as a primary mechanism whereby the voices of counterpublics, as Nancy Fraser discusses them (see below), have been sustained in the midst of the exclusionary practices of the "official" bourgeois public.

In talking about the ways in which alternative, parallel public spheres have always existed in the United States, Fraser cites the work of others (Ryan 1990; Eley 1992; Brooks-Higginbotham 1993) and reinforces the notion that groups who are not politically powerful by "official" definitions (such as African Americans and women) construct, nevertheless, their own access to public political life and to public discourse:

Thus, the view that women and blacks were excluded from "the public sphere" turns out to be ideological; it rests on a class- and gender-biased notion of publicity, one that accepts at face value the bourgeois public's claim to be *the* public. In fact, the historiography of Ryan, Brooks-Higginbotham, and others demonstrates that the bourgeois public was never *the public*. On the contrary, virtually contemporaneous with the bourgeois public there arose a host of competing counterpublics, including nationalist publics, popular peasant publics, elite women's publics, black publics, and working-class publics. (Fraser 1997:75)

The construction of a public sphere was essential to African American protest and to the amelioration of conditions for progress and change. Newspapers and magazines helped the community articulate its own problems, deliberate its own needs, celebrate its own achievements, and identify strategies capable of effecting change in the larger sociopolitical context. In this specific function, the periodical press has been a magnetizing force in generating knowledge about the range of issues and concerns affecting the group and in directing this knowledge toward available strategies. The process enabled both individuals and groups to form opinions and engage in appropriate, often resistant, action. Periodical publications have served as a constant forum for the voices of African Americans to be heard. They have constituted a counterforce to the more dominant "official" voices that define the public agenda in a manner that usually excluded African American interests.

While acknowledging that the African American periodical press was a vibrant arena for public discourse, we need also to emphasize how dynamic, not one-dimensional, the genesis and development of these countervoices were. In particular, we need to interrogate the dominant opinion that *the* arena for African American discourse was the church, that *the* influential voices were those of the clergy, that deliberation was initiated and operated under the specific influence of the church and its interests alone. My view of the historical record, especially if the examination includes antebellum activities, suggests that the variable interests of the African American community and the rhetors who actually participated in rhetorical action across the decades of the nineteenth century (despite the religious affiliations of particular rhetors) operated in both secular and religious contexts. What becomes more distinctive after the Civil War is the dynamic merging of sociopolitical interests, more broadly defined, and the interests of the church. As the most stable community institution, the African American church functioned to provide financial support, an ongoing cohort of educated leadership, and by the end of the century, indeed, a central arena for political participation. The point, however, is that while there has been a merging of interests, there is, nevertheless, a need to distinguish between these two historical threads so that political activism as a literate enterprise and as a gendered one can be better theorized. Viewing both the church and the press as complex community institutions permits an analysis that seems more adequate to account both for a multiple agenda and for multiple voices.

Even without concentrating on the complexities of relationships between the African American periodical press and the church, there is no doubt that, as a public domain with varying participation, the periodical press was successful in making room for African American community interests in political decision-making processes. In 1891, I. Garland Penn in *The Afro-American Press and Its Editors* recognized the critical leadership role of the press in the progress and achievements of African Americans. Penn carefully documented the history of specific publications and their editors, from 1827 (when John B. Russwurm and Samuel E. Cornish began the very first publication, *Freedom's Journal*) through 1891 (when Penn published his book):

> Certainly, the importance and magnitude of the work done by the Afro-American Press, the scope of its influence, and the beneficent results accruing from its labors, cannot fail of appreciation. . . . The object in putting forth this feeble effort is not for the praise of men or for the reaping of money, but to promote the future welfare of Afro-American journalism by telling to its constituents the story of its heroic labors in their behalf. (Penn 1988:Preface)

His desire was to have the African American press better supported within the African American community. His history establishes the multiple ways in which these organs opened public discourse to the participation and the points of view of African American people in public deliberation.

What is most interesting about the functioning of the African American press given the focus of this analysis, however, is the extent to which African American women—particularly the members of the educated elite of the late nineteenth century—were very much involved, if not quite co-equal, in these enterprises. Penn, for example, even in 1891 includes a chapter on women in journalism and cites twenty-nine women: "These are by no means all of our women in journalism who have made themselves felt in that sphere of life. A host of them are doing local work upon newspapers and magazines" (1988:426).[29] Examples of this local work are evident from the beginning. David Ruggles, for example, published the *Mirror of Liberty* (established in 1838) and included a section called the "Ladies Mirror."[30] The mission of the paper was to report on the activities of the interracial New York Committee of Vigilance, a political reform organization of which Ruggles was the secretary. Ruggles, obviously, saw the need for women to have a place in this enterprise, even though he envisioned that place as separate.

The periodical press was established right from the beginning as a primary mechanism whereby African American women participated in public discourse, demonstrated their desires to be agents of change, and were enabled by this forum to act on these desires. Among the most famous of this nineteenth-century group of women journalists and writers is Ida B. Wells, known by her fellow journalists as the "princess of the press."[31] Wells's journalistic experience began in 1884 when she became a contributor to the *Living Way,* a paper in Memphis, Tennessee, associated with the Baptist Church. From her days with the *Living Way,* Wells went on to own her own newspaper, to hold national office in her professional organization as secretary of the National Press Convention, and to build an excellent career as an outspoken investigative reporter, particularly concerning her lifelong anti-lynching campaign.

Wells was neither first nor alone in this work. There were literally dozens of women who, since the 1830s, found the African American periodical press to be the platform from which they could speak and be heard both as creative writers of poetry, short stories, and serialized novels, and as nonfiction writers of informative prose, persuasive essays, personal narratives, biographical sketches, tributes, opinion pieces, and so forth. Their pens became the instruments through which their voices were amplified and their agendas for action were brought to the table of public opinion.

Most of the African American periodicals had women editing the women's page, and significant numbers of women contributors. Women participated variously in the publishing arena (see appendixes).[32] Many of them (for example, Ida B. Wells, Gertrude Mossell, and Pauline Hopkins), as professional journalists, were involved in more than one role, sometimes serving as editor of one paper and contributor to several others. On the other hand, several members of this group did not consider themselves professional journalists. They were women who had professional commitments in other areas, as medical doctors, educators, or community organizers, but who (as Susan Smith McKinney Steward, described earlier) filled roles that extended the definitions of obligation and work and gave rise to practices similar to what we have named in the contemporary context "the public intellectual." These women took responsibility, regardless of their professions, for engaging actively in public discourse— as people with intellectual, problem-posing and- solving abilities. They raised their voices in public discussion and deliberation and thus helped to reconfigure an arena in which the community could receive the attention it deserves.

Coming to Voice: The Pen as a Mighty Sword

Essay writing in the periodical press was a critical mechanism for African American women to participate in public discourse. One prime example of their use of the periodical press is a special issue of the *Voice of the Negro*, a monthly magazine that had a circulation of fifteen thousand within a few months of its founding in 1904 in Atlanta, Georgia. John Wesley Edward Bowen and Jesse Max Barber served as coeditors, although the magazine was funded by J. L. Nichols, a white subscription book publishing company with an African American book department. Despite the controversy surrounding the paper's connection to the white community, and its subsequent cessation in 1907 because of the controversy, during the years of its publication the *Voice of the Negro* was the major African American periodical publication in the South and was well received throughout the country. Barber, who became the principal editor, was affiliated with militant civil rights organizations, including the Niagara Movement (which led to the formation of the National Association for the Advancement of Colored People [NAACP]) and the National Negro American Political League, organized by William Monroe Trotter and Alexander Walters. No matter its controversy or its progressive connections, the *Voice of the Negro* was a periodical that consistently included the voices of African American women.

The July 1904 issue of the *Voice of the Negro* is a stellar example (Special Collections, Clark Atlanta University). It was a special women's issue and may actually be the first anthologizing in a thematic way of the nonfiction, issues-oriented voices of African American women, in this case writing for a broader audience than usual. Newspapers and magazines typically directed women writers toward a women's page despite their topics of interest including both sociopolitical issues and other concerns, such as fashion and home decorating. Generally, though certainly not exclusively, women wrote for women and were published in women's sections. This issue of the *Voice* was different. With some apparent need to justify the issue, Barber advertised it with this comment: "Anybody will profit by reading after these women. The women will occupy the greater portion of the Magazine, but variety is the spice of life."

The contributors included prominent members of the National Association of Clubwomen from across the country: Nannie H. Burroughs,

Addie Waits Hunton, Josephine Silone-Yates, Margaret Murray Washington, Mary Church Terrell, Josephine B. Bruce, Sylvaniz Francoz Williams, and Fannie Barrier Williams. The articles included "Not Color But Character (Burroughs), "Negro Womanhood Defended" (Hunton), "The National Association of Colored Women" (Silone-Yates), "Social Improvement for the Farm Women" (Washington), "The Progress of Colored Women" (Terrell), "What Is the Educated Colored Woman Doing?" (Bruce), "Good Out of Nazareth" (S. F. Williams), and "An Extension of the Conference Spirit" (F. B. Williams). As the article titles indicate, central focal points for the writers were the advocacy of social, educational, and economic issues relevant for African American women, a defense of their character, and a celebration of their achievements.

Among the voices presented was that of Addie Waits Hunton (1866–1943). At the time the articles were written, Hunton was living in Atlanta, Georgia. She was married to William Alphaeus Hunton, the first African American to serve as international secretary for the Young Men's Christian Association. She had grown up in Norfolk, Virginia, the eldest of three children. She graduated from Boston Girls Latin School and from the Spencerian College of Commerce in Philadelphia and, a few years later, attended Kaiser Wilhelm University in Germany. During her professional career, Hunton served as a teacher in the public schools of Virginia; as a principal at the State Normal and Agricultural College in Normal, Alabama; as registrar and accountant at Clark College in Atlanta; in various positions with the Young Women's Christian Association; and as field secretary for the NAACP. She was active in women's organizations, not only the NACW, but others as well. She was a member of the Women's International League for Peace and Freedom, through which she served as the principal organizer of the 1927 Pan-African Congress in New York City, her permanent home. She was president of the Empire State Federation of Women's Clubs and a member of the International Council of Women of the Darker Races.[33] She was a frequent contributor to the periodical press, and in 1938 she published a biography of her husband, *William Alphaeus Hunton: A Pioneer Prophet of Young Men,* who had contracted tuberculosis and died twenty-two years before.

In her article, "Negro Womanhood Defended," Hunton proclaims that her role was not as supplicant or apologist but as defender:

Out of that ever vexing and mysterious hydra-headed evil we name the "race problem," there seems to have grown of late a sentiment, if you will, whose particular function it is to magnify the moral weakness of Negro womanhood. . . . To her, at this time, is being charged every weakness of the race, even though this weakness may have been common to humanity since the days of Adam. Everywhere, her moral defects are being portrayed by her enemies; sometimes, veiled in hypocritical pity, and again, in language bitter and unrelenting. . . . We are neither unconscious [n]or unmindful of our shortcomings; we are simply asking now that, in the clear light of truth and justice, her case be given a hearing by all who are interested in moral and social problems, and who value the principles of justice, freedom and fraternity, or even by those who regard all humanity as something above the common clod. (*Voice of the Negro,* July 1904, 280)

Hunton is hard-hitting in her non-acceptance of the charges against African American women. She takes a proactive stance, discussing how condition and environment are implicated in the negative reputations of African American women, and pointing out by implication the extent to which culpability has clearly been misapplied to African American women instead of to white men and to the systems of power and authority operating in the nation. She acknowledges, in subsequent paragraphs, human variety, even in moral action, and how African American women exhibit as much of a range of behavior as anyone else; and she underscores how vilifications of African American women's character are rooted in ignorance of their lives and work:

It is not strange that those whose prey she had been for so long should have followed her into her new environments. . . . With a blighted past, no fireside training nor home life, driven to and fro at will in a world of poverty and ignorance, it would have been strange and unusual had she not, in many cases, fallen by the wayside. (*Voice of the Negro,* July 1904, 281)

Hunton makes a special point of saying, however, that, whatever incidences of immorality might be in evidence, it was no indication of "wholesale," rather than particular, immorality, even in the South where the majority of African American people were living. She then proceeds to discuss fair wages for women and the need for opportunities for their development. She ends by redefining the problem, reestablishing ethical responsibility, and setting new roles and relationships:

Finally, we are confronting new conditions which make stern demands upon the wisdom and conscience of both races. Let it not be forgotten that the high virtue of the South has its basis on the souls and bodies of Negro women; therefore, it is now time that Southern chivalry, which ever proclaims its right to "keep pure and undefiled the spirit that worships at the family shrine," should extend itself to the protection of the Negro man who seeks to establish the same principle for his home. In the light of Christianity all women must be protected if for no other reason than that they are akin to the Christ-mother. Until this is done, it would, at least, be charitable to leave the discussion of the morality of the Negro woman to those who are earnestly laboring for her uplift. (*Voice of the Negro,* July 1904, 282)

Hunton advocates protection for African American men and their families, in keeping with patriarchal expectations, and she also suggests in evident outrage, "If you—whoever you are—are not helping to solve the problem—as you should be doing, do shut up and get out of the way of those of us who are."

Another view comes through in the article written by Fannie Barrier Williams (1855–1944).[34] Williams grew up in an affluent family in Brockport, New York, one of three children. She attended the local schools and graduated from the State Normal School at Brockport in 1870. After graduation, Williams joined the groups of northern teachers who went south to teach the African Americans recently freed from slavery. She found intolerable her positioning as racially inferior in the South and soon left to accept a teaching position in Washington, D.C., where she met and married S. Laing Williams, a lawyer. The couple moved to Chicago where both of them built reputations as community leaders. Williams was very active in African American women's clubs and in dismantling the barriers between this work and the work of white women in white women's clubs.

Williams was an active community organizer and fundraiser. She was the Chicago reporter for *Woman's Era,* and she was a frequent speaker before many different types of audiences, most notable perhaps for her address at the Chicago World's Fair in May 1893 when she spoke before the Departmental Congress of the National Association of Loyal Women of American Liberty at the World's Congress of Representative Women. Her speech was entitled, "The Intellectual Progress and Present Status of the Colored Women of the United States since the Emancipation Proclamation." Her article in the *Voice* was entitled, "An Extension of the Conference Spirit."

In this article, Williams wrote about a three-day conference held in

Chicago by the Chicago Woman's Club, an elite white women's group in which she became the first African American member. The purpose of the conference was to study "Women in Modern Industrialism." In her essay, Williams connects this work immediately to the annual conferences in the African American community that had been held at Tuskegee, Hampton, and Atlanta Universities and positioned the Chicago conference as "the extension," rather than the core of such work. She highlighted the resonant calls during the conference for attention and action. She cites particularly the call for equal pay for equal work and the agreement of this conference with the Hampton conference and asserts: "there is no reason why a woman of character, graciousness and skill should not change the whole current of public opinion in regard to the respectability of domestic service" (*Voice of the Negro,* July 1904, 302), where, of course, many African American women were employed. In effect, Williams's essay connected the concerns of African American women, and the African American community at large, to a national agenda, underscoring the worthiness of the struggles of African American women, in terms of both race and gender, for justice, equity, and empowerment. She finishes:

> The strong language used in this conference by those who are oppressed in various ways and compelled to live below their rights as citizens, sounded at times like the lamentations we so often indulge in. The interest taken in these high and perplexing questions, by women of wealth and position, and the sympathy revealed for those who are without the power to protect themselves, happily show that the forces that are to solve both the black and white problems, are in course of preparation. The largeness of soul and breadth of conception that are now enlisted in these economic problems, must certainly include within the range of their corrective influence, the wrongs under which we smart and suffer and justly complain. (*Voice of the Negro,* July 1904, 303)

Williams was advocating ongoing struggle, but she was also acknowledging a recontextualizing of that struggle as one that connected us all, African Americans and others.

This special collection of African American women's essays is a showcase, albeit only the tip of the iceberg, of African American women's rhetorical talents and sociopolitical interests. The issue serves as a firm foundation from which to suggest a developing expertise among African American women as writers of essays. Further, it constitutes a twentieth-century marker of the predilection for this form of women who came of age as activists in the nineteenth century. It simultaneously serves as a foreshadowing, indicating that the essay would continue to be a form of choice for public engagement throughout the twentieth century. This collection also does more, however.

This issue of the *Voice of the Negro* suggests that African American women's nonfiction writing, as preserved in the periodical press, is a source for recognizing the manner and means by which African American women actually created on this continent three noteworthy traditions. As their resources expanded, with increasing levels of knowledge and experience, nineteenth-century African American women (and those before them) laid the groundwork for traditions of intellectualism, community leadership, and rhetorical prowess. In this way, the women's issue of the *Voice* at the turn of the twentieth century (and in the company of other nonfiction writing across the decades since the 1830s and the emergence of Maria Stewart) serves as a milestone. Both before and after this moment, a steady stream of contributions have constituted and reconstituted the cultural sea of rhetorical knowledge and experience, the body of richly defined community resources that have given rise to the manifold achievements of contemporary African American women writers.

The Essayist Tradition Among African American Women

One tradition to be highlighted among this configuration of African American women's achievements is the tradition of essaying itself. The first point to make about the essayist tradition, as Claire De Obaldia says, is that "corpuses and traditions tend to be constituted retrospectively" (1995:7). Typically, a tradition is not actually defined solely on what practitioners at the founding moments of the tradition were doing, from their own points of view. In other words, it is not typical for someone to say, "I'm going to start a tradition now." Instead, we embody a tradition by invoking a sense-making process—after whatever is perceived to be the starting point is identified and deemed meaningful enough to replicate. So, it is the looking back, the retrospective eye, that sets the possibility. A tradition operates in the resonating heart and eye of a beholder, and in the commitment of that beholder to affirm by word or deed what the tradition upholds. Potential practitioners of ways of seeing, being, and doing can be influenced or inspired by others—and subsequently their ability consciously or even tacitly to continue the perceived practice or adhere to the values and concepts is enabled or nurtured, thus demonstrating the continuity that we acknowledge as a defining feature of this term.

My view is that for researchers—rather than practitioners—the notion of a tradition is inverted. While we too are looking with a retrospective eye, the term *tradition* functions more as an analytic category than as a label or even an enabling identity. Through the use of this term, we signal a moment in time when we can garner evidence for coalescing forces, events, and interests, a moment in which we can discern features and see continuities in practice. With the tools of scholarship we can make, then, a case for the existence of a tradition by documenting the manifestations of it. At that point we are called upon to apply the identified features to practitioners over time. The basic goal of such an analysis, as in this case, is not to romanticize the experiences of forebears but to observe and document behavior and to contextualize that behavior within meaningful frameworks.

After more than a century and a half of productivity, we can cite the beginning of the use of the essay by African American women in 1831 with the publication of Maria Stewart's "Religion and the Pure Principles of Morality." Now, we can look from that point, make connections, and see patterns, even though the women themselves, especially the pioneers, quite probably did not think about whether they were participating in such an endeavor or not. The first feature to be acknowledged is contextual. There has been a continuity of oppression of African American women over time. The consistency of social, political, and economic encumbrances in the lives of African American women has been noteworthy, if not simply amazing. What is also noteworthy is the continuity of African American women's resistance to these constraints and the manifestation of this resistance in essaying practices.

The nagging question, however, is not about continuities in oppressions and resistance, but the question of delivery, that is, the transmission of practices, beliefs, and values from one generation to the next. We know what the basic message was. In effect, all of them mainly asserted, "Use language by whatever means of persuasion available to you to engage in sociopolitical action in support of community mandates in order to create a better world for yourself and for others." The question is how these messages, especially about rhetorical expertise, were transmitted when we have presumed that mainstream mechanisms so clearly operated against such privileges. After all, it has been only recently that we have recovered, in sasa time, even the names of Maria Stewart, Frances Ellen Watkins Harper, Ida B. Wells-Barnett, Anna Julia Cooper, Mary Church Terrell, Fannie Barrier Williams, and the hundreds of other nineteenth-century women pioneers of these achievements. How could we receive advice and counsel if we do not know the women? For many, many decades we have not even known their shadows, for example, their general achievements even without their names. They have been absent from mainstream history books. They have not been included as American heroines. They have not been included in literature anthologies as models of rhetorical genius. Evidence of their lives and work was only sprinkled, here and there. How could we have a sense of *tradition* when presumably our information about these types of activities is so limited?

This question has indeed been a challenging one, especially if we keep to the mainstream perspective. However, if we shift the viewpoint to the lives of the women as we have come to discover them through more recent scholarship, we can see a different story. We can begin by assigning credibility to the tradition of community leadership among African American women, a leadership that often does not get inscribed in history books but, rather, in the hearts and minds of the people served. It is a leadership that gets encoded often anecdotally by our images of African American women as "strong," "regal," "no nonsense," even "mean." With an acknowledgment of African American women as community leaders, we can see that a major mechanism for the transmission of practices is in the body itself. As Carla L. Peterson inscribes in the title of her analysis, African American women are *Doers of the Word* (1995). They do language and action. They embody it by their presence as people who use their resources, including rhetorical resources, to get things done. With this perspective the scope and the possibility of transmission changes.

Because of the constraints imposed on them by race, gender, and class, African American women have not had easy access to the mechanisms for credibility and national visibility in historical mainstream arenas, although some among them have managed to attain such visibility anyway. Neither have they been able to easily sustain a historical presence, even in the case of the few that have attained high levels of visibility. Ida B. Wells's achievements illustrate this point. Although Wells attained national and international recognition in the nineteenth century for her anti-lynching campaign, by the twentieth century she was "disappearing" as an easily recognizable figure. Her prominence and scope as a heroine faded, such that by the 1980s her name was not on the tip of most people's tongues as a woman of achievement. She needed to be "recovered," except in two arenas: in Chicago, where she lived and continued to be active until her death, and in particular circles such as the Black Clubwomen's network, where her achievements are recorded in the historical records. In Chicago Wells's leadership was celebrated when that city named a housing project in her honor. In sources connected to the Black Clubwomen's Network, references to her contributions are referenced in a variety of records, and she exists in this history to be re-rendered by others.

In local arenas, therefore, Wells remained a physical presence. At this level, her achievements were incorporated in community lore as part of the general fabric of cultural life. In Chicago, especially, her life contributed to the building of images of African American women, perhaps not so specifically as a speaker and writer, but certainly as a strong woman whose actions, including speaking and writing, were deemed valuable. Local communities recognize many women in this way as people dedicated to the survival and progress of the community, assigning to them as "public" women places of status and respect.

By rendering Wells's achievements in global contexts that are so persistently unaccommodating, she becomes invisible. By a rendering of her in a more local context, her impact as a public woman of excellent reputation in her own community becomes clearer. In the localized version, Wells was deemed valuable throughout her life, not just while she occupied a national and international limelight. I am suggesting with this example that hundreds, if not thousands, of nineteenth-century women activists were possibly also in this category, thus making the transmission of critical messages (including messages about the uses of literacy) from one generation to the next into an ordinary rather than an extraordinary experience. African American women speak and they write whenever they need to, and often in public. These speaking/writing women have lived and worked in and for their communities, doing what they do, using their speaking and writing abilities in schools, in churches, in other community organizations, in various walks of life, with whatever impact they can manage to achieve. These women embody the rhetorical performances that form the tradition.

Sometimes African American women have operated in larger circles, with women similarly involved in local, regional, national, and international organizations. Sometimes they have not. In other words, I suspect, from the anecdotes publicly acknowledged about women as local models, mentors, and friends, that the stories of the local transmission of women's traditions by both formal and informal mechanisms are actually manifold, not few. Consider, as an instructive example, the rhetorically effective women who have been cited as inspiration by any number of contemporary African American women writers, including Maya Angelou, bell hooks, and Paule Marshall (just to name a few). My sense is that messages of the uses of literacy for action have not been dependent, therefore, on our knowledge of extraordinary models in national and international arenas alone (such as the women cited in this book), but on the local examples of language and action, as these outstanding women have been connected and have connected themselves to the day-to-day practices of women who lived their lives and did their work among us in close-up and very personal ways.

At the end of the twentieth century with the actual recovery of specific names and practices, however, the potential to benefit from both ordinary and extraordinary stories of achievement shifts the landscape dynamically. With our current hindsight, we can see that indeed traditions exist and we can be made wiser by knowledge of this history and the habits of performance and achievement. Contemporary African American women essayists have the opportunity to operate in awareness of an ancestry and in a context informed by meta-knowledge and experience and meta-narratives as they continue to do what African American essayists have always done, to read and write the world.

A second feature of essaying practices to be acknowledged is that African American women writers used language to disrupt sociocultural expectations strategically and to defy predominant interpretive frameworks. This process of disruption and defiance made the essay a particularly accommodating expressive form, one which they used frequently to be both read and heard (since as rhetors they often presented their ideas from written texts).[35] To review some of the generic elements of the essay: it is self-authorized; it privileges the first-person "I" perspective; it is grounded in experience; it shows a mind at work; it is exploratory; it recognizes a listening audience and expects response; it invites skepticism; it is situated in a particular time and place and responsive to the material realities of that time, place, and writer; it permits the writer's knowledge, experience, and insight to merge; it is protean in form.

With the essay as a primary instrument for action, nineteenth-century African American women found two specific arenas for exercising their rhetorical abilities. They wrote for the periodical press; and they spoke before varied audiences such as church groups, club groups, community organizations, political gatherings, professional organizations, and so forth. Through these two practices, in particular, they acquired rhetorical experiences within their own circles of expression, large and small, but particularly within the African American community and within local, regional, national, and international women's communities.[36] My attention in this analysis, therefore, has been particularly drawn to the development of rhetorical prowess in public domains.

In focusing on African American women's participation in public discourse, I acknowledge the predominant view that official mainstream public discourse formed originally in European cultures as a bourgeois male domain. I acknowledge also that when this type of public sphere was constructed in the United States, as a new European-centered nation, it excluded African American interests, gendered interests, and several other types of interests as well. These acknowledgments, in fact, make it easier to see how, historically, African American women were multiply positioned in society as not entitled to speak. They were not even entitled to listen. By these constructions of the public sphere, they were rendered unimportant and invisible. It is no wonder, then, that making a case for literacy and social change among this group at the end of the twentieth century would begin with essentially unnoticed trace evidence, rather than with evidence that has been preserved and valued as part of mainstream knowledge-making processes.

By taking into account the circumstances and conditions of African American women's lives over time, we cannot help noticing that their rhetorical activities have had greater visibility in what might be called either counterdiscourses or (as I prefer to consider them) simultaneous discourses, rather than in the discourses of the powerful and privileged. To the extent that mainstream arenas have permitted African American women a presence, these systems have most habitually relegated them to positions of powerlessness and basic disregard. If they are noticed at all, they are viewed typically as outsiders or interlopers in the conversation, rather than as official participants. In not permitting status and authority, such positioning encourages the sense that their voices are ephemeral, disembodied, muted. Their words float on the wind or are experienced as "the random brushings of birds" (Lorde 1990:xi).

The ongoing task of African American women, therefore, has been to create a space where no space "naturally" existed and to raise voices that those who *were* entitled to speak did not welcome and were not particularly compelled to acknowledge. As Victoria Earle Matthews stated:

if this woman who stood upon the auction block possessed of no rights that a white man was bound to respect, and none which he did respect, if there had been no other awakening of the Afro-American woman than this, that she made a home for her race, and abiding place for husband, and son, and daughter, it would be glory enough to embalm her memory in song and story. As it is [given the many other achievements cited in the essay], it will be her sufficient monument through all time that out of nothing she created something. (Logan 1995:152–53)

Matthews was herself born a slave, but she, like the women she celebrates in the essay, was a woman who raised her voice for others to hear and focused her energy on social welfare and political action. Her life and the lives of others of her generation illustrate in full measure an assertion by contemporary writer bell hooks, "To speak then when one was not spoken to was a courageous act—an act of risk and daring" (hooks 1989:5).

Historically, African American women have held within themselves what hooks describes as "the craving to speak, to have a voice, and not just any voice but one that could be identified as belonging to me" (1989:5). In speaking and writing, nineteenth-century African American women claimed for themselves, as hooks does today, a "legacy of defiance, of will, of courage" (9). They embraced their own sense of reality, assumed positions as agents of change, and responded, not in defeat but in defiance—speaking up and out, in their case quite consistently, in the interests of peace, justice, equality, and empowerment. As William Cook articulates this type of marginality (1993), as rhetors positioned in the margins of public discourse African American women were able to see what was represented in official discourse and what was not. With this insight, given the traditional social roles they were indoctrinated to fill, these women accepted the social obligation to act in the interest of the community, and they used language and literacy to do just that.

This group blazed trails into uncharted space. Not only did they present themselves as distinctive voices, they also brought in their own topics. Through the lenses of race, gender, and class, Maria Stewart and Mary Shadd Cary brought forth political and economic autonomy; Ida B. Wells, anti-lynching reform and woman suffrage; Anna J. Cooper, the right of women to higher education; Gertrude Mossell, the rights of women to time and space in their own lives and the contributions of African American women to the professions; and so on. In blazing such trails in terms of both the speaking subject and the subject spoken, these women created legacies of power, richly endowed practices in using language while fully aware of their own locations as language users and while sharply attuned to the interests of the communities around them.

Ultimately, then, within a context of inhospitable circumstances, nineteenth-century African American women used language and literacy as a tool to authorize, entitle, and empower themselves; as an enabler for their own actions; and as a resource for influencing and inspiring others. They set a lively pace in taking the authority to look at, define, discuss, and suggest solutions to all manner of problems, and to hold accountable for their words, actions, and inactions all manner of public figures and social institutions. In this regard African American women's voices can be envisioned, not just as revolutionary, but as evolutionary. They have spoken often against the grain, but they have just as often engaged in positive recovery—that is, in the identification and construction of places from which to begin making the world anew. This approach as a general practice becomes, therefore, interestingly inclusive, healing, and generative. These features—inclusive, healing, generative—are particularly evident in the places which they construct as starting places for communicating with others and making a difference. Often, these women began by posing solutions in which all of their targeted constituencies can be encouraged to think again or to have a role to play in negotiating common interests and implementing them.

This latter practice typically manifests itself in their habit of speaking to several audiences at once. They may recognize and call the name of a first audience, as Stewart does the African American community of Boston. But they are just as likely to shift the gaze, in order to speak to others whom they apparently recognize as also present or implicated, as Stewart does African American men, white women, African American women, the American public (that is, white men). This recognition of audiences behind the primarily targeted audience permits no one who can be held responsible—either in the problem or in the solutions—to go unaddressed.

In keeping with Freire and Macedo's analysis of literacy and critical consciousness (1987), nineteenth-century African American women "read" and rewrote the world. They succeeded in developing a critical consciousness by which they envisioned their context, shaped their realities, and charted courses of action. They redefined their sphere of operation, imagining intersections for themselves among private, social, and public domains, and inventing ways to effect change using whatever platform was available to them. For example, as public speakers, Stewart authorized herself as the instrument of God and Wells authorized herself as a Christian woman who was obligated by righteousness to speak the truth. Each of them invented an intellectual ancestry through women and men who had gone before: Stewart through women in the Bible and in history and through radical activist David Walker; Wells through the heritage of loving parents who were politically active and within a community of activists such as Frederick Douglass, various African Methodist Episcopal Church (AME) bishops, poet and activist Frances Ellen Watkins Harper, and others. As evidenced by the various recovery projects and the efforts to re-historicize these women and their contributions, the result of such legacies is the identification of enabling resources for ongoing rhetorical action: people, practices, and events that have offered both inspiration and remarkable models for ongoing action.

As we approach a third century of African American women's uses of language and literacy for sociopolitical purposes, we see behind us:

• traditions of ethos formation shaped by the materiality of their relationships to work and by the material conditions of the world around them;

• patterns of rhetorical engagement that have been shaped by mandates that have emerged from those very material conditions;

• traditions of community leadership that have been rendered invisible by gendered and racialized views of what constitutes the concept of leadership but that are now being unearthed and made available for scrutiny and replication;

• traditions of intellectualism from which contemporary African American women and others can draw in response to ongoing needs to solve complex problems and to create a better world.

From this fertile ground, we have the advantage of the shifting analytical paradigms that have invited in recent research and scholarship new and different interpretations of reality and achievement. These paradigms push us toward a more multidimensional view, one that offers a broader, deeper, more dynamic sense of the implications of social and political location. With frameworks that take into account a gendered and racialized experience and an economically and ideologically sensitive viewpoint, we are much better positioned than we have ever been in the past to make visible the literate practices of African American women (and others), to note the impact and the consequences of these practices, and to take into account their ongoing viability.

Herein lies an immediate benefit of this shifted historical view, an enhanced capacity to see the current practices of African American writers more dynamically. One feature of current practice that is gaining integrity as a site of inquiry, for example, is a notion that is well articulated by Stacey Young in *Changing the Wor(l)d: Discourse, Politics, and the Feminist Movement*. In discussing the concept of "discursive political activism," particularly as it relates to the women's movement, Young states:

The defining characteristics of these texts are that their authors engage in theoretical reflection, grounded in feminism and anti-essentialist attention to diver-

sity and historical and cultural specificity; and that they turn that theoretical reflection to their experiences of domination and resistance as they are shaped by
the particular combination of gendered, racial, sexual, economic, and cultural
requirements and restrictions they face. These writings are part of a feminist
strategy of discursive struggle. (1997, 236)

Contemporary African American women essayists are using their autonomous experiences to articulate theoretical positions and to make
those positions speak to the hearts, minds, and souls of others in vivid,
lively ways. Their theories are well rooted in and grow organically from
the subjectivities of their lives with a sense of "I-ness"—that is, autobiography and autoethnography. They are demonstrating a capacity to exca-
vate the terrain of experience and to create from these excavations textual
space. They are creating a speaking self and a listening and responsive
community. They are certifying a viewpoint, articulating a mandate, and
clarifying a mode, manner, and direction for action. Although an au-
totheoretical perspective is not new to African American women's essays,
writers in contemporary arenas seem to be using this strategy with both
presence of mind and particular eloquence.

This feature is one example. Another is the frequency with which the
writers are not writing across genres necessarily, as their foremothers did,
but blurring genres in one text, using multiple forms, as Walker does for
instance, to engage with expressive distinction. A richly defined historical
view permits us to locate these variations in practice as part of a meaningful matrix of activities, as we discern with greater clarity that contemporary African American writers are indeed traces of a stream. With an
enhanced view we can see meaningful connections over time, as we determine with greater interpretive power the extent to which African American women writers of nonfiction are still pushing boundaries. We can see
that they are still questioning who is entitled to speak, as bell hooks does
throughout most of her essay collections; still broaching topics that are
taboo, as Toni Morrison does in her edited collection, *Race-ing Justice and
En-gendering Power* (1992); still going against prevailing sentiments, as
Morrison does with literary analysis in *Playing in the Dark* (1992). They
are re-creating traditional spaces, as Lani Guinier does with the nature of
equitable political representation in *The Tyranny of the Majority* (1994);
or, as Patricia Williams does in *The Alchemy of Race and Rights* (1991), in

interrogating the social construction of race and rights within the law. Contemporary African American women writers are breaking new ground, a ground that will apparently be no less suggestive than the ground their nineteenth-century progenitors traversed. What remains clear is that those of us who have been fascinated by the making of African American women's literate traditions will continue to have much to think about, and much more to do. Apparently, two centuries signal that these women have only just begun.

Photographic Essay

African American Women Rhetors, When and Where They Enter

Only the Black Woman can say "when and where I enter, in the quiet, undisputed dignity of my womanhood, without violence and without suing or special patronage, and there the whole Negro race enters with me."

Anna Julia Cooper, *A Voice from the South*, 31

African American Women speak and write in public arenas, so the saying of when and where they enter, they certainly did. They entered every arena they could, with Anna Julia Cooper being one of the most eloquent among them in articulating their rights and abilities to do so. Cooper was born a slave in 1858 in Raleigh, North Carolina. Despite such humble beginnings, however, over the course of her life and work her accomplishments were manifold. She became one of the first African American women to receive a doctorate degree, the first African American woman to be named president of a college, and she built a national reputation as an educator, scholar, and community leader. Cooper made the statement above in an essay entitled "Womanhood a Vital Element in the Regeneration and Progress of a Race," which was included in her 1892 collection *A* Voice from the South. *This statement was representative of the sentiments of African American women during her era who saw the opening doors of opportunity in the late nineteenth century to be a godsend but who recognized that the progress of the race as a whole depended on the ability of those at the very bottom in terms of esteem and access (that is, the women) to achieve and to be respected.*

Cooper's generation was keenly aware of the burden of opportunity and their obligations, therefore, to "do good" in the interest of social and political change and the survival and progress of the race. Because of this work and commitment, these women were called the "race" women, women who found many ways to use their talents and abilities in various and sundry public arenas. They were recognized by their communities for their astute abilities to see problems, for their tenacity in solving them, for the eloquence with which they used their language abilities in speaking and writing to convey their viewpoints and sociopolitical commentary, for getting critical jobs done, and for inspiring others to take responsibility both for themselves and for sociopolitical action.

We talk about this generation using many terms (race women, club women, professional women, elite women, community organizers/workers, activists, and so on) but the term most appropriate for this book is that they were rhetors, people who engaged actively and with consequence in public as speakers and writers. Highlighted on the following pages are just a few among them, the traces of a stream, as we continue to recover names and lives, recount stories, and become inspired by their work and achievements for a new day.

By 1881 and the founding of the Spelman Seminary (later Spelman College), African American women were already acting on their desires to educate themselves, as opportunity permitted, but the opening of institutional doors more generally to women after the Civil War constituted a critical moment. The photograph above (courtesy of the Spelman College Archives) shows the first graduating class of Spelman (1887), including Clara Howard (front row, middle, seated in chair). Howard and others of her generation, as indicated by the photograph to the right (Quarles Memorial Library, courtesy of the Spelman College Archives) were enhancing their knowledge and skills through formal training and building a more broadly based sociocultural experience, processes that facilitated the development of rhetorical prowess.

Featured on the left of the page is Charlotte Forten Grimké (courtesy of the Schomburg Center for Research in Black Culture, the New York Public Library, Astor, Lenox and Tilden Foundations); on the right is Lucy Stanton, and on the facing page is Blanche V. Harris (both courtesy of Oberlin College Archives, Oberlin, Ohio). All were among the first African American women to complete post-secondary education, Grimké at Salem Normal School in Salem, Massachusetts, and Stanton and Harris at Oberlin. All were also among the first waves of courageous northern teachers who went to the South to teach recently freed African Americans during and after the Civil War. The later achievements of Harris are unclear, beyond her continuing to teach, but records clearly indicate that Grimké and Stanton were successful in building excellent reputations as community activists, and in Grimké's case as a poet and contributor of essays to the periodical press.

Mary Jane Patterson (above), a highly respected educator who spent most of her career in Washington, D.C., was the first African American woman to receive a bachelor's degree from an accredited college in the United States when she graduated in 1862 from Oberlin. Patterson was followed in this accomplishment by Fanny Jackson Coppin (facing page, top left) in 1865. While still a student, Coppin opened an evening school for freed people in Oberlin; upon graduation she became the principal of the female department at the prestigious Institute for Colored Youth in Philadelphia, making her the most highly placed African American woman educator of her day. She wrote children's books, maintained a woman's column in the Christian Recorder *(the news-*

paper of the AME church), and contributed to other periodical publications. Anna Julia Cooper (top right) and Mary Church Terrell (bottom right), also renowned educators, were both in the Oberlin class of 1884. All these women were active leaders in the NACW and other community organizations. Coppin, Cooper, and Terrell, especially, spoke frequently in public and wrote frequently for the periodical press, establishing themselves among the most well-known women of their day. (All four photographs courtesy of the Oberlin College Archives, Oberlin, Ohio.)

The nineteenth century was an era that witnessed the rise of African American women in the professions. Pictured on the left is Mary Shadd Cary (courtesy of the National Archives of Canada), the first African American woman to edit and write for her own newspaper, the Provincial Freeman, in Canada. She was an outspoken political activist and businesswoman who went on to complete a law degree from Howard University and to advocate through various community organizations for women's rights.

Pictured on the right is Susan Smith McKinney Steward (courtesy of the Schomburg Center for Research in Black Culture, The New York Public Library, Astor, Lenox and Tilden Foundations). Steward was one of the first African American women to complete a medical degree in the United States and also a very active member of the NACW and other community organizations.

The Black Clubwomen's Movement was an incomparable
mechanism for the sociopolitical
work of African American
women and for their development of rhetorical experience
and expertise. Maritcha Lyon,
right, was a well-respected educator in Brooklyn, New York,
and Victoria Earle Matthews,
below, was founder of the White
Rose Mission, a settlement
house for African American girls
and women. These two activists
organized the first tribute to

Ida B. Wells in 1892 in support of her anti-
lynching campaign, an event that served
also as an occasion for energizing the formation of a national political organization
among African American women. This effort resulted in the emergence of the
NACW in 1896. (Both photographs are
courtesy of the Schomburg Center for Research in Black Culture, the New York Public Library, Astor, Lenox and Tilden Foundations.)

The most striking record of African American women's participation in public discourse in the nineteenth and early twentieth centuries is in the periodical press, especially the African American periodical press. Women activists of this era owned newspapers and magazines, served as general editors, editors of women's pages, staff writers, and contributors. They were also active in women's and other community organizations, functioning frequently as provocative voices in support of both their gendered and their racialized groups. Pictured at the top is Ida B. Wells-Barnett (courtesy of the Schomburg Center for Research in Black Culture, The New York Public Library, Astor, Lenox and Tilden Foundations), the best-known African American woman journalist of her day. On the bottom is Josephine St. Pierre Ruffin (Moorland-Spingarn Research Center, Howard University), the founding editor of Woman's Era, *the first official publication of the NACW.*

Part 3

An Ideological View

Chapter 6

A View from a Bridge

Afrafeminist Ideologies and Rhetorical Studies

One key role for Black women intellectuals is to ask the right questions and investigate all dimensions of a Black women's standpoint with and for African-American women. Black women intellectuals thus stand in a special relationship to the community of African-American women of which we are a part, and this special relationship frames the contours of Black feminist thought. . . . While Black feminist thought may originate with Black feminist intellectuals, it cannot flourish isolated from the experiences and ideas of other groups. The dilemma is that Black women intellectuals must place our own experiences and consciousness at the center of any serious efforts to develop Black feminist thought yet not have that thought become separatist and exclusionary.

Patricia Hill Collins, *Black Feminist Thought*

In resonance with this epigraph, my goal here is to share knowledge and experience, not about the literate practices of African American women as in the previous chapters but about my own standpoint as a researcher and scholar in the process of completing this book. The first and most consistent challenges have come hand in hand with the very choosing of the work itself, that is, with identifying myself as a researcher who focuses on a multiply marginalized group; whose interests in this group center on topics not typically associated with the group, such as nonfiction and public discourse rather than imaginative literature and literary criticism; and who is called upon by the material conditions of the group itself to recognize the necessity of employing a broader, sometimes different range of techniques in garnering evidence and in analyzing and interpreting that evidence. In declaring my interest in a non-mainstream academic area, I have benefited from an array of practices in rhetorical studies, literacy studies, and feminist studies. However, I have not been privileged to have a guide in identifying appropriate analytical frame-works for the use of such practices with my targeted group or in either choosing or developing a set of methodologies that were actually ade-quate to the task.

In forging ahead in uncharted territory, I have also had to confront di-rectly, in the rendering of text, my own status as a researcher who identi-fies unapologetically with the subjects of my inquiries. In terms of my own invented ethos, within contexts that would position me otherwise because of the "marginality" of what I do, I have had to create proactive spaces rather than reactive spaces from which to speak and interpret. The task of creating new space, rather than occupying existing space, has en-couraged in me the shaping of a scholarly ethos that holds both sound scholarly practices and ethical behavior in balance and harmony and that consistently projects this balancing in research and in writing.

As I have discussed in the essay "When the First Voice You Hear Is Not Your Own" (1995), despite my constructions of a proactive scholarly self, many who have responded to presentations of my research have resisted viewing my work in this way. They have consistently demanded, subtly and not so subtly, that I prove my worth and the worth of my subject matter using measures that seem to me to suggest the reader's or listener's own needs to contain, limit, and control both definitions of authenticity and rights to interpretive authority. For example, in the early days, when I explained my focus on nineteenth-century African American women, re-sponses were often a statement of surprise, "Oh!" or statements of in-credulity, "Were African American women really writing anything back then?" "How large a body of texts could we be talking about here?" "Who would have been their reading audience? After all, very few African Amer-icans could read back then, right?" These responses were typically con-veyed with more an intonation of declaration than inquiry. Such reac-tions suggest that the questioners expected me to fail in talking back to them, in making my case, rather than succeed in establishing my interests and viewpoint as reasonable and indeed valuable.

Further, whatever my counter-response, I have occasionally con-fronted a "so what?" factor, which seems to emerge in the guise of ques-tions related to the saliency of evidence. In other words, given the source of the evidence I use (that is, the experiences and achievements of African

American women), I have heard, between the lines, "How instructive could African American women possibly be in the grand scheme of things?" "How could the lives of *these* women possibly suggest anything important enough to notice that has not already been noticed by looking at others?"

Interpretations such as mine that take African American women into account as being not just redundant but valuable—or as agents of change rather than simple victims of oppression and dominance—seem particularly vulnerable to requests, even now in contemporary academic discourse, for comparisons with African American men, white women, and white men, comparisons in which the parameters of comparison are set by the other group.[1] My sense of the attitudes motivating such calls for comparison is that they arise all too often, still, not simply in the interest of comparative analyses (which have the potential to inform) but more from a belief that the marginal status of African American women in society requires that anything related directly to us is "naturally" inconsequential in larger interpretive frameworks. In effect, African American women are perceived to occupy positions, especially historically, of sociopolitical unimportance, which inevitably dictate that whatever point is made about such a low-status group gains credibility, validity, and reliability only as it can be redefined through the lives and contributions of others more credible, more legitimate, and more salient. The uniqueness of African American women's standpoint from such a view becomes a sign of weakness, not strength.

In other words, Charlotte Forten's story becomes secondary to Laura Towne's story. The significance of Anna Julia Cooper translates not by means of her own scholarship but through the master narratives of William E. B. DuBois or Alexander Crummell as preeminent African American male scholars. The political actions of Margaret Murray Washington or Amy Jacques Garvey become minor themes in accounts of their more highly esteemed husbands, Booker T. Washington and Marcus Garvey. The essayist traditions among African American women become absorbed and neutralized by our habits and practices in valuing Emerson, Thoreau, and their more recognizable progeny.

The mandates of this type of questioning have appeared to be in the interest of sustaining predominant views of material reality and resisting interpretations that might permit the emergence of alternative realities, such as the ones inherent in my research. From my point of view, I have operated, therefore, within systems of deep disbelief, which go beyond the doubts rooted in mere ignorance to those seemingly more deeply rooted in arrogance. Deep disbeliefs seem so ingrained they actually short-circuit a more inclusive knowledge-making process and limit the impact of challenges, however large or small, to predominant interpretive frameworks. The result is that researchers such as I have spoken, but we have not been believed, and our viewpoints have remained largely unacknowledged and unincorporated into predominant ways of knowing and valuing. The circles of people who are well informed about African American women and their work remain relatively small and specialized.

Over the years I have come to view the systems of deep disbelief as contending forces, as prevailing winds that push against scholarly proactivity and toward a continual reinscription of the status quo. My response has been to resist being circumscribed. Although I recognize that responding to disempowering sociopolitical mandates is unavoidable, I also recognize that responding only to these mandates would just as inevitably mean positioning myself as a defender of African American women's experience, rather than an interrogator of it. I prefer the latter since my own deep beliefs are keyed to the notion that African American women's achievements are fully capable of standing on their own merit, once that merit is articulated.

In a fundamental way, therefore, my response has been to define my own mandates. As a researcher and a scholar, I seek to develop scholarly practices that are theoretically sound, systematic, and generative. I recognize as valuable the perspectives of the scholarly fields in which I operate; simultaneously I respect the wisdom of the community with which I identify. I seek to position myself in academic writing, therefore, in a way that merges membership in two communities: the one I am studying and the ones in which I have gained specialized knowledge. A central task is to establish a sense of reciprocity between my two homes and to keep in the forefront of my thinking the sense that negotiations of these territories are ongoing.

My role as a researcher has been to look theoretically and philosophically at the data, to bring meaning to it. The very first order of business by necessity has been to establish an interpretive viewpoint that clearly places African American women at the center of our own story. The assumption is that viewpoint matters. As Anna Julia Cooper stated in 1892 in *A Voice from the South,* "what is needed, perhaps, to reverse the picture of the lordly man slaying the lion, is for the lion to turn painter!" (1988:225). In scholarly research and analysis, the question to be addressed is more than whether African American women occupy a passive position of object or an active position of subject. Rather, the question, at the level of interpretation, is how—as objects or subjects—we are placed on a landscape or within a material reality.

In this analysis, I rejected images of African American women that would position us interpretively as a mirror or a reflection of others, or as a room accessed by other people's doors and windows, or even as a backdrop against which other stories are told, invigorated, or clarified. Instead, this analysis positions African American women as the "lions" in a "lion's tale." My intent has been to consider African American women as the embodiment of our own dreams and aspirations, our own created and re-created selves, in a world with others, certainly, but without the need at critical points in the analytical process (that is, in the initial stages) to be filtered through the experiences of others, no matter how resonant or dissonant those experiences might be. In making such a commitment to creating a working space amid dualities, I believe I have acquired an understanding of both scholarly positioning and knowledge production in this arena from which advice to others might be abstracted. In choosing an appropriate mechanism for sharing advice in a more direct manner, however, without suggesting the notion of easy prescriptions, I realize once again that theory, like history, also begins with a story.

Theory Begins with a Story Too

My first archival project on African American women began without much fanfare in 1979 when I was named coordinator of the Spelman College centennial celebration. Over the next two years of preparation for the celebratory year of 1981, I had the good fortune of discovering women about whom I had previously known precious little or nothing, and about whom (I was quite certain) most others knew even less than I. I was so amazed by these women's stories of life and learning that I wanted to do more research. When the centennial celebration was over, I requested and was granted release time by the college to become in the fall of 1982 the first research associate of our new Women's Research and Resource Center.

The project I constructed focused on seven women from among the first graduates of Spelman, all of whom were missionaries, health-care providers, and/or teachers. My first opportunity to share my discoveries was in the form of a low budget photodocumentary exhibit and an exhibit catalog, which I developed for the First National Conference on Black Women's Health, held in June 1983. The exhibit was entitled *Women as Healers: A Noble Tradition.* This project actually catapulted me into the world of Black feminist scholarship. Despite the title of the exhibit, however, the project actually pushed me in an identifiable way, not as a general researcher on African American women but as what I now refer to as an afrafeminist researcher in the field of rhetoric and composition.[2]

In setting up the lines of inquiry for the project, I chose women who were generally unknown in the annals of history but who were stellar in terms of their contributions to and impact upon the communities in which they lived and worked. My task was to consider factors such as race, gender, class, historical period, and cultural context as I tried to clarify and interpret their pathways to learning and achievement. As I became more knowledgeable of who they were, what they did, and how they did it, it became clearer to me that the lives of these women actually told quite a representative story among women of African descent, in terms of their collective quest for literacy and of the mechanisms whereby women who are marginalized in multiple ways might still find a means of participating in public domains and ways of working to make the world a better place.

With this insight I refined the task, which by this point had become a lifelong project. First, as I explained in the introduction of this book, I wanted to recover, flesh out, and reconstruct the ways in which women of African descent generally, and African American women in particular, came historically to acquire written language. I was even more curious, however, to figure out and document the texture of these women's lives and their patterns of behavior, not just in terms of their being hard-working people, which they certainly were, but more directly in terms of their being literate women who, regardless of their life's work, helped to form the first critical mass of college-educated women, many of whom demonstrated by their productivity as speakers and writers that they valued language well used.

My basic questions were: Under what circumstances did these women acquire literacy? What did literacy and learning mean to them? In what ways were they empowered to act in the world by their knowledge of language and how it might be useful in achieving particular rhetorical effects? Most of all, after they acquired these tools and abilities, what did they actually choose to do? What did their actions show evidence of? What differences did their actions make?

To answer these questions, I realized I had to operate quite differently as a researcher than I ever had before. I was no longer a person examining a literary text in terms of a theory of literary criticism, or even a person examining linguistic data in terms of a theory of language. Instead, I was looking at a collection of documents, various print and visual texts (photographs, for example), and other artifacts, the material evidence of lived experience, and I was trying to make sense of the lives of the people with whom these materials were connected. I saw it as my task to extend the base of specific details available on their lives, and to talk about this base in a useful way for our understanding of women's education in general and of their use of literacy for sociopolitical action in particular.

The project required that I learn something about history, economics, politics, and the social context of women's lives. For the first time, I had to spend more time considering context than text. I had to take into account insights and inquiry patterns from disciplines other than those in which I was trained. I had to take into account the specific impact of race, class, gender, and culture on the ability to be creative and to achieve—not in some generic sense, but in terms of a particular group of human beings who chose deliberately to write and to speak, often in public. This shift in analytical perspective toward a multi-lensed approach is in keeping with techniques that are now quite recognizably interdisciplinary and feminist.

I had set myself on a pathway that strikes me now as more transdisciplinary than interdisciplinary and more afrafeminist than feminist. By all accounts, my basic vision as a researcher was deeply affected, changing rather significantly the paradigm through which, from that time forward, I would draw meaning from women's experience. Before the shift, I had understood that there was much to know about these women because they were people of African descent. After the shift, I became conscious of how much *more* there was to know because these people were women and mostly poor, held certain cultural values, and can be placed at a particular point in time within a particular set of socioeconomic conditions. In this latter case, the women were all either employed outside the home or very actively involved in community service. In keeping with what Hill-Collins indicates in her analysis of Black women's experiences, the relationships of this group of women to material reality were unique.[3]

In becoming sensitized for the first time to a fuller understanding of this uniqueness, I conclude all these years later that I was developing the habit of caring as a rhetorician (as a researcher who centralizes the use of language), but I was constructing meaning with a transdisciplinary view in defiance of clearly rendered disciplinary boundaries. I pulled into my rhetorical schema a richly defined material world and brought texture to the conditions for learning and rhetorical action.

By coincidence, two other sets of activities supported the development of these transdisciplinary and afrafeminist habits. The first occurred in 1983 when I became a founding member of the editorial collective of *SAGE: A Scholarly Journal on Black Women* with Beverly Guy-Sheftall, Patricia Bell-Scott, and Janet Sims-Wood. We came together from across four disciplinary areas (American literature, sociology, history, and of course rhetoric and composition) to edit a semi-annual interdisciplinary journal focused on women of African descent.[4] By participating in this collaborative, I was privileged to read and to become intimately involved in knowledge production from across disciplinary boundaries, and to do so in ways that centralized the conditions, lives, and achievements of women of African descent wherever they might reside. I was required by this work to read more broadly than was my habit or training, and thus to think more comprehensively about women of African descent. My responsibilities as editor created systematic opportunities for me to participate in lively discussions around interdisciplinary issues. This work changed dramatically the terms by which I engaged with text. My perspectives for raising questions and perceiving details to be instructive were made clearer, more open-ended, and more inclusive, positively affecting both my research habits and my writing, that is, how I composed lives and drew meaning from written expression.

Essentially, as a researcher I used my linguisitic training to center concerns within a conceptual frame that is rooted still in traditions of rhetorical criticism (see chapter 2). Simply stated, I retained my interests in looking at who says what to whom under what circumstances and with what motives, intentions, impact, and legitimacy. From a more complex view, however, I became more curious about the ways in which knowledge, experience, and language merge, as African American women, through language, make decisions that have sociopolitical consequence. I became curious about how these women gain access to knowledge, construct new knowledge, and operate with a sense of agency. I became concerned with issues of authority, certification, validation, power, privilege, and entitlement. These concerns led me to pay closer attention to discourse communities and to constructions of voice and vision within those communities. I look now (as this book demonstrates) at the acquisition, uses, and consequences of literacy, at African American women's rhetorical expertise, at their use of language as a tool for living and working alone and in communities.

In reflection, I think it significant that at the same time as I was engaging in the intellectual work of my research project and with the *SAGE* editorial team, I was also teaching and coordinating the Spelman College Comprehensive Writing Program, a writing across the curriculum program that included a writing center. All three activities—research, editorial team activities, program administration—worked together in creating a generative environment in which I was able to discover new ways of being as a researcher and scholar. A remarkably synergetic dimension of this interface was that, at the same time as I was coming to understand that the convergence of gender, race, class, and ethnicity offered a provocative point of departure for considering historical issues of literacy and learning for African American women, I was also responsible for coordinating systems for developing the literate abilities of contemporary African American women through the activities of the Writing Program. One project in particular becomes instructive in demonstrating this point.

In 1985, I became the co-coordinator (with Beverly Guy-Sheftall, coeditor of *SAGE* and director of the Women's Research and Resource Center) of a new program we had created, the SAGE Writer/Scholars Internship Program.[5] It was a cooperative endeavor of the college Women's Research and Resource Center, the Comprehensive Writing Program, and *SAGE: A Scholarly Journal on Black Women.* By its very definition this program sought to support women who indicated a desire to work on their writing. It sought also to support the development of an intellectual pipeline that would carry forward the traditions of productivity and leadership that I had found so compelling in my work on nineteenth-century women. The program was supported during its first few years by the Fund for the Improvement of Post Secondary Education and then continued throughout the remainder of my tenure at Spelman with support from the United States Office of Education.[6] The goals of the project were various:

1. to introduce undergraduate women students to the process of writing as part of scholarly inquiry;

2. to provide opportunities for students to develop their critical and analytical skills and to demonstrate these through their writing;

3. to expose students to women of African descent who are writer/scholars and who would serve as mentors;

4. to provide opportunities for students to participate in the writing, editing, proofreading, and supportive research necessary for the production of a scholarly, interdisciplinary journal.

Fundamentally, the project was designed as an enrichment experience for students who had demonstrated academic excellence but who needed to build strength in scholarly writing as opposed to creative writing. In 1985, in the midst of the new attention being afforded African American women writers, we were acting against a prevailing image of African American women writers as writers of novels, short stories, poems, plays, and so on, rather than as writers of scholarly books, articles, and essays. Our intent was to shape the program by definitions of African American women as intellectual beings and not just creative beings.

In keeping with statistics at that time documenting the paucity of African American scholars across the nation, this program sought to encourage people with intellectual potential to rethink the territory of writing, and to consider graduate school rather than professional school. We sought to enrich their understanding of what it feels like to engage seriously, if not passionately, in research and scholarship, including scholarly publication. Students who participated in the program were generally self-selecting, based on their desires to enhance their critical skills and to know more about themselves as writers in a scholarly arena. Generally, they were quite active in several other classroom experiences and in extra-classroom work on and off the campus, such that a constant challenge for the program was finding times to schedule meetings. Over the years, the "culture" that emerged in the program encouraged me to name and respect this "busy-ness" as in keeping with the lives of African American women intellectuals.

Our administrative response was to adjust the definition of what "interning" with the program meant. Over the course of the project, we continued to offer an ever-growing array of experiences, as originally planned, but we developed an escalating sense of what we were really trying to do. We encouraged the students to be deliberative and selective about the level and intensity of their participation. We considered this process to be practice for the decision-making and juggling we anticipated they would be doing for the remainder of their lives. In essence, we shifted from a sense of the program as an "internship," designed to extend experiences, to a clearer sense of it as a "mentoring" program, designed to help developing scholars think about what it means to be a writer/scholar.

The students responded variously. Typically over the course of a year, there was a small core of students who participated in almost everything. There were others who picked and chose. There were others who became occasional participants. Some students called themselves SAGE Interns; some did not. All were welcome whenever they came. All were kept on the active roster and received announcements and updates about activities. Without a prescription for participation, however, our new challenge became finding ways to counteract our sense of disintegration in the program. We noted, though, that we were not the ones setting parameters; the students were. We came to see that we were not "structuring" an internship as such. We were helping students to engage in a particular kind of inquiry. We were advising them, directing them toward various and sundry opportunities for growth and inspiration, and offering ourselves

to them as resources in support of particular needs that we all identified—together. We had placed the authority to shape, define, and measure in their hands. There were no grades. There was no credit. The idea
was that, in as nonexclusive a manner as possible, we were nurturing intellectual potential and the students were developing it. This model—
given the more structured ways in which such programs typically proceed—did not come automatically.

Very early in the project, I happened to ask the student interns two obvious questions: How many of you consider yourselves writers? How
many consider yourselves scholars, intellectuals? The answers to the second question caught me off guard. I found (as I expected to find) that the
interns were quite comfortable claiming themselves as writers, and as
competent and capable people who expect to be successful. But in 1985
they were not so eager to claim and name themselves as scholars or intellectuals. I was surprised. Given the workings of gender, race, and culture
in this country, though, I should not have been.

At this college in 1985, a women's college, there were no pedagogical or
curricular structures in place to encourage these women to claim space as
"intellectuals." We did not yet have, as a reflective model, the African
American woman scholar who became president two years later. We did
not have, as the writing program developed later, a Thinking Across the
Curriculum project designed to raise intellectual development from tacit
levels of understanding to conscious awareness and systematic attention.
The "Life of the Mind" series had not yet begun; and at that point the Liv-
ing-Learning Program did not operate as an extra-classroom experience
to nurture relationships between faculty and other mentors and students.
In effect, then, when the SAGE Writer/Scholars Internship Program began, there were no programs on the campus that directly "mentored" intellectual development. There were internship programs of various sorts,
but they were designed to broaden the horizon (as this program was originally intended to do) but not to nurture specifically intellectual potential.

In essence, campus discourse did not include, in any systematic way,
talk about women of African descent as intellectuals. What we talked
about and nurtured was an image of women as achievers, as creative and
ingenious beings, as leaders—not really as thinkers, or scholars, or intellectuals. So, I should not have been surprised that the students in this

program were able to talk about themselves as writers, as achievers, as academically talented, but were not so comfortable talking about themselves as scholars and intellectuals. Fortunately, times and images change, however. Shortly after 1985 the intellectual lives and actions of women in general and women of color in particular came to bolder relief across the landscape of higher education, and particularly through the research and scholarship in feminist studies.

At the inception of the internship program, however, I considered it very good fortune that I actually asked the students questions about these self-perceptions.[7] If I had not, we could have assumed too much about them and contributed unwittingly to a sort of stereotyping that could have been just as disintegrating to progress and development as the more negative stereotyping of women of African descent has been. Without such questions, I may not have given much conscious thought at all to the actual workings of education and literacy in people's lives. Having asked those questions, however, I was able to use the students' hesitations at that moment to inform and to energize how we went about operating the program. We became more conscious of the actual people before us and of the task at hand. This tidbit of information, this moment, became a window of opportunity that we used consistently to maintain clarity and direction.

One of our fundamental assumptions about how the program should work was intensified. We were much clearer about the need for change in the material conditions of the students' institutional lives—that is, changes in the cultural context of the institution and changes in their material relationships to academic work. We became more determined than ever to use the program as a testing ground. We felt the extra-classroom environment of the program could provide a lower-risk place to think about how to enhance learning and to operationalize learners. We were strengthened in our hopes that such efforts would be useful: in the classroom environment, in other activities of the Writing Program, and in institutional planning. We assumed also that—even though this project was designed especially for a specific group of students in a specific context—the experience still might have implications for other students, both marginalized and nonmarginalized.

Basically, we sought to enliven the intellectual atmosphere through a specific array of extra-classroom activities. We coordinated workshops on writing, thinking, and publishing; visits with mentors; trips to scholarly conferences. We encouraged students to submit manuscripts to *SAGE*. We encouraged students and faculty in joint research efforts. We structured dialogues on issues that impact upon our contemporary lives. We encouraged them to use their classroom experiences more boldly, to listen carefully, to read broadly, to question, to take authority and responsibility for themselves as learners. We urged them to be self-directed—to listen to the voices from within for what Howard Thurman, a noted theologian, called "the sound of the genuine" (1981). In actuality, we freed ourselves to structure a program we wish someone had structured for us as young women two decades before. The internship program became essentially a mentoring program, which recognized the advantages of joining hands collaboratively with other programs around the campus that sought to engage with students along complementary lines (by this point in time, the list of mentoring activities on the campus had grown exponentially).

With the interns, we were inspired to shape mentoring experiences based on the implications of questions such as the following: What sociocultural influences have shaped African American women to the extent that academically successful students would readily claim authority as learners and as creative writers but would be more reluctant to claim a comparable authority as scholars or intellectuals? What historical conditions and circumstances have given rise to how African American females feel about themselves and about scholarly achievement? What resonates about these conditions and circumstances in the lives of other women or people in general? How have those who have found degrees of comfort as writers, scholars, and/or intellectuals come to feel and operate as they do? What kinds of instructional practices have enhanced and hindered students who are well centered as intellectuals in terms of their comfort with the power and authority to write, to speak, to think, to learn, and to produce? How can students, female students, female students of African descent, assume the authority to speak, to think, to learn, to write, to claim anything? What is the genesis of authority? What are pathways to personal power and achievement?

These questions encoded the interface that I felt between my work with nineteenth-century African American women and my work with contemporary women. I was able to identify resonant patterns of engagement with issues of authority, agency, privilege, and entitlement across time. Moreover, seeing the continuity of African American women's mandates supported the shaping of my administrative style in the program in a way that I suggest now is very much in keeping with afrafeminist practices. From my point of view, this categorization of my administrative style gains integrity in two specific ways:

1. We relinquished our exclusive authority to define the program and our control of its sense-making with each act of listening to the students and responding actively to the material realities of their lives.

2. We centralized the notion of reciprocity in the roles and relationships that we were nurturing as mentors and participants each time that we shifted dialectically between program (that is, specialized perspectives) and participants (that is, the individual perspectives among this particular community of women).

In other words, the SAGE Writer/Scholars Internship Program, as we developed and refined it, was begun with a Black feminist standpoint, as the objectives indicate, and it grew stronger in this standpoint over time.[8] In pedagogical terms, I became more focused on what I thought it meant to help students gain authority and move productively toward intellectual empowerment. My strategies were designed to enhance the literate resources of young African American women who would potentially join the stream of their rhetorically productive ancestors. The impact of trying to carry out these strategies in terms of my own ideological development, however, is that I was led to two conclusions that now form constitutive parts of my ways of thinking and operating from an afrafeminist view: people who do intellectual work need to understand their "intellectual ancestry"; and people who do intellectual work need to understand power and how they are affected by it.[9]

People Who Do Intellectual Work Need to Understand Their Intellectual Ancestry

In the beginning, we thought of the SAGE Internship Program as a rather innocuous enrichment experience, but the time we spent on consciously structuring mentoring activities proved an ongoing strength.

The central task became the structuring of specific experiences that might move these women toward a more concrete sense of their personal power as writers, scholars, and intellectuals. After all, each of them already had a claim to a history of academic success. We did not need to convince them they were competent and capable women. Instead, a critical task became helping them to broaden their definitions of their strengths—in ways that, at the time, women in general and women of African descent in particular did not habitually do so. Our task initially was to help them situate themselves within a community of women (especially women like themselves, that is, of African descent) and to help them see a historical continuum within which they were participating, consciously or not. Based on our own personal experiences as women scholars, we operated on the hypothesis that the students' pursuit of intellectual authority can be informed and sanctioned by their conscious and specific awareness of the historical conditions and circumstances of others like themselves. As Deirdre David (1987) terms it, "inventing and discovering intellectual ancestry" becomes an "informing event" (226).

Dialogue was a basic strategy. There was talk one-to-one, between the students and myself. There were periodic meetings for the full group, and conversations between the students and visiting mentors and faculty mentors about research, scholarship, life choices, life experiences. There were all manner of workshops, seminars, conferences, which formed a community of discourse wherein the students could participate actively. We talked and talked and talked in dialectical ways, with springboard resources and experiences and without them. We looked closely and critically at a broad range of issues that seemed to relate to what the students were observing, reading, writing, and also to how they were thinking, feeling, and believing. We encouraged them—always—to place their own sense of reality at the center and to question this sense of reality intensely, using various analytical frames without fear of accountability outside of their own accountability to themselves. The students benefited from this community. So did I.

The most frequent types of responses to the internship experience were affective. Generally, the students reported they had previously had little or no idea that African American women through the years had done all the things that they read about in the journal or that they learned about through internship-supported and -encouraged activities. The students particularly liked getting to know Beverly Guy-Sheftall and me better, since we were the faculty most centrally involved with the program, and getting to know other faculty who worked with us periodically. In these interactions they gained a more concrete appreciation of faculty as scholars, with intellectual lives of their own, over and above their previous recognition of faculty as teachers in classrooms. They were encouraged and inspired by the visiting mentors who participated in the program. The periodic opportunity to talk with other students who cared about the same issues, problems, and concerns as they cared about helped them to feel less "singular" or "different" as developing intellectuals—feelings they might have characterized earlier in the life of the program, as feeling alone and isolated. The change in vocabulary from "alone" and "isolated" to "singular" and "different" offers evidence of a change in awareness for both self and situation. They came to understand that their intellectual desires were not so singular or different. They belonged to a community. They also began to understand that their lives as African American women intellectuals ran a high risk of placing them in worlds that might indeed contribute to their feeling alone and isolated. They began to notice the systems and forces surrounding them, many of which are hostile.

An advantage during the formulation of this model was the growing body of scholarship across the disciplines on African American women. The students were able to use this type of scholarship to contextualize their own experiences and to be strengthened by the knowledge that others have gone before. With a combination of historical and contemporary mentors, we found that the students could identify specific torchbearers, pathfinders, heroines, women before them who have endured, who have soared, who have traversed, if not the same territory, at least similar paths. They could see what success looks and feels like and be energized and strengthened for their own struggles.

In addition to making use of this type of information, however, we found that the interns also needed the ability to contextualize their personal genesis as writers and scholars within the broad cloth of human experiences globally. We operated on the belief that students are in a much stronger position to fashion for themselves their own authority to speak, to write, to learn, and to produce when they can determine, not just the resonance of their own lives with others, but also the dissonance. The general result was that we developed a three-pronged approach as an operational model, determining that students need to:

1. reconstruct their pathways to the present point in time, to think specifically about how they have come to be as they are and to think, believe, and act as they do;

2. situate their experiences within the historical context of the lives of others like themselves, in this case the multidimensional lives of African American women generally; and then

3. examine the specifics of global conditions, circumstances, systems of oppression and privilege so that they can see more fully what possibility and productivity mean and often do not mean across communities.

Our assumption was that if students can take stock of the maze of material realities in various communities and cultures, taking into account both the ties that bind and the lines that divide people, then, perhaps, they can have a clearer sense of their own *psychic wholeness* and also of those factors that can contribute to fragmentation.[10]

People Who Do Intellectual Work Need to Understand Power and How They Are Affected by It

The second conclusion I drew from the internship program is that fleshing out intellectual ancestry reveals a need for students to articulate oppression and the making of victims in both personal and systemic ways.[11] Within models that traditionally operate in curricula and classrooms, the history, experiences, and achievements of marginalized people are, to a significant degree, imperceptible and uncredited. Marginalized students find ways of adjusting to these contexts, but sometimes their adjustments are more intuitive than conscious, making it more difficult upon occasion to maintain a positively defined sense of self and potential. My experiences have convinced me that students can more easily maintain balance when they understand power and how individuals, including themselves, are affected by it. This type of understanding is facilitated by the examination of conceptual models beyond Eurocentric, patriarchal ones (the examination of afrafeminist and feminist models, for example) and by the application of such models to varieties of human experiences.

In their explorations of power, authority, and privilege, feminist scholars (Lerner 1986; McIntosh 1988, for example) have been particularly helpful in clarifying factors and conditions that constitute systems of power and others that support the formulation of strategies for personal and group empowerment. Such research constantly reminds us that women in pursuit of learning, African American women in this case, are operating within instructional environments that are not designed for the personal benefit and interest of learners marginalized by race, class, or gender. This scholarship, therefore, echoes questions about whose knowledge is being privileged in schools and about whose interests are being served.[12] Fundamentally, these scholars question, as Lois Weis has done,

[the] ideological analysis of the strategic implications of school knowledge, its
silences, and its deletions of the self-affirming history of the oppressed. . . . The
attempt to explicitly link knowledge to power also partially opened up a fecund
ground of possibilities for the investigation and exploration of school life
around issues of the formation and constitution of racial and sexual identities
and representations. . . . For writers such as Baldwin and Shange, American
schools are principal sites for the production and naturalization of myths, half
truths, silences and obfuscations about the socially disadvantaged. (1988:19–26)

Speaking to the dynamics of race, class, and gender, such analyses take note directly of how these factors interact consistently as traditional patterns of power, authority, and privilege are made manifest in curricula and in classrooms. These analyses also acknowledge complicity and resistance in how the marginalized inevitably internalize prevailing values despite their needs to resist these same values.

This type of dichotomous existence between margin and center was powerfully articulated in 1903 by W. E. B. DuBois in *The Souls of Black Folk* when he talked about the *two-ness* of being Black *and* American. Bell hooks extended our thinking in *Feminist Theory: From Margin to Center* (1984) when she focused on the insights and resiliency that can be engendered by such thinking. On one level, like the African American women who are the objects of my research, marginalized students who are well centered in their personhood seem to learn a type of multiconsciousness, a consistent awareness of otherness. They fashion multiconscious mechanisms (information, skills, strategies, attitudes) that support academic work while simultaneously building up a resistance against oppositional forces to positive and productive personal development. Even in the face of opposition, they seem able to create for themselves a proactive rather than a reactive vision of reality.[13] They see sources of possible fragmentation and find a way to transcend them. Because we are just beginning to document this type of transcendence,[14] empirically documented patterns of proaction and reaction are yet to be established.

In working simultaneously with historical case studies and with contemporary students, I noticed that, when African American women define and empower themselves, they often think and operate from the margins—in opposition to central authority. They see, for example, what is marginalized or ignored in their own lives, as well as in the lives of others. Dialectically, however, they think and operate from the center in resonance with that authority. They are able to find and use their strengths, to bring their fully recognizable selves into the focus of mainstream values and expectations. These women are called upon to create a place of comfort in a stream that seems—by nature, but more likely by design—to seek to drown or, at the very least, to dilute them. Typically, they fashion for themselves their own authority to speak, to write, and to produce. Yet they also look at themselves, as DuBois says, "through the eyes of others . . . measuring one's soul by the tape of a world that looks on in amused contempt and pity" (1994:45). What seems central to creating a sense of *place*—that is, the space to be productive—seems to be an informed understanding of power, authority, and privilege.

What I learned from this program as an administrator and teacher was that the continuum of African American women's uses of literacy as professional women created learning occasions for the students, especially since these professional arenas were often the ones in which the students envisioned themselves participating as leaders. I learned that making intellectual ancestry more explicit helped the students to a more visceral understanding of struggle—and (given the intent of this program) intellectual struggle. The students could see connections and disconnections between themselves and others and fashion within the context of their historical knowledge lines of authority, privilege, and entitlement.[15]

What I realized in terms of my own development, as we fashioned intellectual experiences for the interns and created a community of engagement for them, was that this work and the privilege of sharing culturally engaging experiences with the students were creating material connections for me as well. I was being nurtured and affirmed in my own ideological transformation. Being a codirector of the program, engaging in my research project on nineteenth-century women, working with *SAGE*, all contributed to my sense of ideology in action, and thereby to the dynamic evolution and transformation of my own ideology, an ideology that was manifesting itself at this point not only in my research and scholarship but also, by means of the internship program, in my work as a teacher and administrator.

Within this highly charged context, I became more conscious of how my own authority as researcher, scholar, and teacher was transforming into the afrafeminist ideology that now shapes my professional practices. I view the African American women that I study (and by extension the varieties of students that I teach) as sentient beings who are capable of proactive engagement in the world. I deal consciously with the world as a place that is materially defined by social, economic, and political relationships. I continue to struggle in determining an appropriate place for myself in performing research. At the same time, however, I have become more comfortable with the notion that "place"—especially in the participant/observer roles I often take on—is continually negotiated and renegotiated, a process that offers peculiar challenges when (as in my case) many of my subjects are no longer living and the time frame for them is obviously the past.

There is a constancy in the need for negotiation, beginning with the uncomfortable question of how much I actually do share identities with the women I study and how much I do not. I share what I claim as a cultural heritage. I share in kind, though perhaps not in degree, some of their material realities. I do not share their time or place. I have known, for example, the oppression and domination of the segregated South, but not slavery or Reconstruction. I write about northern, mostly urban women, and I grew up in the rural South. I recognize the important cultural resonances that exist across African diasporic communities, but I understand also the existence of dissonance, especially as these distinctions become complicated by the passage of time and by cross-cultural fusions that I have experienced, and which they may have experienced differently. I am continually reminded, however, of two points. The first point, in keeping with Kenneth Burke's view of "identification" (see chapter 2), is the notion that identity is not natural. It is constructed. I have indeed identified multiple connections between these women and myself, despite our not being perfectly matched. The second point is that the need for negotiation is, therefore, not arbitrary. It is part and parcel of the consubstantial process. The need for negotiation is yoked to the need for a well-balanced analytical view that takes into account shifting conditions, values, and circumstances between human beings. This materiality for scholarly production and representation brings me recursively to two questions: What is an afrafeminist ideology? How does this viewpoint facilitate good practices in scholarship?

The Construction of an Afrafeminist Ideology

In "The Social Construction of Black Feminist Thought," an essay that preceded the book from which I draw the epigraph at the beginning of this chapter, Patricia Hill-Collins presents a compelling case for the emergence of a Black feminist standpoint. As she explains, she does not intend to suggest either a uniformly shared experience for all African American women or a uniformly articulated and recognized consciousness among us. Instead, she posits a plurality of experiences within an overarching concept that supports the idea that African American women have not passively accepted their domination or oppression but actively resisted it. She theorizes that these acts of resistance nourish the development of sensibilities among African American women as a variable group, sensibilities that form collectively a cultural worldview.[16]

In explaining this idea, Hill-Collins presents two interlocking characteristics of this standpoint. One is that African American women's political and economic status, as enacted through the paid and unpaid work we do, has provided us with a material reality that is unique. The second is that having a unique relationship to material reality inevitably shapes across a spectrum of political and economic conditions a comparably unique way of perceiving the world and ourselves in it. The relationships of African American women to the material world have yielded, at minimum, tacit perceptions of that world and the "places" we occupy. These perceptions, in turn, have enabled us to define ourselves in counterdistinction to the externally defined perceptions that have been assigned to us over the generations. Hill-Collins names this counterdistinction a Black feminist consciousness; I have been calling it an afrafeminist ideology.

In positing a theory of Black feminist consciousness, Hill-Collins acknowledges that making tacit connections between the "work" one does, paid and unpaid, and what one thinks, especially about self and possibility within the world, does not lead automatically to a clear theoretical articulation of this positioning as an intellectual standpoint, or as ideology. Quite the contrary. The expression of an afrafeminist ideology within a sociopolitical milieu set up to privilege other ideologies is inherently problematic. Societal apparata support other standpoints, which because of their places of power, prestige, and privilege are hegemonic. The central systems of belief, the predominant systems of practice, the master narratives of the social order do not invite the creation of counter-ideologies that would by their very existence have the potential to subvert prevailing authority or to resist domination. Hegemonic systems by their very nature are set up to limit resources for resistance, to absorb the momentum generated by resistance, and to maximize the resources for resilience in maintaining the status quo.

In light of hegemonic systems that give rise to a hostile environment for the development of afrafeminist ideologies, my sense of the challenge to an afrafeminist theorist is twofold. On one hand, the task is basic. The challenge is to make overt connections, as Hill-Collins emphasizes, between the everyday understanding of African American women as they live their lives by whatever means and the specialized understanding that an African American woman intellectual might bring as she contextualizes these lives within meaningful frameworks. My goal as an afrafeminist researcher in rhetorical studies is to interrogate the literate practices of women of African descent in ways that enable me to find and collect data; to sort through, interrogate, and assess those data meaningfully; to draw implications that are well centered in the knowledge and experience of the group; and also to render interpretations that are recognizable by the group itself as meaningful, instructive, and usable.

On the other hand, the task is more complex. The challenge is not simply to operate well in terms of scholarly enterprises but to articulate an ideological view. Hill-Collins articulates this task as an identification of an overarching concept based on a collectivity of Black feminist standpoints. The purpose of fulfilling such a task is to use the concept, the ideology to enable action despite hostility. In intellectual pursuits, the effort is to assume a viewpoint that permits African American women to be imagined as embodied by our own values and beliefs; to root that viewpoint in both community knowledge (recognizing and valuing the specificity of the material context of African American women) and in specialized knowledge (recognizing and valuing the extent to which critical perspectives of that context become imperative). The idea is that afrafeminist theories permit Black women intellectuals to paint the contours of research and scholarship with a different brush and with a different scenario in mind. An afrafeminist approach, as an enabling site of operation for both thought and action, suggests in rhetorical studies a paradigm shift. The shift begins with a reconsideration of *who* the primary and secondary audiences of the scholarship are and *who*, even, the *agents* of research and scholarship include.

My intent in this book, for example, is to acknowledge and credit community wisdom and the roles that this knowledge might play directly and indirectly in affirming validity, reliability, and accuracy. My tendency has been to assign the women a point of view, authority, and agency in their intellectual work. The women emerge not just as subjects of research but also as potential listeners, observers, even co-researchers, whether silent or voiced, in the knowledge-making processes themselves. In contrast to their being the slates on which I write, I permit them to assume a *presence*. I think of them as real and not controlled by me. My job in analysis and interpretation is to account for their point of view and interests.

Critical to such methodological practices, therefore, is the idea that, whatever the knowledge accrued, it would be both presented and represented with this community, and at least its potential for participation and response, in mind. This view of subjects as both audiences and agents contrasts with a presentation and representation of knowledge in a more traditional fashion. Typically, subjects are likely to be perceived in a more disembodied way, that is, without allowing a central place of consideration for the material interests of the subjects in the knowledge-making. The differences here between approaches might be signaled by the contrasts between two questions: "How is this knowledge informative to or representative of the group on whose lives the knowledge is based?" in the first paradigm; and "How is this knowledge abstractable and relatable to larger meaning-making structures?" in the second. The first approach, which I claim not as exclusively afrafeminist but centrally so, assumes that the researcher has obligations to the community. The second, a more traditional approach, does not.

The contrast is one of values and assumptions. Afrafeminist models, in recognizing direct connections to lives and experiences of African American women, situate the intellectual work within the values and assumptions of this specific racialized and gendered group.[17] As African American women intellectuals doing this work, we are obligated, as are our counterparts within the community, to be holistic, to remember our connectedness in both places. We are free to do our own intellectual business, and at the same time we are also obligated to have that work respond to sociopolitical imperatives that encumber the community itself. We, like our sisters (the African American women whom we study), are accountable ultimately to the merging of the interests of mind, body, and soul as part and parcel of the wholeness of the knowledge-making enterprise, which includes accounting for our own social obligations as members of the group. We speak and interpret *with* the community, not just *for the* community, or *about* the community.

In other words, as participant/observers within the community, African American women intellectuals are accountable to those with whom and about whom we speak.[18] As I see the challenge, our work is expected by this view to recognize that research and scholarship have the potential to empower and disempower, that a primary site for the validation of knowledge is the community itself, and that there is an inherent expectation that knowledge carries with it a mandate for appropriate action, again, in the interest of the general welfare of the community, both narrowly and broadly defined, a mandate on which the research and scholarship quite literally rest.

Further, my view of afrafeminist thought is that African American women intellectuals as participant/observers are indeed the obvious originators of afrafeminist ideologies (as compared with nonmembers of the community), because of the very fact of our participant/observer status.

We have deeply vested interests, which, by their very subjectivity, lay claim, not to biases as an abnormal condition but to biases as a normal condition and to levels of commitment to the work that such biases are likely to engender. Because of our potential as researchers with both insider knowledge and outsider knowledge, it seems obvious that we should be central to the formation and development of knowledge production in this arena. African American women intellectuals are the ones within intellectual circles who should generally care (and, I would venture to say, do generally care) the most. I suggest, then, that afrafeminist ideologies acknowledge a role for caring, for passionate attachments. In effect, the status of participant/observer suggests interests that cover a wide and deep range of caring. This range certainly includes our own reflexive interests as part of the group, but also it includes concerns centered as well in our disciplinary and transdisciplinary needs to know in keeping with typical scholarly practices and pursuits.

In positioning ourselves in this work as central players, African American women intellectuals are charged with creating *bridges* from which to speak and interpret, as compared with the *bridges* by which African American women in general have envisioned the world and operated within it.[19] This distinction relates more directly to the merging of specialized knowledge and community knowledge. As researchers and scholars who identify with the subjects of our scholarly gaze, Black women intellectuals occupy positions in the synergetic space at the in-between. From this bifocal standpoint, we have a primary responsibility for seeing, defining, naming, and interpreting our own reality within a sense-making schema (such as the theory for language and sociopolitical action I propose in chapter 2) and also for suggesting and taking appropriate actions in our own interests and in the interests of whatever alliances for progress and change across the sites and sources of knowledge-making that we may be able to forge.

In this latter regard, the second part of the epigraph at the beginning of this chapter becomes cautionary advice. I agree with Collins that afrafeminist ideologies cannot flourish in isolation from the ideas and experiences of others outside the group. A recurring question in ethnic and gender "studies," however, is whether researchers and scholars who do not share the identities of the subjects are capable of assuming an appropriate standpoint and of operating well. Is it possible, in this case, for someone who is not an African American woman to do good work in afrafeminist scholarship? I think most people would answer affirmatively, but the real question in this scenario is how is this so? In my estimation, the answers to such questions are multidirectional.

From one perspective, with special insider/outsider knowledge-making potential, African American women intellectuals are challenged to build bridges between afrafeminist insights within the group and the visions and experiences of others. The objective of such bridge-building is to maximize the interpretive power of various standpoints, by bringing all that we know together kaleidoscopically.[20] The assumption is that the whole of a kaleidoscopic view has greater interpretive power than a singularly defined view would have. The forging of knowledge-making coalitions and alliances, therefore, becomes an important dimension of a long-range developmental process for knowledge-making.

To restate the point, the work of making sense of the lives of African American women originates as a territory perfectly—if not naturally— suited to African American women. It is our work. However, as full-fledged members of humanity, this work is not by necessity ours alone. Others can also have interests and investments in it that can be envisioned from their own standpoints, from their own locations. What becomes critical to good practice, however, is that these researchers—who are indeed outsiders in the communities they study—have special obligations that begin with a need to articulate carefully what their viewpoints actually are, rather than letting the researchers' relationships to the work go unarticulated, as is often the case with practices of disregard. My view is that noncommunity scholars are called upon by their outsider status to demonstrate respect for the communities they study. They are obligated (by afrafeminist ideologies anyway) to recognize overtly their ways in which their authority, as it may be drawn from dominant systems of power and privilege, intersects with the authority of others. They are obligated to hold themselves, rather than just their subjects, accountable for and responsive to disparities.

In other words, the intellectual work of afrafeminist scholarship is multidirectional. By the measure of this analysis, it originates with African American women intellectuals, and it can be extended and/or nuanced by the work of others. The idea is that scholarship can handle mutual interests, without setting aside the politics and privileges of "first voice" (Royster 1996). The concept of first voice acknowledges a need for scholarly practices to show a deliberate sense of both analytical and ethical regard. Given this dialectical expectation a persistent dilemma, however, continues along methodological lines. How do we clarify the distinctive roles of participant/observers, that is, those who speak and interpret as members of the community and those who speak and interpret as non-members? On what bases do those of us who are community members articulate our own locations in the research and in the rendering of scholarship? How do others engage likewise from their own locations? How do we each find "credible" places to stand? How do we develop methodologies that are both "credible" and accessible as touchstones for each other? In other words, what does it mean to do good work in researching the lives, conditions, and contributions of women of African descent and in interpreting that information in both insightful and respectful ways?

"Ways of Doing" in Afrafeminist Scholarship

The actual articulation of an ideological perspective, as in my own case, may not be a task that can be done alone and in isolation. I suspect that ideology grows in the material world and in the company of others with similar interests and concerns (for example, in the ways I was enabled in my thinking and practices by the specificity of my work with the *SAGE* editorial team and, among other experiences, by my advisory role with the SAGE Interns). In other words, ideology formation, as a knowledge-making process, is socially constructed.

Moreover, as evidenced by the stories of African American women writers,[21] there is also a lively notion of apprenticeship, a sitting at the feet or by the side of others as we develop habits of seeing, doing, and in many cases also of being. We find "teachers," "mentors," "guides," many of them indirectly rather than directly related to our specific goals, but who nonetheless have necessary advice and insights for us to complete our transformations. Octavia Butler, for example, enacts this need for "guidance" in her *Dawn* trilogy (see chapter 2) by illustrating that effective transformation is possible in the good and loving hands of others who assist in whatever ways the transforming subject needs the help.

In the case of the researcher who is more outsider than insider in relation to the community targeted for study, such guides are invaluable. With or without guides, however, it may be helpful to distinguish between the construction of personal identity (ways of being) and the articulation of research and scholarly methodologies (ways of seeing and doing) as we try to imagine a fuller spectrum of how participation in knowledge-making might optimally function. My sense is that, despite the coincidence of being or not being an insider, researchers and scholars still have systematic behaviors (habits of seeing and doing) in which they can engage that demonstrate a commitment to both scholarly and ethically responsible actions, such as those indicated in this explanation.

Setting aside the value of apprenticeship, my view of afrafeminism is very much definable in material terms. This approach embodies the notion that the mind, heart, body, and soul operate collectively and requires intellectual work to include four sites of critical regard: *careful analysis, acknowledgment of passionate attachments, attention to ethical action,* and *commitment to social responsibility.* From my perspective, these sites operate together to create a well-functioning whole with each site involving practices forged in light of critical ways of doing that are also capable of being touchstones for critical ways of being.

Careful analysis suggests typical concerns about scholarly behavior. I see the necessity of using systematically the vocabulary, theories, and methodologies of our field or fields of study, with attention to clarity, accuracy, and precision. In other words, it makes good sense to me that we should not discard the disciplinary views we have refined over the years, as they have helped us to draw out meaning in abstract and concrete terms. Instead, my view is that we can take supreme advantage of this specialized knowledge, merge it with the knowledge of the community, and then build interpretive frames that have more generative power, that is, the power to be dynamic and to have within their purview both general landscapes that speak to the whole and specific ones that account for varieties within the whole.

In other words, when I use a particular analytical model my caution is to make sure it is well rooted in the accumulated knowledge of the field and also useful in shedding light on the subject. Questions come in, however, through the application of the model. The opportunity for inquiry emerges at points where the subject of analysis exhibits characteristics that are likely to be specific rather than general, local rather than global, or outside the assumed and the valued. The imperative is both to use the framework and to interpret it. The act of both using and critically questioning the analytical framework makes it possibile to notice both the predictable and the unpredictable and of taking note, thereby, of discrepancies and distortions between the expected and whatever might be unseen. By this process, I am suggesting that discrepancies and distortions can be perceived as normal rather than abnormal, and that the degree and extent of discrepancy and distortion often depend on the point of view. Paying attention to point of view clarifies the notion that any analytical framework reveals some characteristics and obscures others, a process that often opens up secondary questions: How can we make adjustments or refinements to the sight line and to the value system that sets the sight line? How can we see both more and differently? How can we engage in analysis in a more thorough way and develop interpretations that are more useful and meaningful?

An *acknowledgment of passionate attachments* reminds us that knowledge has sites and sources and that we are better informed about the nature of a given knowledge base when we take into account its sites, material contexts, and points of origin. My point here is that knowledge is produced by someone and that its producers are not formless and invisible. They are embodied and in effect have passionate attachments by means of their embodiments. They are vested with vision, values, and habits; with ways of being and ways of doing. These ways of being and doing shape the question of what counts as knowledge, what knowing and doing mean, and what the consequences of knowledge and action entail. It is important, therefore, to specify attachments, to recognize who has produced the knowledge, what the bases of it are, what the material circumstances of its production entail, what consequences or implications are suggested by its existence, and for whom the consequences and implications hold true.

Thus, *attention to ethical action* acquires considerable significance. This site suggests, on one hand, a scholarly mandate to be theoretically and methodologically sound, but on the other hand, it also indicates a need to sustain a sense of accountability. As researchers, scholars, and teachers, we are accountable to our various publics. We are challenged to think metacognitively about lines of accountability throughout the intellectual process. We see the importance of monitoring and measuring our methodologies from the beginning to the end of our actions. Based on this ongoing assessment, we recognize the need to negotiate working space and working relationships within this context of ongoing critical reflection. What also becomes clearer is the need to represent our work (whether in textual form or otherwise) in conscious regard of our ethical obligations.

In this paradigm, therefore, a *commitment to social responsibility* (and, I might add, social action) reminds us that knowledge does indeed have the capacity to empower and disempower, to be used for good and for ill. As researchers and scholars, we are responsible for its uses and, therefore, should think consciously about the momentum we create when we produce knowledge or engage in knowledge-making processes. Our intellectual work has consequences. I believe the inevitability of these consequences should bring us pause as we think not just about what others do but about what we are obligated to do or not do.

In being useful, however, ideology should be able to translate into action. In my own articulation of an afrafeminist ideology, I note the need for researchers and scholars to articulate their own ideological standpoints systematically, not simply as a personal or professional flag to wave at a convenient moment but in support of ideological clarity; in recognition of how our viewpoints are implicated in scholarly presentation and representation; and also in support of "humility," as we locate ourselves within the text as scholars, and thereby as people who have interpretive power. In addition to seeing one's own standpoint, however, I note also the need to look for the standpoints of others; to be sensitive to the importance of "location" as a specific scholarly value; and to be prepared, therefore, to reconstruct the standpoints of others as we analyze and interpret data, and construct a sense of audience or spectator. My sense of the advantage of such practices is that being able to articulate a standpoint ideologically makes use of an understanding of both self and others as both historical and sociopolitical beings and, more important, as people in specific relationships to power, privilege, authority, and entitlement.

To re-state the idea, my use of an afrafeminist approach centralizes the need to develop and consistently enact a regard for material reality, which in turn shifts the inquiry toward a more multidimensional viewpoint. The imperative is to recognize that, by its very existence as a concept, *point of view* means that some things become visible while others are cast in shadow. We benefit, therefore, from an intentional shifting of perspectives. In my work, I have sought to demonstrate this commitment by triangulating types of evidence. See, for example, the attention I assign in chapter 2 to an examination of the formation of ethos, the context for action, and the rhetorical expertise of a given writer. I garner evidence from transdisciplinary sources; look diachronically, not just synchronically, at literate practices; and look across genres for resonances among a given writer's habits and concerns.

In other words, I consider myself to be operating ethnographically. What I find challenging, though, is using such an approach with historical subjects who can no longer be interviewed. Ethnography and historical subjects, in fact, make strange bedfellows. For me the combination has meant that the crisscrossing of available data becomes a necessity, not simply an option. The practice of merging sight lines, regardless of my inability to gather data as I would with contemporary subjects, is the key to what makes these practices fit within an ethnographic schema. The goal with historical subjects strikes me as the same. As a researcher I seek to reduce distortion by positioning various views in kaleidoscopic relationships to each other.

One type of evidence that gains authority in this type of triangulation of data is personal experience, or more accurately stated, the reporting of personal experience. The imperative in seeing and using reports of personal experience as evidence becomes a function of finding substantive and systematic ways to interrogate it and particularly to have a discriminating view of the behaviors that constitute it. In literacy studies, we have developed inquiry paradigms (such as the analytical model I posit in chapter 2) that permit an exploration of the physicality of experience, and, in the case of rhetorical studies, permit us to examine in context specific behaviors related to literate production. The focus is on material culture, on (1) the researcher's capacity to be specifically attuned to the material context and (2) the conditions for meaning-making. Ethnographic methodologies, therefore, are useful, since interrogating experience and discriminating among specific behaviors demand typically that we make the familiar strange and the strange familiar. We need, as Clifford Geertz established, "thick" descriptions from which we develop the ability to see more of what is really there and what is actually going on.

In addition to embracing the disciplinary methodologies that are current in my field (such as trends and practices in rhetorical criticism, discourse analysis, ethnographic analysis, and so forth), I acknowledge, still, the need to be responsive both to the community that is the object of my scholarly gaze and to that community's own articulations of values, beliefs, and protocols. I look at and listen to what the women say and have said in writing over time. When I have the opportunity, I speak before contemporary African American women and listen to their responses to my work. I take their responses as advice, as wisdom to be consciously regarded as I make decisions about scholarly presentation and representation.

In recognizing the intersections of specialized and community knowledge, the afrafeminist paradigm that I am suggesting also makes room for the in-between, the liminal spaces where the threshold for new possibilities is high. New possibilities suggest there is a room in this viewpoint for imagination to enter and to find a useful place as an interpretive tool. In my work, the deliberated use of imagination has been eye-opening. In constructing a place for the imagination (in chapter 3), I was able to traverse the cavernous space between the known, the unknown, and, in the case of African American women's history, quite probably the unknowable.

In offering these sample practices of how I manifest an afrafeminist ideology, I emphasize that I have encoded careful analysis, an acknowledgment of passionate attachments, attention to ethical action, and a commitment to social responsibility (and action) as touchstones. While I have discussed them as discrete points for consideration, I am aware there is nothing to indicate that these touchstones actually operate pristinely. Reinvoking the metaphor of the kaleidoscope, my sense is that these sites of regard merge and blend in various configurations as we take our intellectual work seriously, whatever our personal locations might be. The point is that afrafeminist ideologies, in my opinion, invite researchers and scholars to think of ourselves as whole in intellectual processes, rather than as disembodied, destabilized, or deconstructed. They permit wide-ranging choices because they centralize relationships to material reality, which inevitably reveals variations in context and condition. In these approaches similarity and generality matter; but simultaneity, specificity, and variability also matter.

In terms of the history of African American women's literacy, afrafeminist ideologies permit us to see the connections of these women's literate practices within the landscape of literate practices generally. In addition, however, they also permit us to see how these connections have been forged. We can see how these women with their unique voices, visions, experiences, and relationships have operated with agency and authority; defined their roles in public space; and participated in this space consistently over time with social and political consequence. Using this type of approach, with a group that by other lenses has been perceived as inconsequential, we have a provocative springboard from which to question what "public" means, what "advocacy" and "activism" mean, what rhetorical prowess means, even what "literacy" means. With this type of analysis, the ferreting out of actions and achievements in the alternative terrain are instructive for an interrogation of contemporary public discourses, debunking the myth that public discourse is a ground only for institutionally sanctioned voices. With African American women, we have a cautionary tale, one that speaks volumes for the historical habits and practices of rhetoric and composition.

These women's stories suggest that, as users of language, we construct ways of being, seeing, and doing in recognition of the materiality of the world around us and of who and how we are in our sundry relationships to it. Their work suggests that we should not automatically discount the discordant, revolutionary, or evolutionary voices of the unsanctioned or un-institutionally authorized. It also suggests that, in order to be generative in our interpretations of contemporary language practices, we need analytical models of discourse that are flexible enough to see the variability of the participants and their worlds, to draw meaning from the shifting contours of rhetorical negotiation across and within material relationships, and to imagine the possibility of building bridges. A basic advantage of more imaginative models, given the volatility of our contemporary era, is that we can see how connections are merging between private, social, and public space. We can understand the simultaneity of competing and conflicting agenda. We can think more carefully about what bridge-building—that is, coalition, alliance, codes of conduct and communicative practice in "public"—might more imaginatively mean as we solve complex problems. Most of all, we can imagine, as African American women have traditionally done, that the "public" arena is a place where negotiation can be with words rather than with weapons, and we can commit ourselves, as African American women writers have done, to turning our thoughts toward action in making a better world for us all.

Appendix 1

Appendix 2

Bibliography

Notes

Index

Appendix 1

Some Early African American Women Contributors, Editors, Publishers, and Owners of Periodical Publications

Please note that this list is intended to be preliminary, not exhaustive or comprehensive. It is designed to underscore that, from the beginning, African American women have been active participants in the African American periodical press, and to bring into bolder relief the fact that they filled multiple roles, including leadership roles. Note also that this list compiles only African American periodical publications. It does not include the white press. (The list was compiled using information from the Clark Atlanta University Special Collections, Bullock [1981], and Penn [1988].)

Name	Roles
Lucinda Bragg Adams	Associate editor of the *Musical Messenger* with Amelia Tilghman; sister to Rev. George F. Bragg, Jr.; publisher of the *Afro-American Churchman* and the *Church Advocate*.
Fanny Alexander	Editor of *Alexander's Magazine*, a medium for political campaigning, from May 1905 to April 1909; second editor of women's section after Carrie W. Clifford.
Sada J. Anderson	Ohio editor of *Woman's Era*.
Anna DeCosta Banks	Editor for Department of Nurses' Training in the *Hospital Herald* with Dr. Alonzo Clifton McClennan and Lucy Brown. Head nurse at Hospital and Teaching School for Nurses in Charleston.
Carrie A. Bannister	Editor of the *Future State*, journal of Negro progress, with Ernest D. Lynwood, which started in 1891 in Kansas City as a newspaper and then became a magazine.
Ida Wells-Barnett	Contributor to the *African Methodist Episcopal Zion Quarterly, Howard's American Magazine,* and the *AME Church Review;* editor of Home Department for *Our Women and Children*.

Name	Roles	*(Continued)*
Florence C. Bentley	Contributor to the *Voice of the Negro*.	
Mary E. Bibb	Named corresponding editor of the *Afro-American Repository*, but there is no evidence of its publication.	
Ariel Serena Bowen	Contributor to the *Voice of the Negro*.	
Rosa Dixon Bowser	Virginia editor for *Woman's Era*.	
Lucy H. Brown	Associate editor of the *Hospital Herald* with Dr. Alonzo Clifton McClennan, who established the Hospital Training School for Nurses in 1897 and published the *Hospital Herald* to support it. The publication later became the official organ of the Association of Colored Physicians of South Carolina, the organization that later became the Palmetto Association of Physicians, Pharmacists, and Dentists of South Carolina.	
Josephine B. Bruce	Contributor to the *Voice of the Negro*.	
Nannie Helen Burroughs	Contributor to the *Voice of the Negro;* corresponding secretary of the Women's Auxiliary of the National Baptist Convention.	
Agnes Carroll	Editor of the *Negro Music Journal* from 1902 to 1903, with J. Hillary Taylor, in Washington, D.C.	
Mary Ann Shadd Cary	Contributor to the *Anglo-African Magazine;* editor and publisher of the *Provincial Freeman,* a newspaper in Toronto and Chatham.	
Carrie W. Clifford	Editor of the women's section of *Alexander's Magazine*, a Boston-area political magazine; contributor to the *Colored American*.	
Dora J. Cole	Pennsylvania editor for *Woman's Era*.	
Anna Botsford Comstock	Contributor to the *Voice of the Negro*.	
Mary Virginia Cook	Education Department editor of *Our Women and Children;* principal of Normal Department in Simmons's (the editor's) school.	
Anna Julia Cooper	Contributor to *McGirt's;* woman's editor for the *Southland*.	
Fanny Jackson Coppin	Contributor to the *AME Review*.	
Julia Ringwood Coston	Cleveland editor and publisher of *Ringwood's Afro-American Journal of Fashion*.	

Name	Roles	*(Continued)*
Henrietta Vinton Davis	Contributor to *Negro America*.	
Irene DeMartie	"Social News" columnist, with Marian Ridley, for *Woman's Era*.	
Mrs. Howard Diggs	Contributor to the *Voice of the Negro*.	
Sarah Mapps Douglass	Contributor to the *Repository* and the *Anglo-African Magazine*.	
Alice Moore Dunbar Nelson	Contributor to the *Future State;* New Orleans editor for *Woman's Era*.	
Elizabeth Piper Ensley	Denver editor for *Woman's Era*.	
Jessie Redmond Fauset	Editor for DuBois's *Brownie's Book,* a monthly magazine for children, and *Crisis*.	
Jessie Fortune	Contributor to the *New York Age*.	
Medora Gould	Literature columnist for *Woman's Era*.	
Arianda V. Gray	Pharmaceutical editor for the *National Medical Association Journal* (1909).	
Madame E. Azalia Hackley	Contributor to the *Colored American* and the *AME Review*.	
Gertrude L. Hadnott	Contributor to the *Voice of the Negro*.	
Frances E. W. Harper	Contributor to the *Repository,* the *Anglo-African Magazine, McGirt's,* and the *AME Review*.	
Adrienne E. Herndon	Contributor to the *Voice of the Negro*.	
Theodora Holly	Nonfiction contributor to the *Colored American: Life and Customs in Haiti*.	
Pauline Elizabeth Hopkins (pseudonym Sarah A. Allen)	Editor of and contributor to the *Colored American;* contributor to the *Voice of the Negro;* editor of the *New Era Magazine,* with Walter Wallace.	
May Howard Jackson	Contributor to the *AME Review*.	
C. M. Hughes	Editor of the Christmas issue of the *Colored Woman's Magazine* (1907).	
Addie Waits Hunton	Contributor to the *Voice of the Negro* and the *Colored American;* president of Atlanta Women's Club.	
Elizabeth Johnson	Contributor of "Women at Home" column in *Woman's Era*.	

Name	Roles	*(Continued)*
M. A. Johnson	Kansas editor of the *Colored Woman's Magazine* from 1907 to 1920.	
Anna H. Jones	Contributor to the *Voice of the Negro*.	
Molly E. Lambert	Literary Department editor for *Ringwood's Afro-American Journal of Fashion*.	
S. Willie Layton	California editor of *Woman's Era*.	
Lena Garrett Lewis	Contributor to the *Voice of the Negro*.	
Gussie Mims Logan	Contributor to the *Voice of the Negro*.	
Alice W. McKane	Georgia editor of *Woman's Era*.	
Sylvia Mann Maples	Tennessee editor of *Woman's Era*.	
Victoria Earle Matthews	Editor of *Woman's Era* and the *New York Age*.	
Emma Frances Grayson Merritt	Contributor to the *Voice of the Negro*.	
Sarah Mitchell	Home Department editor of *Ringwood's Afro-American Journal of Fashion* in Cleveland.	
Mary B. Monroe	Publisher of the *Southern Teachers' Advocate*.	
Gertrude Bustill Mossell	Contributor to the *AME Review* and columnist for *Woman's Era*.	
Ernestine Clark Nesbitt	Cincinnati contributor of "Mother's Corner" column in *Ringwood's Afro-American Journal of Fashion*.	
Hallie E. Queen	Contributor to the *School Teacher*.	
Florida Ruffin Ridley	Editor and publisher of *Woman's Era*, with her mother, Josephine.	
Marian Ridley	"Social News" column contributor, with Irene DeMartie, in *Woman's Era*.	
Minna K. Ross	Editor, with her husband, of the *Gazetteer and Guide*.	
Josephine St. Pierre Ruffin	Editor and publisher of *Woman's Era*, with her daughter, Florida.	
Susie I. Shorter	Editor of "Plain Talk to Our Girls" in *Ringwood's Afro-American Journal of Fashion*.	
Martha A. Sissle	Contributor of women's column with a theatrical focus for the *National Domestic*.	
Alice Ward Smith	Contributor to the *Voice of the Negro*.	
Amanda Berry Smith	Publisher of the *Helper*, in the early 1900s, to support Amanda Smith Industrial Home in Harvey, Indiana.	

Name	Roles	(Continued)
Cora L. Smith	Texas editor for *Woman's Era*.	
Hannah Smith	Departmental editor for *Woman's Era*.	
Lucy Wilmot Smith	Department of Women's Work editor for *Our Women and Children*.	
Waterloo B. Snelson	Editor of the *Negro Educational Journal*, with her husband, from 1895 to 1896.	
Maria W. Stewart	Contributor to the *Repository*.	
Adah M. Taylor	Editor of "Our Women and Children" column in the *Afro-American Budget*.	
Mary Church Terrell	Contributor of biographical sketches to *Ringwood's Afro-American Journal of Fashion*; contributor to the *Voice of the Negro*; D.C. editor of *Woman's Era*; contributor to *McGirt's, Ebony, Howard's American Magazine*, the *AME Review*, and the *School Teacher*.	
Amelia L. Tilghman	Publisher and editor of the *Musical Messenger*.	
Katherine Davis Tillman	Contributor to the *Voice of the Negro*.	
Florence Lee Thomas	Contributor to the *Voice of the Negro*.	
Aida Overton Walker	Contributor to the *Colored American*.	
Josephine Turpin Washington	Contributor to the *Voice of the Negro* and the *Colored American*.	
Margaret Murray Washington	Contributor to the *Voice of the Negro* and the *Colored American*; editor of *Woman's Era* and *National Association Notes*, the publication of the NACW.	
Adina E. White	Art Department editor for *Ringwood's Afro-American Journal of Fashion*.	
Lida Keck Wiggins	Contributor to the *Voice of the Negro*.	
Sylvania Fracoz Williams	Contributor to the *Voice of the Negro*.	
Leslie Wilmot	Contributor of "Chats with Girls" column in *Woman's Era*.	
Fannie Barrier Williams	Contributor to the *Voice of the Negro*; Chicago editor of *Woman's Era*, the *Colored American*, and the *AME Review*.	
Josephine S. Lord Yates	Contributor to the *Voice of the Negro*; Kansas City editor of *Woman's Era*; columnist for the *Colored American* and the *AME Review*; on editorial staff of the *Negro Educational Review*; president of the NACW.	

Some Early Periodical Publications with Which African American Women Writers Were Associated

General

Mirror of Liberty (1838)

AME Church Review (1841)

Repository (1858)

Anglo-African Magazine (1859)

New York Age (1884), formerly the
    New York Freeman

Negro American (1887)

Afro-American Budget (1889)

AME Zion Quarterly (1890)

Southland (1890)

Future State (1891)

Howard's American Magazine (1895)

Colored American Magazine (1900)

Helper (c. 1900)

Gazetteer and Guide (1901)

McGirt's Magazine (1903)

Voice of the Negro (1904)

Alexander's Magazine (1905)

American Magazine (1905)

National Domestic (1905)

Ebony (1906)

New Era Magazine (1920)

By and for Women

Ladies' Magazine (1880)

Our Women and Children (1888)

Ringwood's Afro-American Journal of
    Fashion (1891)

Woman's Era (1894)

National Association Notes (1897)

Woman's World (1900)

Colored Woman's Magazine (1907)

Special Interest

Musical Messenger (1886)

Negro Educational Journal (1894)

Hospital Herald (1898)

Negro Music Journal (1902)

Southern Teachers' Advocate (1905)

National Medical Association Journal
    (1909)

School Teacher (1909)

Notes

Notes to Introduction

1. See Royster (1996).

2. For an explanation of the impact of the cult of true womanhood on African American women, see Giddings (1984); Helly and Reverby (1992); Matthews (1992); Hall (1993); Royster (1997).

3. Amy Shuman discussed this concept in a talk delivered at Ohio State University during the Colloquium on Women in the History of Rhetoric (1997).

Notes to Chapter 1

1. I will use the term African American to designate people of African descent in the United States, and the term Black to designate more generally people of African descent who may reside elsewhere.

2. See, for example, Giddings (1984); Joseph and Lewis (1981); Lorde (1984); Caraway (1991).

3. For a more specific sense of literary criticism during this era related to African American women writers, see, for example, Christian, (1980); Carby, (1987); Gates (1988); Awkward (1989).

4. Henderson (1992) attributes this term to Barbara Smith, who used it in her introduction as editor of *Home Girls: A Black Feminist Anthology* (1983:xxxii).

5. In Royster (1990), I explain this pattern as being significant to an understanding of both African American women's literary traditions and their intellectual history.

6. De Obaldia (1995) cites Klaus (1991) as a scholar who is invoking the essay as a fourth genre.

7. For examples of actual essaying practices, see the next two sections of this chapter, and "The Essayist Tradition Among African American Women" in chapter 5.

8. See chapters 2 ("Toward an Analytical Model for Literacy and Socio-Political Action") and 6 ("A View from a Bridge: Afrafeminist Ideologies and Rhetorical Studies") for my twofold theoretical perspective.

9. See Mittlefehldt (1993) as one example of the scholarship that is becoming available on African American women essayists.

10. See Butrym (1989), one of the first collections in recent years devoted to essay analysis; also the more recent Freedman and Medway (1994); De Obaldia (1995); and Heilker (1996).

11. Contemporary research in literacy studies has taken us well beyond a narrow envisioning of oral and literate practices as a continuum; see, for example, Street (1995); Fair-

clough (1992); and Shuman (1986). See chapter 3 for a more direct explanation of how paradigms have been shifting over the last fifteen years.

12. Patterns of argumentation that value logical, pathetic, and ethical appeals seem to hold an importance comparable with the notion of "truth" in the nonfiction writing of African American women. See chapter 2 for a fuller discussion of this point.

13. Street (1995) analyzes long-standing assumptions about literacy and orality. He posits that distinctions between these two practices, rather than being evident in actual language use, have essentially been rhetorically crafted at the hands of researchers and scholars. See chapter 3 for more discussion of shifting paradigms in literacy studies.

Notes to Chapter 2

1. In chapter 1, I discuss the blurring of oral and literate practices, using the essays of Alice Walker as a case in point.

2. For a similar definition of literacy, see Jerrie Cobb Scott's (1990) address to the Louisiana Literacy Forum.

3. In this explanation I refer to the following scholars: Dell Hymes, sociolinguistics; Brenda Dervin and Kathleen D. Clark, communications; Lev Vygotsky, philosophy; Mikhail Bakhtin and Mae Gwendolyn Henderson, literary criticism; Hans-Georg Gadamer, linguistics; Kenneth Burke, rhetoric.

4. Hymes (1972b).

5. For an earlier version of this argument, see Royster (1990).

6. See "Coming to Voice: Maria W. Stewart, a Case in Point," in chapter 4 for a more thorough analysis of Stewart's essays.

7. In chapter 1, I use Henderson (1992) to explain in general terms the concept of multivocality as it applies to womanist essayists.

8. For a more thorough analysis of the rhetorical practices of Ida B. Wells in her anti-lynching campaign, see my introductory essay in Royster (1997).

9. Frances Ellen Watkins Harper (1825–1911) was a poet, a novelist, and a leader in women's organizations, building over the decades of her social advocacy and activism a national and international reputation as an excellent public speaker who championed many causes, including civil rights, women's rights, temperance, and woman suffrage.

10. Portelli (1999) has discussed narrative perspectives in similar terms, using as contrasts stories told from "above" versus stories told from "below," terms he uses to distinguish between local points of view and distant points of view in history telling.

11. See chapter 1 for a fuller discussion of characteristics of the essay as a genre that seem to support the preferred use of this form by African American women.

Notes to Chapter 3

1. Some of the difficulties encountered in historical research on women of African descent have been discussed in Terborg-Penn (1992); Brown (1989); Hine (1993:xix–xxii).

2. Compare this explanation with the passage in Toni Morrison's *Beloved* in which she discusses "rememory" and the way in which we "bump into a rememory that belongs to somebody else" (1987:36). Momaday suggests the ways in which we create "reality"; Morri-

son suggests the ways in which experience/reality never dies but keeps reverberating as memory, which repeats and becomes experience/reality again and again as we keep "bumping" into it. In this chapter, I wish to embrace both notions of the role of "memory" (time, space, history, truth) and notions of imagination in the making of knowledge and the garnering of understanding.

3. In a reading at Spelman College on November 14, 1990, Erna Brodber made this statement during a discussion of the role of imagination in the making of history.

4. See n. 2 for a passage in *Beloved* in which Morrison discusses "rememory."

5. Bohannan and Curtin (1988) report that African nations permitted Europeans to build and maintain "forts" or "factories" from which they engaged in slave-trading activities. They also report that "27 were constructed on the Gold Coast over a distance of only about 220 miles" (287). Goree Island was one of several such holding stations. For more information about these activities, see also Postma (1990); and Lovejoy (1986).

6. For a more extensive explanation of the trans-Atlantic slave trade, see Bohannan and Curtin (1988); Davidson (1980); Postma (1990); Lovejoy (1986).

7. See the next subsection for a more detailed explanation of typical women's roles in West African communities.

Notes to Chapter 4

1. See "Coming to Voice: Maria W. Stewart, A Case in Point," at the end of this chapter for a more detailed discussion of Stewart's life and work.

2. For a more detailed explanation of the history of education among African Americans, see Woodson (1991); Jones (1980); Vaughn (1974); Anderson (1988).

3. For a more detailed explanation of the negative images imposed on African American women, see Davis (1981); Giddings (1984); King (1988); Royster (1997); White (1999).

4. I am not suggesting these early generations of women would have labeled their beliefs and practices in this way. What I am suggesting is that they were able to retain a tacit sense of similarity, even normalcy, about self and self-in-society, since there were continuities between their relationships with others and the work roles they fulfilled in both African and American contexts.

5. This notion of spiritual resiliency is captured well by the title of Septima Clark's personal narrative, *Ready from Within* (1990), which chronicles her participation as an activist in the civil rights movement.

6. The details of this account of Lucy Terry Prince's life and work are drawn from Shockley (1988); Greene (1959); and Stetson (1981).

7. See Porter (1971) for more examples of early documents that show this type of sociopolitical activity.

8. James Forten was Charlotte Forten's grandfather and the patriarch of an affluent, very politically active family in which both men and women became well known in the abolitionist movement. See "Charlotte Forten and the Port Royal Commission" in this chapter for an explanation of the important role she played in the history of educational opportunity in the South during the Civil War.

9. See Nash (1990) and Tise (1988) for a more extensive explanation of the failure of the new American Republic to end slavery and of the rising racial animosity of white America at the turn of the nineteenth century.

10. For an accounting of the anglocentric biases in histories of American literacy, see Greene (1994). Greene explains that Spanish was the first European literacy in North America, not English.

11. Woodson's work in this publication, which includes the gathering of a remarkable collection of early documents, forms the basis of information from which this section is written. Page references in the next few paragraphs are to this work. Cornelius (1991) also examines the connections between literacy, slavery, and religion during this era.

12. See Postma (1990) for an explanation of the complex role played by the Dutch in establishing and shaping the flow of the Atlantic slave trade.

13. For an accounting of literacy development activities among African American women who worked as missionaries in foreign mission fields, see Williams (1982); Jacobs (1982, 1995); Royster (1993a). See also the story of Clara Howard later in this chapter in the section entitled "Schools of Their Own."

14. The first institution to open its doors to African American women without their petitioning was Oberlin College, Ohio, in 1833 (see chapter 5).

15. See chapter 5 for a more detailed explanation of the participation of Black club-women as advocates and as activists in public discourse.

16. Although a thorough treatment of free Blacks in the South is not possible in this analysis, we should not lose sight of the delicate balance (which involved keeping a very low profile and often required the protection of whites) that had to be maintained for free Blacks to exist unmolested in a slaveholding society.

17. Resources for this account include Grimké (1988); Westwood (1986); Westwood and *CWTI* (1986); Newman (1984); Foner (1983); Jacoway (1980); Holland (1969); Rose (1964); Basler (1953:vol. 6), and the library and archives of the Penn Center.

18. Details about the life and work of Charlotte Forten are drawn from Grimké (1988); Billington (1981); Maloney (1990); archival materials at the Salem State College archives, the Peabody Essex Museum, and the library and archives of The Penn Center. The Port Royal Commission foreshadows the activities associated later with the American Missionary Association (AMA), an organization that sent several thousand men and women into the South to establish schools and to serve as teachers. These activities were known as "home" mission (as compared with "foreign" mission) activities. For more discussion of the participation of African American women missionaries in "home" mission activities during this era, see in this chapter, "The Opening Doors of Opportunity."

19. Forten's mother died when she was three years old, and she spent most of her younger years with her grandmother (for whom she was named), her aunts, uncles, and cousins. Her father remarried and had more children, but Charlotte was never really a part of this arrangement. Her father loomed large in her life, however, and she made constant efforts to please him and to keep a father-daughter relationship.

20. Forten's departure from the Penn School was not prompted by her own discom-

forts. Her father, a sergeant major in the Union Army, contracted typhoid fever, and Forten, his oldest child, went home to help with nursing him, as she had the habit of do- ing for most of her relatives when they became ill. Her father died from the illness, and Forten did not return to St. Helena.

21. *Playing in the Dark* is a collection of three essays in which Morrison interrogates the problem of writing literature in a racialized society. She suggests that race becomes a mechanism for enabling meaning without its being directly addressed itself.

22. The information in this section was gathered from my research at the archives of Clark Atlanta University, Spelman College, and the Atlanta public schools.

23. Information for this list comes from the Spelman College archives and from Roys- ter (1983).

24. All references to the writings of Maria W. Stewart are to this edition.

25. See Howard-Pitney (1990) for an explanation of the Jeremiad tradition among African Americans.

26. See chapter 2 for an explanation of Kenneth Burke's terms *consubstantiality* and *identification:* Burke uses these terms to explain various negotiations in successful rhetori- cal action that are illustrated well by Stewart's choices.

Notes to Chapter 5

1. In 1892, Anna Julia Cooper (1988) reported on a survey she had conducted of U.S. colleges and universities, both white and African American, to determine how many African American women had by that time received college degrees. Between 1892 and 1956, there were general publications on African American education, see Woodson (1919); on women's education, see Woody (1929); on women's master's theses, see Butcher (1936); and on women's doctoral dissertations, see Cuthbert (1942). However, before Noble there was no scholarly book in the mainstream arena that focused on the history of African American women's education.

2. For more detailed information about the cult of true womanhood, as an ideology that confined women's sphere and authority to domestic environments, and for informa- tion about how the polarities of public and private space are being questioned, see Vance (1984); Giddings (1984); Ryan (1990); Helly and Reverby (1992); Matthews (1992); Hall (1993); Fraser (1997).

3. See "Cooperative Endeavor and Sociopolitical Mandates" in this chapter for addi- tional information on the work of the National Association of Colored Women.

4. For resources that draw attention to the priorities and issues of African American women's education and to the efforts of educators to manage the moral behavior of African American women students, see Guy-Sheftall and Stewart (1981); Bell-Scott (1979); Guy-Sheftall and Bell-Scott (1989); and Shaw (1996).

5. See Shaw (1996:68–92) for an explanation of the White Shield Society and its prac- tices, and for a discussion of other practices at colleges and universities that generally show concern about the behavior of African American women.

6. I presented an earlier version of this analysis in Royster (1993b).

7. Information for this section, unless otherwise noted, was obtained from documents in the Oberlin College archives.

8. The information in this section on Oberlin alumnae is based on documents in the Oberlin College archives and in Lawson (1984).

9. I have published a more detailed account of Sarah Margru Kinson in Swearingen and Pruett (1999).

10. The American Missionary Association became the largest organization for social reform in the United States during the nineteenth century and (see chapter 4) served as a major source of teachers for African Americans in the South after the Civil War.

11. This information offers an opportunity to consider the extent to which women of African descent were internalizing their own oppression (in terms of race, class, gender, and ethnicity) and supporting notions of respectability in which they positioned themselves negatively.

12. By common practice, and more often by common mandate, after a female teacher married, she resigned her teaching position. The place of married women was in the home with husband and children.

13. For more information on rhetorical training in the nineteenth century, see Berlin (1984); Knoblauch and Brannon (1984); Kitzhaber (1990); Murphy (1990); Johnson (1991).

14. For additional information on the Black Clubwomen's Movement, see "Cooperative Endeavor and Sociopolitical Mandates" in this chapter.

15. All information on Atlanta University is taken from documents in the Special Collections Department of the Clark Atlanta University and from Bacote (1969) and DuBois (1969).

16. This account of Lucy C. Laney is based on information collected from the Clark Atlanta University Special Collections; Hine (1993); and Rouse (1989).

17. Public high school educational opportunities in the South were generally not available to African American students during this era (see chapter 4), and even after 1870, when opportunities became more available, the education provided in public schools was often deemed by African American parents to be inadequate and non-academic in its orientation.

18. Information on Sarah Winifred Brown is also from materials from the Cornell University archives.

19. The profiles of the two women are based on information from Bullock (1981); Davis (1982); Sterling (1984); and Hine (1993).

20. The New York Medical College for Women was a homeopathic medical school, founded in 1863 by Clarence Sophia Lozier, an abolitionist. Homeopathic medical schools were more accommodating to women than other medical schools. Medicine, of course, was considered a male domain.

21. As Sterling (1984) documents, during this decade more than 15,000 U.S.-born African Americans, including Cary's father, emigrated to Canada.

22. Simpkins's (1999) recent dissertation chronicles the conflict between Cary and the Bibbs, and presents a rhetorical analysis of both Cary and Mary Bibb's participation in public arenas.

23. In 1856, three years after Cary began her journalistic activities with the *Provincial Freeman,* she married Thomas F. Cary, and they made a home in Chatham, Ontario.

24. Organizing publicly in this way before the Civil War and the ending of slavery was a privilege of free—not enslaved—African Americans. Common practice in slaveholding states did not permit slaves to assemble without supervision. These restrictions, for obvious reasons, required that community action be more subversive. Note also the population estimates made by some history scholars: for example, Franklin (1980:158–9) reports 59,000 free African Americans with the first decennial census in 1790, with 32,000 of these living in the South; an increase of 82 percent to 107,400 by 1800; an increase to 319,000 by 1830; an increase to 488,000 by 1860, with 44 percent living in the south Atlantic states.

25. For more information on African American women and organized social reform, see White (1999); Salem (1990); Hine (1993); B. Jones (1990); and Wesley (1984).

26. For a more extended discussion of the participation of African American clubwomen in the Wells campaign and in anti-lynching activities more generally, see Royster (1997).

27. Josephine St. Pierre Ruffin was born in Boston in 1842, was educated in Salem and Boston, and at sixteen married George Lewis Ruffin, an 1869 graduate of Harvard Law School who served in the state legislature of Massachusetts and became the first African American to serve as a municipal court judge in Boston. Ruffin was mother to four children and was extremely active as a journalist, a leader among African American club women, and later a suffragist.

28. For a more extensive discussion of his viewpoint, see also Habermas (1990, 1971).

29. Another nineteenth-century book that showcased women's achievements, including their journalistic achievements, is Monroe A. Majors, *Noted Negro Women: Their Triumphs and Activities* (1986; first published in 1893). For a preliminary list of nineteenth-century African American women who were active journalists, see appendix 1.

30. David Ruggles (1810–1849), was born in Norwich, Connecticut, of free-born parents, moved to New York City in 1827, and made a name for himself as a businessman, abolitionist, Underground Railroad conductor, anti-colonizationist, journalist, printer, hydropathist, and the first-known African American bookseller. Ruggles achieved notoriety as a militant African American activist.

31. For more information on the life and work of Ida B. Wells, see Duster (1970); Thompson (1990); DeCosta-Willis (1995); and Royster (1997).

32. The charts in the appendixes do not include the numerous women who contributed poetry and short stories. I certainly do not seek to represent these lists as being exhaustive but, rather, as demonstrating the substantive participation of African American women in this arena.

33. The details of Hunton's life and work are from Maclachlan (1993:596–97). Hunton's alliances with international organizations illustrate how her generation envisioned themselves and their interests in global terms. Part of this history of international involvement is referenced in a short article by Hoytt (1986:54–55).

34. Details of Williams's life and work are from Hendricks (1993:1259–61).

35. See chapter 2 for an explanation of the triadic relationships among context, ethos formation, and rhetorical decision-making in African American women's writing.

36. Logan (1995) and Loewenberg and Bogin (1976) are two anthologies that illustrate the range of African American women's essays and speeches during this era. Guy-Sheftall (1995), which thematically chronicles the history of African American feminist thought, is also an invaluable resource for examining the uses African American women have made of the essay over time.

Notes to Chapter 6

1. The problem of African American women's studies being treated as redundant was poignantly articulated in Hull, Bell-Scott, and Smith (1982).

2. See the next section for a more thorough explanation of the term *afrafeminist*. My sense here is that I operate with a Black feminist consciousness, supported by an ideological frame or worldview in which my awareness has been shaped by the experiences I cite in this chapter and others.

3. See the next section, "The Construction of an Afrafeminist Ideology," for a more detailed explanation of the unique relationships of African American women to the material conditions of work.

4. For an account of the founding of *SAGE,* see Royster (1995).

5. I chronicle my experiences with this program in similar fashion in Royster (1992, 1988). The collaboration for this project involved two people directly: Beverly Guy-Sheftall (director of the Women's Center and cofounder/coeditor of *SAGE*) and myself (director of the Writing Program and senior associate editor of *SAGE*). However, we also received support through the years from the other members of the editorial team.

6. I left Spelman in 1992. The program, however, has continued to flourish and has been renamed the Bambara Writers Program in honor of African American woman writer Toni Cade Bambara.

7. In planning the program, I had administered an attitudinal survey to them about writing, but this instrument did not include questions related to their sense of "intellectual" self or to the "intellectual" dimensions of their lives. It focused mainly on writing and reading practices and their general attitudes concerning performance and abilities.

8. I acknowledge here the wisdom and experience of Beverly Guy-Sheftall in this collaboration. I credit much of my view of Black feminism to her, the more experienced Black feminist, and to the collegial relationships that developed from our work together on this and other projects. I benefited greatly from the consistency with which Beverly exercised a critical perspective on everything she came in contact with, and from the occasions that this intellectual companionship provided for me to exercise my own critical abilities more consistently.

9. See, for example, Chodorow (1978); Heilbrun (1981); O'Brien (1984); David (1987); Hansen and Philpson (1990); Haraway (1991).

10. For an explanation of "psychic wholeness," see Royster (1990). For a discussion of fragmentation, see Dubois (1994); and hooks (1984).

11. Examples of scholarship in this area include Hall and Sandler (1982); *SAGE* (Spring 1984); Solomon (1985); Hill-Collins and Anderson (1988); Pearson, Shavlik, and Touchton (1989).

12. Woodson (1990) raised similar questions.

13. See chapter 2 for a more extended discussion of the use of language in forging a proactive vision.

14. Examples of this type of scholarship include James and Farmer (1993); Wear (1993); and Kirsch (1993).

15. For an explanation of the concepts of "entitlement" and "privilege" as used here, see Coles (1977).

16. Compare this with my explanation (chapter 2) of how African American women's habits of action and belief have systematically supported uses of language and literacy. A significant difference between this chapter and chapter 2 is in the actual naming of the analytical approach I use in developing a theory of language and sociopolitical afrafeminist action. This chapter focuses on the approach. Chapter 2 is a demonstration of a theory that can emerge from such a standpoint.

17. My goal in this chapter is to explain how I have sought to make an afrafeminist approach manifest in my own work. My assumption is that this way constitutes one way of working, not the only way, and that there are other methodologies that would also be appropriate to this ideological view.

18. Interrogating the roles and practices of the participant/observer in research and scholarship is an area of considerable activity in several fields at the present time. For an example of how issues are being articulated and addressed in the field of rhetoric and composition, see Mortensen and Kirsch (1996).

19. See chapter 2 for my explanation of how experience, knowledge, and language converge in the lives of African American women to focus behavior and action.

20. See chapter 2 for an explanation of the use of a kaleidoscopic approach in knowledge construction.

21. hooks (1989) and Marshall (1981) are two examples of writers who discuss how young African American girls learn in the company of their "elders."

Bibliography

This bibliography is organized according to the following themes:
    African History and Culture
    African American Education
    African American History
    African American Women's History and Culture
    The Black Clubwomen's Movement
    The Essay and African American Women Essayists
    Literacy, Language, and Rhetoric
    The Public Sphere and the Periodical Press

African History and Culture

Achebe, Chinua. 1959. *Things Fall Apart.* New York: Fawcett Crest.

Arens, W., and Ivan Karp, eds. 1989. *Creativity and Power.* Washington, D.C.: Smithsonian Institution Press.

Bohannan, Paul, and Philip Curtin. 1988. *Africa and Africans.* 3rd ed. Prospect Heights, Ill.: Waveland Press.

Curtin, Philip D. 1969. *The Atlantic Slave Trade: A Census.* Madison: University of Wisconsin Press.

———. 1990. *The Rise and Fall of the Plantation Complex.* New York: Cambridge University Press.

Davidson, Basil. 1980. *The African Slave Trade.* Rev. ed. Boston: Back Bay/Little, Brown.

Diop, Cheikh Anta. 1974. *The African Origin of Civilization: Myth or Reality.* Trans. Mercer Cook. Westport, Conn.: Lawrence Hill.

Egejuru, Phanuel A., and Ketu Katrak. 1997. *Nwanyibu: Womanbeing and African Literature.* Trenton, N.J.: Africa World Press.

Hafkin, Nancy, and Edna Bay, eds. 1976. *Women in Africa: Studies in Social and Economic Change.* Stanford: Stanford University Press.

Hay, Margaret J., and Sharon Stichter, eds. 1984. *African Women South of the Sahara.* New York: Longman.

Karp, Ivan, and Charles S. Bird, eds. 1980. *Explorations in African Systems of Thought.* Washington, D.C.: Smithsonian Institution Press.

Kiple, Kenneth F. 1984. *The Caribbean Slave: A Biological History.* New York: Cambridge University Press.

Kolawole, Mary. 1997. *Womanism and African Consciousness.* Trenton, N.J.: Africa World Press.

Lovejoy, Paul E. 1986. *Africans in Bondage: Studies in Slavery and the Slave Trade.* Madison: African Studies Program/University of Wisconsin Press.

Mazrui, Ali A. 1986. *The Africans: A Triple Heritage.* Boston: Little, Brown.

Mbiti, John S. 1969. *African Religions and Philosophy.* New York: Praeger Press.

Mohanty, Chandra T., ed. 1991. *Third World Women and the Politics of Feminism.* Bloomington: Indiana University Press.

Mokhtar, G., ed. 1990. *General History of Africa.* Abr. ed. Berkeley: UNESCO/University of California Press.

Postma, Johannes Menne. 1990. *The Dutch in the Atlantic Slave Trade, 1600–1815.* New York: Cambridge University Press.

Richardson, David, ed. 1987. *Bristol, Africa and the Eighteenth Century Slave Trade to America.* Vol. 2: *The Years of Ascendancy.* Bristol: Bristol Record Society.

Robertson, Claire C., and Iris Berger, eds. 1986. *Women and Class in Africa.* New York: Africana.

Robertson, Claire C., and Martin A. Klein, eds. 1983. *Women and Slavery in Africa.* Madison: University of Wisconsin Press.

Rodney, Walter. 1972. *How Europe Underdeveloped Africa.* London: Bogle L'Ouverture Press.

Thompson, Robert Farris. 1983. *Flash of the Spirit: African and Afro-American Art and Philosophy.* New York: Vintage/Random.

Thornton, John. 1992. *Africa and Africans in the Making of the Atlantic World, 1400–1680.* New York: Cambridge University Press.

African American Education

Aisenberg, Nadya, and Mona Harrington. 1988. *Women of Academe: Outsiders in the Sacred Grove.* Amherst: University of Massachusetts Press.

Anderson, James D. 1988. *The Education of Blacks in the South, 1860–1935.* Chapel Hill: University of North Carolina Press.

Armstrong, Mrs. M. F., and Helen W. Ludlow. 1875. *Hampton and Its Students.* New York: G. P. Putnam's Sons.

Bacote, Clarence A. 1969. *The Story of Atlanta University: A Century of Service, 1865–1965.* Atlanta: Atlanta University/Princeton University Press.

Ballantine, W. G., ed. 1883. *The Oberlin Jubilee, 1833–1883.* Oberlin, Ohio: Goodrich.

Bell-Scott, Patricia. 1979. "Schoolin' 'Respectable' Ladies of Color: Issues in the History of Black Women's Higher Education." *Journal of National Association of Women Deans and Counselors* (1979): 22–28.

Bigglestone, W. E. 1971. "Oberlin College and the Negro Student, 1865–1940." *Journal of Negro History* 56, no. 3: 198–219.

Bolton, Ina. 1948. "Problems of Negro College Women Graduates." Ph.D. diss., University of California.

Butcher, Beatrice. 1936. "The Evolution of Negro Women's Schools in the United States." Master's thesis, Howard University, Washington, D.C.

Clark Atlanta University Special Collections. Atlanta, Ga.

Cheyney University. 1999. [About Cheyney University]. http://www.cheyney.edu/aboutcu.html.

Cuthbert, Marion. 1942. "Education and Marginality: A Study of the Negro Woman College Graduate." Ph.D. diss., Teachers College, Columbia University, New York.

Du Bois, William E. B. [1905] 1969. "Atlanta University." *From Servitude to Service.* Westport, Conn.: Negro Universities Press.

Fairchild, James H. 1871. *Oberlin: Its Origin, Progress and Results.* Oberlin, Ohio: Butler.

———. 1883. *Oberlin: The Colony and the College.* Oberlin, Ohio: Goodrich.

Fisk University Special Collections. Nashville, Tenn.

Fleming, Jacqueline. 1984. *Blacks in College.* San Francisco: Jossey-Bass.

Fletcher, Robert Samuel. 1943. *A History of Oberlin College: From Its Foundation Through the Civil War.* 2 vols. Oberlin, Ohio: Oberlin College.

Guy-Sheftall, Beverly. 1982. "Black Women and Higher Education: Spelman and Bennet Colleges Revisited." *Journal of Negro Education* 51, no. 3: 278–87.

Guy-Sheftall, Beverly, and Jo Moore Stewart. 1981. *Spelman: A Centennial Celebration.* Atlanta: Spelman College.

Guy-Sheftall, Beverly, and Patricia Bell-Scott. 1989. "Finding a Way: Black Women Students and the Academy." In *Educating the Majority: Women Challenge Tradition in Higher Education,* ed. Carol S. Pearson, Donna L. Shavlik, and Judith G. Touchton, 47–56. New York: American Council on Education.

Hosford, Frances Juliette. 1937. *Father Shipherd's Magna Carta: A Century of Coeducation in Oberlin College.* Boston: Marshall Jones.

Jacoway, Elizabeth. 1980. *Yankee Missionaries in the South: The Penn School Experiment.* Baton Rouge: Louisiana State University Press.

Jones, Jacqueline. 1980. *Soldiers of Light and Love: Northern Teachers and Georgia Blacks, 1865–1873.* Chapel Hill: University of North Carolina Press.

Lawson, Ellen NicKenzie. 1984. *The Three Sarahs: Documents of Antebellum Black College Women.* Studies in Women and Religion 13. New York: Mellen.

Lawson, Ellen NicKenzie, and Marlene Merrill. 1983. "The Antebellum 'Talented Thousandth': Black College Students at Oberlin Before the Civil War." *Journal of Negro Education* 52, no. 2: 142–55.

———. 1990. "Antebellum Black Coeds at Oberlin College." In Hine, *Black Women in United States History,* 3:827–35.

Maloney, Joan M. 1990. *Salem Normal School, 1854–1905: A Tradition of Excellence.* Acton, Mass.: Tapestry.

Noble, Jeanne L. 1956. *The Negro Woman's College Education.* New York: Columbia University Press.

Oberlin College Archives. Oberlin, Ohio.

Pearson, Carol S., Donna L. Shavlik, and Judith G. Touchton, eds. 1989. *Educating the Majority: Women Challenge Tradition in Higher Education.* New York: American Council on Education.

Read, Florence Matilda. 1961. *The Story of Spelman College.* Atlanta: Atlanta University/Princeton University Press.

Richardson, Joe M. 1980. *A History of Fisk University, 1865–1946.* Tuscaloosa: University of Alabama Press.

Spelman College Archives. Atlanta, Ga.

Vaughn, William Preston. 1974. *Schools for All: The Blacks and Public Education in the South, 1865–1877.* Lexington: University Press of Kentucky.

Weiss, Lois, ed. 1988. *Class, Race, and Gender in American Education.* Albany: State University of New York Press.

Willie, Charles V., and Ronald R. Edmonds, eds. 1978. *Black Colleges in America: Challenge, Development, Survival.* New York: Teachers College Press.

Woodson, Carter G. [1933] 1990. *The Miseducation of the Negro.* Trenton, N.J.: Africa World Press.

———. [1919] 1991. *The Education of the Negro Prior to 1861.* Salem, N.H.: Ayer.

Woody, Thomas. 1929. *A History of Women's Education in the United States.* New York: Science.

African American History

Alexander, Adele Logan. 1991. *Ambiguous Lives: Free Women of Color in Rural Georgia, 1789–1879.* Fayetteville: University of Arkansas Press.

Bain, David. 1999. *The College on the Hill: A Browser's History for the Bicentennial.* Middlebury, Vt.: Middlebury College Press.

Basler, Roy P., ed. 1953. *The Collected Works of Abraham Lincoln.* 9 vols. New Brunswick, N.J.: Rutgers University Press.

Blackburn, Robin. 1988. *The Overthrow of Colonial Slavery, 1776–1848.* London: Verso.

Blassingame, John W. 1979. *The Slave Community: Plantation Life in the Antebellum South.* Rev. ed. New York: Oxford University Press.

Blockson, Charles L. 1994. *The Underground Railroad.* New York: Hippocrene Books.

Cain, William E., ed. 1995. *William Lloyd Garrison and the Fight Against Slavery.* Boston: Bedford Books.

Curtin, Philip D. 1990. *The Rise and Fall of the Plantation Complex: Essays in Atlantic History.* Cambridge: Cambridge University Press.

DuBois, W. E. B. [1903] 1994. *The Souls of Black Folk.* New York: Gramercy-Random.

Equiano, Olaudah. [1814] 1987. *The Interesting Narrative of the Life of Olaudah Equiano, or Gustavus Vassa, The African.* In *The Classic Slave Narrative,* ed. Henry Louis Gates Jr. New York: Mentor/New American Library.

Franklin, John Hope. 1980. *From Slavery to Freedom: A History of Negro Americans.* 5th ed. New York: Alfred A. Knopf.

Foner, Philip S. 1983. *History of Black Americans: From the Compromise of 1850 to the End of the Civil War.* Westport, Conn.: Greenwood.

Gaither, Edmund Barry. 1989. "Heritage Reclaimed: An Historical Perspective and Chronology." In *Black Art, Ancestral Legacy: The African Impulse in African-American Art,* ed. Robert V. Rozelle, Alvia Wardlaw, and Maureen A. McKenna, 17–34. Dallas: Dallas Museum of Art.

Genovese, Eugene D. 1969. *The World the Slaveholders Made.* New York: Vintage/Random.

Gilroy, Paul. 1993. *The Black Atlantic: Modernity and Double Consciousness.* Cambridge, Mass.: Harvard University Press.

Greene, Lorenzo Johnston. 1959. *The Negro in Colonial New England, 1620–1776.* New York: Columbia University Press.

Gutman, Herbert G. 1976. *The Black Family in Slavery and Freedom, 1750–1925.* New York: Vintage/Random.

Harding, Vincent. 1981. *There Is a River: The Black Struggle for Freedom in America.* New York: Vintage/Random.

Harrison, Eliza Cope, ed. 1997. *For Emancipation and Education: Some Black and Quaker Efforts, 1860–1900.* Philadelphia: Awbury Arboretum Association.

Herskovits, Melville J. [1941] 1970. *The Myth of the Negro Past.* Gloucester, Mass.: Peter Smith.

Holland, Josiah Gilbert. 1855. *History of Western Massachusetts.* 2 vols. Springfield, Mass.: S. Bowles.

Holloway, Joseph E., ed. 1990. *Africanisms: In American Culture.* Bloomington: Indiana University Press.

Howard-Pitney, David. 1990. *The Afro-American Jeremiad: Appeals for Justice in America.* Philadelphia: Temple University Press.

Huggins, Nathan Irvin. 1971. *Harlem Renaissance.* London: Oxford University Press.

Hughes, Langston. 1997. "The Negro Speaks of Rivers." In *Norton Anthology of African-American Literature,* ed. Henry Louis Gates Jr. and Nellie Y. McKay, p. 1254. New York: W. W. Norton.

Klein, Herbert S. 1978. *The Middle Passage: Comparative Studies in the Atlantic Slave Trade.* Princeton, N.J.: Princeton University Press.

———. 1999. *The Atlantic Slave Trade.* Cambridge, Mass.: Harvard University Press.

Jordan, Winthrop. 1974. *The White Man's Burden: Historical Origins of Racism in the United States.* New York: Oxford University Press.

Locke, Alain. 1925. "The Legacy of the Ancestral Arts." In *The New Negro,* ed. Alain Locke. New York: Albert and Charles Boni.

Logan, Rayford W., and Michael R. Winston, eds. 1982. *Dictionary of American Negro Biography.* New York: W. W. Norton.

Meier, August and Eliot Rudwick. 1970. *From Plantation to Ghetto.* Rev. ed. New York: Hill and Wang.

Mellon, Matthew T. [1934] 1969. *Early American Views on Negro Slavery: From the Letters and Papers of the Founders of the Republic.* New York: Bergman.

Nash, Gary B. 1990. *Race and Revolution.* Madison, Wis.: Madison House.

Newman, Debra L., comp. 1984. *Black History: A Guide to Civilian Records in the National Archives.* Washington, D.C.: General Services Administration.

Nobles, Wade W. 1991. "African Philosophy: Foundations for Black Psychology." In *Black Psychology,* ed. Reginald L. Jones. 3rd ed. Berkeley, Calif.: Cobb and Henry.

Penn Center Library and Archives. St. Helena Island, S.C.

Portelli, Alessandro. 1994. "History-Telling and Time: An Example from Kentucky." In *History and Memory in African-American Culture,* ed. Genevieve Fabre and Robert O'Meally, 164–77. New York: Oxford University Press.

Porter, Dorothy, ed. 1971. *Early Negro Writing, 1760–1837.* Boston: Beacon Press.

Quarles, Benjamin. 1969. *Black Abolitionists.* New York: Oxford University Press.

———. 1987. *The Negro in the Making of America.* 2nd, rev. ed. New York: Collier.

Royster, Jacqueline Jones, ed. 1997. *Southern Horrors and Other Writings: The Anti-Lynching Campaign of Ida B. Wells, 1892–1900.* Boston: Bedford.

Rozelle, Robert V., Alvia Wardlaw, and Maureen A. McKenna, eds. 1989. *Black Art, Ancestral Legacy: The African Impulse in African-American Art.* Dallas: Dallas Museum of Art.

Sobel, Mechal. 1987. *The World They Made Together: Black and White Values in Eighteenth-Century Virginia.* Princeton, N.J.: Princeton University Press.

Sparks, Jared, ed. 1840. *The Works of Benjamin Franklin.* 10 vols. Boston: Tappan, Whittemore, and Mason.

Thurman, Howard. 1981. "The Sound of the Genuine." Centennial Founders Day Service, Spelman College, April, 11.

Tise, Larry E. 1988. *Proslavery: A History of the Defense of Slavery in America.* Athens: University of Georgia Press.

Walker, David. [1830] 1993. *David Walker's Appeal.* Baltimore: Black Classic Press.

Welmers, William E. 1973. *African Language Structures.* Berkeley: University of California Press.

Wertheimer, Barbara Mayer. 1977. *We Were There: The Story of Working Women in America.* New York: Pantheon Books.

Westwood, Howard. 1986. "Mr. Smalls: A Slave No More." *Civil War Times Illustrated* 25:20–23; 28–31.

Westwood, Howard, and *CWTI.* 1986. "A Portfolio: The Port Royal Experiment." *Civil War Times Illustrated* 25:24–27.

Yentsch, Anne. 1996. "Hot, Nourishing, and Culturally Potent: The Transfer of West African Cooking Traditions to the Chesapeake." *SAGE: A Scholarly Journal on Black Women* 9, no. 2: 15–29.

African American Women's History and Culture

Alexander, Adele Logan. 1991. *Ambiguous Lives: Free Women of Color in Rural Georgia, 1789–1879.* Fayetteville: University of Arkansas Press.

Aptheker, Bettina. 1982. *Woman's Legacy: Essays on Race, Sex, and Class in American History.* Amherst: University of Massachusetts Press.

Belenky, Mary Field, et al. 1986. *Women's Ways of Knowing: The Development of Self, Voice, and Mind.* New York: Basic Books.

"Belinda, or the Cruelty of Men Whose Faces Were Like the Moon." 1787. American Museum and Repository of Ancient and Modern Fugitive Pieces, Prose and Poetical. Vol. 1, June.

Billington, Ray Allen, ed. [1953] 1981. *The Journal of Charlotte L. Forten: A Young Black Woman's Reactions to the White World of the Civil War Era.* New York: W. W. Norton.

Boone, Sylvia Ardyn. 1986. *Radiance from the Waters: Ideals of Feminine Beauty in Mende Art.* New Haven, Conn.: Yale University Press.

Braxton, Joanne M. 1989. *Black Women Writing Autobiography: A Tradition Within a Tradition.* Philadelphia: Temple University Press.

Braxton, Joanne M., and Andree Nicola McLaughlin, eds. 1990. *Wild Women in the Whirlwind: Afra-American Culture and the Contemporary Literary Renaissance.* New Brunswick, N.J.: Rutgers University Press.

Brown, Elsa Barkley. 1989. "African-American Women's Quilting: A Framework for Conceptualizing and Teaching African-American Women's History." *Signs: Journal of Women in Culture and Society* 14, no. 4: 921–29.

Brown, Hallie Quinn. [1926] 1988. *Homespun Heroines and Other Women of Distinction.* New York: Oxford University Press.

Bullwinkle, Davis A., ed. 1989. *African Women: A General Bibliography, 1976–1985.* New York: Greenwood.

Butler, Octavia. 1987. *Dawn.* New York: Popular Library/Warner.

———. 1988. *Adulthood Rites.* New York: Popular Library/Warner.

———. 1989. *Imago.* New York: Popular Library/Warner.

Caraway, Nancie. 1991. *Segregated Sisterhood: Racism and the Politics of American Feminism.* Knoxville: University of Tennessee Press.

Carby, Hazel V. 1987. *Reconstructing Womanhood: The Emergence of the Afro-American Woman Novelist.* New York: Oxford University Press.

Christian, Barbara. 1980. *Black Women Novelists: The Development of a Tradition; 1892–1976.* Westport, Conn.: Greenwood Press.

Chodorow, Nancy. 1978. *The Reproduction of Mothering: Psychoanalysis and the Sociology of Gender.* Berkeley: University of California Press.

Clark, Septima. 1990. *Ready from Within.* Trenton, N.J.: Africa World Press.

Connors, Robert. 1992. "Dream and Play: Historical Method and Methodology." In *Methods and Methodology in Composition Research,* ed. Gesa Kirsch and Patricia Sullivan. Carbondale: Southern Illinois University Press.

Cornell University Library, Division of Rare and Manuscript Collections. Ithaca, N.Y.

David, Deirdre. 1987. *Intellectual Women and Victorian Patriarchy: Harriet Martineau, Elizabeth Barrett Browning, George Eliot.* Ithaca, N.Y.: Cornell University Press.

Davis, Marianna W. 1982. *Contributions of Black Women to America.* 2 vols. Columbia: Kenday.

Decosta-Willis, Miriam. 1995. *The Memphis Diary of Ida B. Wells.* Boston: Beacon Press.

Du Bois, Ellen Carol, and Linda Gordon. 1984. "Seeking Ecstasy on the Battlefield: Danger and Pleasure in Nineteenth Century Feminist Sexual Thought." In *Pleasure and Danger: Exploring Female Sexuality,* ed. Carol S. Vance, 31–49. Boston: Routledge and Kegan Paul.

Duster, Alfreada M., ed. 1970. *Crusade for Justice: The Autobiography of Ida B. Wells.* Chicago: University of Chicago Press.

Fox-Genovese, Elizabeth. 1988. *Within the Plantation Household: Black and White Women of the South.* Chapel Hill: University of North Carolina Press.

Giddings, Paula. 1984. *When and Where I Enter: The Impact of Black Women on Race and Sex in America.* New York: Bantam.

———. 1988. *In Search of Sisterhood: Delta Sigma Theta and the Challenge of the Black Sorority Movement.* New York: William Morrow.

Gates, Henry Louis, Jr. 1988. *The Signifying Monkey: A Theory of Africa American Literary Criticism.* New York: Oxford University Press.

Gilligan, Carol, Nona P. Lyons, and Trudy J. Hanmer. 1990. *Making Connections: The Relational Worlds of Adolescent Girls at Emma Willard School.* Cambridge, Mass.: Harvard University Press.

Grimké, Charlotte Forten. 1988. *The Journals of Charlotte Forten Grimké.* Ed. Brenda Stevenson. New York: Oxford University Press.

Hall, Jacqueline Dowd. 1993. *Revolt Against Chivalry.* New York: Columbia University Press.

Hall, Roberta, and Bernice Sandler. 1982. *The Classroom Climate: A Chilly One for Women?* Washington, D.C.: Association of American Colleges.

Hansen, Karen V., and Ilene J. Philipson, eds. 1990. *Women, Class, and the Feminist Imagination.* Philadelphia: Temple University Press.

Haraway, Donna. 1991. *Simians, Cyborgs, and Women: The Reinvention of Nature.* New York: Routledge.

Hartsock, Nancy M. 1983. "The Feminist Standpoint: Developing the Ground for a Specifically Feminist Historical Materialism." In *Discovering Reality,* ed. Sandra Harding and Merrill Hintikka, 283–310. Boston: Reidel.

Hay, Margaret Jean. 1988. "Queens, Prostitutes and Peasants: Historical Perspectives on African Women, 1971–1986." Working Papers in African Studies 130. Boston: African Studies Center, Boston University.

Heilbrun, Carolyn G. 1979. *Reinventing Womanhood.* New York: W. W. Norton.

Hill-Collins, Patricia, and Margaret L. Anderson, eds. 1987. *An Inclusive Curriculum: Race, Class, and Gender in Sociological Instruction.* Washington, D.C.: American Sociological Association.

———. 1990. *Black Feminist Thought: Knowledge Consciousness, and the Politics of Empowerment.* Boston: Unwin Hyman.

———. 1995. "The Social Construction of Black Feminist Thought." In *Words of Fire,* ed. Beverly Guy-Sheftall, 338–57. New York: New Press.

Hine, Darlene Clark, ed. 1993. *Black Women in America: An Historical Encyclopedia.* 2 vols. Brooklyn, N.Y.: Carlson.

———. 1990. *Black Women in United States History.* 16 vols. Brooklyn, N.Y.: Carlson.

Holland, Rupert Sargent, ed. [1912] 1969. *Letters and Diary of Laura M. Towne, Written from the Sea Islands of South Carolina, 1862–1884.* New York: Negro University Press/Greenwood.

Hull, Gloria T., Patricia Bell-Scott, and Barbara Smith, eds. 1982. *All the Women Are White, All the Blacks Are Men, but Some of Us Are Brave: Black Women's Studies.* Old Westbury, Conn.: Feminist Press.

Ihle, Elizabeth L. 1986. *History of Black Women's Education in the South, 1865–Present.* Washington, D.C.: U.S. Department of Education.

Jacobs, Sylvia M. 1995. "The Sons and Daughters of Africa: Nancy Jones, Missionary in Mozambique and Southern Rhodesia, 1888–1897." *SAGE: A Scholarly Journal on Black Women* 9, no. 2: 88–89.

Jacobs, Sylvia M., ed. 1982. *Black Americans and the Missionary Movement in Africa.* Westport, Conn.: Greenwood.

James, Joy, and Ruth Farmer, eds. 1993. *Spirit, Space and Survival.* New York: Routledge.

Johnson, Audreye. 1993. "Catherine Ferguson." In Hine, *Black Women in America,* 1:426.

Jones, Jacqueline. 1985. *Labor of Love, Labor of Sorrow.* New York: Vintage.

———. 1990. "'My Mother Was Much of a Woman': Black Women, Work, and the Family Under Slavery." In Hine, *Black Women in United States History,* 3:737–71.

Jordan, Judith V., et al. 1991. *Women's Growth in Connection: Writings from the Stone Center.* New York: Guilford.

Joseph, Gloria I., and Jill Lewis. 1981. *Common Differences: Conflicts in Black and White Feminist Perspectives.* Boston: South End Press.

King, Deborah K. 1988. "Multiple Jeopardy, Multiple Consciousness: The Context of a Black Feminist Ideology." In *Black Women in America: Social Science Perspectives,* ed. Micheline R. Malson et al., 265–95. Chicago: University of Chicago Press.

Kirsch, Gesa. 1993. *Women Writing the Academy.* Urbana, Ill.: National Council of Teachers of English.

Ladner, Joyce. 1971. *Tomorrow's Tomorrow: The Black Woman.* Garden City, N.J.: Doubleday.

Lengermann, Patricia Madoo, and Ruth A. Wallace. 1985. *Gender in America: Social Control and Social Change.* Englewood Cliffs, N.J.: Prentice-Hall.

Lerner, Gerda. 1986. *The Creation of Patriarchy.* New York: Oxford University Press.

———. 1993. "Sarah Mapps Douglass." In Hine, *Black Women in America,* 1:351–52.

Lorde, Audre. 1990. Foreword to *Wild Women in the Whirlwind: Afra-American Culture and the Contemporary Literary Renaissance,* ed. Joanne M. Braxton and Andree Nicola McLaughlin, xi–xiii. New Brunswick, N.J.: Rutgers University Press.

Loth, Heinrich. 1987. *Woman in Ancient Africa.* Trans. Sheila Marnie. Westport, Conn.: Lawrence Hill.

Loewenberg, Bert James, and Ruth Bogin. 1976. *Black Women in Nineteenth-Century American Life: Their Words, Their Thoughts, Their Feelings.* University Park: Pennsylvania State University Press.

Majors, Monroe A. [1893] 1986. *Noted Negro Women: Their Triumphs and Activities.* Salem, N.H.: Ayer.

Malson, Micheline R., et al., eds. 1988. *Black Women in America: Social Science Perspectives.* Chicago: University of Chicago Press.

Marrow, Gloria. 1993. "Anne Marie Becroft." In Hine, *Black Women in America,* 1:105–6.

Marshall, Paule. [1959] 1981. *Brown Girl, Brownstones.* Old Westbury, Conn.: Feminist Press.

McIntosh, Peggy. 1988. "White Privilege and Male Privilege: A Personal Account of Coming to See Correspondences Through Work in Women's Studies." Working paper no. 189. Wellesley, Mass.: Wellesley College, Massachusetts Center for Research on Women, ED335262.

Mitchell, Jacquelyn. 1988. "Three Women: Cultural Rules and Leadership Roles in the Black Community." *SAGE: A Scholarly Journal on Black Women* 2 (Fall): 9–19.

Morrison, Toni. 1987. *Beloved.* New York: Alfred A. Knopf.

———, ed. 1992. *Race-ing Justice, En-gendering Power: Essays on Anita Hill, Clarence Thomas, and the Construction of Social Reality.* New York: Pantheon.

O'Brien, Mary. 1984. "The Commutization of Women: Patriarchal Fetishism in the Sociology of Education." *Interchange* 15:43–60.

Patton, June O. 1993. "Lucy Craft Laney." In Hine, *Black Women in America,* 2:693–95.

Phillips Library. Peabody Essex Museum. Salem, Mass.

Ricoeur, Paul. 1984–88. *Time and Narrative.* 3 vols. Trans. Kathleen McLaughlin and David Pellauer. Chicago: University of Chicago Press.

Robertson, Claire C. 1988. "Never Underestimate the Power of Women: The Transforming Vision of African Women's History." *Women's Studies International Forum* 2, no. 5: 439–53.

Rose, Willie Lee. 1964. *Rehearsal for Reconstruction: The Port Royal Experiment.* Indianapolis: Bobbs-Merrill.

Royster, Jacqueline Jones. 1983. *Women as Healers: A Noble Tradition.* Atlanta: Spelman College.

———. 1990. "Perspectives on the Intellectual Tradition of Black Women Writers." In *The Right to Literacy,* ed. Andrea A. Lunsford, Helene Moglen, and James Slevin, 103–12. New York: MLA.

———. 1993a. "Clara A. Howard." In Hine, *Black Women in America,* 1:586–87.

———. 1993b. "Time Alone, Place Apart: The Role of Spiracy in Using the Power of Solitude." In *Women in Solitude,* ed. Delease Wear. Albany: State University of New York Press.

———. 1995. "Capping a Sage Stone: The Final Issue." *SAGE: A Scholarly Journal for Black Women* 9, no. 2 (Summer): 2–4.

————. 1999. "Sarah's Story: Making a Place for Historical Ethnography in Rhetorical Studies." In *Rhetoric, the Polis, and the Global Village: Proceedings from the 1998 Rhetoric Society of America Conference,* ed. C. Jan Swearingen and Dave Pruett. Mahwah, N.J.: Erlbaum.

SAGE: A Scholarly Journal on Black Women. 1984–96. 9 vols.

Salem State College Archives, Salem, Mass.

Sargent, Lydia, ed. 1981. *Woman and Revolution.* Boston: South End Press.

Schomburg Center for Research in Black Culture, New York Public Library. New York.

The Schomburg Library of Nineteenth Century Black Women Writers. 1988. 28 vols. New York: Oxford University Press.

Scott, Joan W. 1991. "The Evidence of Experience." *Critical Inquiry* 17, no. 4: 773–97.

Shaw, Stephanie J. 1996. *What a Woman Ought to Be and Do.* Chicago: University of Chicago Press.

Sheldon, George. 1895–96. *History of Deerfield, Massachusetts.* 2 vols. Deerfield, Mass.: Lippincott.

Shockley, Ann Allen. 1988. *Afro-American Women Writers, 1746–1933.* Boston: G. K. Hall.

Smith, Barbara. 1983. *Home Girls: A Black Feminist Anthology.* New York: Kitchen Table/Women of Color Press.

Solomon, Barbara Miller. 1985. *In the Company of Educated Women: A History of Women in Higher Education.* New Haven, Conn.: Yale University Press.

Steady, Filomina Chioma, ed. 1985. *The Black Woman Cross-Culturally.* Cambridge, Mass.: Schenkman.

Sterling, Dorothy, ed. 1984. *We Are Your Sisters: Black Women in the Nineteenth Century.* New York: W. W. Norton.

Stetson, Erlene. 1981. *Black Sister: Poetry by Black American Women, 1746–1980.* Bloomington: Indiana University Press.

Tate, Claudia. 1992. *Domestic Allegories of Political Desire.* Oxford: Oxford University Press.

Terborg-Penn, Rosalyn. 1992. "Women and Slavery in the African Diaspora: A Cross-Cultural Approach to Historical Analysis." *SAGE: A Scholarly Journal on Black Women* 6, no. 2 ("Africa and the Diaspora"): 11–15.

Terborg-Penn, Rosalyn, Sharon Harley, and Andrea Benton Rushing, eds. 1989. *Women in Africa and the African Diaspora.* Washington, D.C.: Howard University Press.

Turner, Lorenzo Don. 1949. *Africanisms in the Gullah Dialect.* Chicago: University of Chicago Press.

Vance, Carole S. 1984. *Pleasure and Danger: Exploring Female Sexuality.* Boston: Routledge and Kegan Paul.

Voice of the Negro. Special Collections, Clark Atlanta University. Atlanta, Ga.

Walker, Alice. 1983. *The Color Purple.* New York: Harcourt Brace Jovanovich.

Walker, Sheila S. 1990. "Walled Women and Women Without Walls Among the Fulbe of Northern Cameroon." *SAGE: A Scholarly Journal on Black Women* 7, no. 1: 13–17.

Washington, Mary Helen. 1987. *Invented Lives: Narratives of Black Women, 1860– 1960.* Garden City, N.J.: Anchor.

Wear, Delese, ed. 1993. *The Center of the Web: Women and Solitude.* Albany: State University of New York Press.

Williams, Walter L. 1982. *Black Americans and the Evangelization of Africa, 1877–1900.* Madison: University of Wisconsin Press.

Wilson, Harriet E. [1859] 1983. *Our Nig; or, Sketches from the Life of a Free Black.* New York: Random House.

Woodard, Charles L. 1989. *Ancestral Voice: Conversations with N. Scott Momaday.* Lincoln: University of Nebraska Press.

Woman's Era. Boston Public Library. Boston, Mass.

The Black Clubwomen's Movement

Alexander, Adele Logan. 1990. "How I Discovered My Grandmother . . . and the Truth About Black Women and the Suffrage Movement." In Hine, *Black Women in United States History,* 1:15–23.

Berkeley, Kathleen C. 1990. "'Colored Ladies Also Contributed': Black Women's Activities from Benevolence to Social Welfare, 1866–1896." In Hine, *Black Women in United States History,* 1:61–83.

Brooks-Higginbotham, Evelyn. 1993. *Righteous Discontent: The Women's Movement in the Black Baptist Church, 1880–1920.* Cambridge, Mass.: Harvard University Press.

Cash, Foris Barnett. 1993. "Victoria Earle Matthews." In Hine, *Black Women in America,* 2:759–61.

Dickson, Lynda F. 1990. "Toward a Broader Angle of Vision in Uncovering Women's History: Black Women's Clubs Revisited." In Hine, *Black Women in United States History,* 9:103–19.

Gilmore, Glenda Elizabeth. 1996. *Gender and Jim Crow: Women and the Politics of White Supremacy in North Carolina, 1896–1920.* Chapel Hill: University of North Carolina Press.

Hendricks, Wanda. 1993. "Fannie Barrier Williams." In Hine, *Black Women in America,* 2:1259–61.

Hoytt, Eleanor Hinton. 1986. "International Council of Women of the Darker Races: Historical Notes." *SAGE: A Scholarly Journal on Black Women* 3, no. 2 (Fall): 54–55.

Jones, Beverly Washington. 1990. *Quest for Equality: The Life and Writings of Mary Eliza Church Terrell, 1863–1954.* Brooklyn, N.Y.: Carlson.

Maclachlan, Gretchen E. 1993. "Addie Waits Hunton." In Hine, *Black Women in America,* 1:596–97.

Perkins, Linda. 1990. "Black Women and Racial 'Uplift' Prior to Emancipation." In Hine, *Black Women in United States History,* 3:1077–94.

———. 1993. "Fannie Jackson Coppin." In Hine, *Black Women in America,* 1:281–83.

Porter, Dorothy. 1936. "The Organized Educational Activities of Negro Literary Societies, 1828–1846." *Journal of Negro Education* 5 (October): 555–74.

Rouse, Jacqueline Anne. 1989. *Lugenia Burns Hope: Black Southern Reformer.* Athens: University of Georgia Press.

Salem, Dorothy. 1990. *To Better Our World: Black Women in Organized Reform, 1890–1920.* In Hine, *Black Women in United States History,* vol. 14. New York: Carlson.

Thompson, Mildred I. 1990. *Ida B. Wells-Barnett: An Exploratory Study of an American Black Woman, 1893–1930.* Brooklyn, N.Y.: Carlson.

Wesley, Charles Harris. 1984. *The History of the National Association of Colored Women's Clubs: A Legacy of Service.* Washington, D.C.: NACW.

White, Deborah Gray. 1999. *Too Heavy a Load: Black Women in Defense of Themselves, 1894–1994.* New York: W. W. Norton.

The Essay and African American Women Essayists

Angelou, Maya. 1993. *Wouldn't Take Nothing for My Journey Now.* New York: Random.

Butrym, Alexander J., ed. 1989. *Essays on the Essay: Redefining the Genre.* Athens: University of Georgia Press.

Cooper, Anna Julia. [1892] 1988. *A Voice from the South, by a Black Woman of the South.* New York: Oxford University Press.

Davis, Angela. 1981. *Women, Race and Class.* New York: Vintage/Random.

———. 1989. *Women, Culture, and Politics.* New York: Random.

De Obaldia, Claire. 1995. *The Essayistic Spirit: Literature, Modern Criticism, and the Essay.* New York: Clarendon Press.

Freedman, Aviva, and Peter Medway, eds. 1994. *Genre and the New Rhetoric.* London: Taylor and Francis.

Giovanni, Nikki. 1994. *Racism 101.* New York: William Morrow.

Guinier, Lani. 1994. *The Tyranny of the Majority: Fundamental Fairness in Representative Democracy.* New York: Free Press.

Guy-Sheftall, Beverly, ed. 1995. *Words of Fire: An Anthology of African-American Feminist Thought.* New York: New Press.

Heilker, Paul. 1996. *The Essay: Theory and Pedagogy for an Active Form.* Urbana: NCTE.

hooks, bell. 1984. *Feminist Theory: From Margin to Center.* Boston: South End Press.

———. 1989. *Talking Back: Thinking Feminist, Thinking Black.* Boston: South End Press.

———. 1990. *Yearning: Race, Gender, and Cultural Politics.* Boston: South End Press.

———. 1994. *Teaching to Transgress: Education as the Practice of Freedom.* New York: Routledge.

Hunton, Addie Waits. 1904. "Negro Womanhood Defended." *Voice of the Negro* (July): 280–82.

Joeres, Ruth-Ellen Boetcher, and Elizabeth Mittman, eds. 1993. *The Politics of the Essay: Feminist Perspectives.* Bloomington: Indiana University Press.

Jordan, June. 1985. *On Call: Political Essays.* Boston: South End Press.

———. 1992. *Technical Difficulties: African-American Notes on the State of the Union.* New York: Pantheon.

———. [1981] 1995. *Civil Wars: Observations from the Front Lines of America.* New York: Touchstone/Simon and Schuster.

Klaus, Carl. 1991. "Essay." In *Elements of Literature*, 4th ed., ed. Robert Scholes and Carl Klaus. New York: Oxford University Press.

Logan, Shirley Wilson, ed. 1995. *With Pen and Voice: A Critical Anthology of Nineteenth-Century African-American Women.* Carbondale: Southern Illinois University Press.

Lorde, Audre. 1980. *The Cancer Journals.* San Francisco: Aunt Lute.

———. 1984. *Sister Outsider.* Freedom, Calif.: Crossing.

———. 1988. *A Burst of Light.* Ithaca, N.Y.: Firebrand.

Mittlefehldt, Pamela Klass. 1993. "'A Weaponry of Choice': Black American Women Writers and the Essay." In *The Politics of the Essay*, ed. Ruth Ellen Boetcher Joeres and Elizabeth Mittman. Bloomington: Indiana University Press.

Morrison, Toni. 1990. *Playing in the Dark: Whiteness and the Literary Imagination.* Cambridge, Mass.: Harvard University Press.

Mossell, Mrs. N. F. [1908] 1988. *The Work of the African American Woman.* New York: Oxford University Press.

Peterson, Carla L. 1995. *Doers of the Word: African American Women Speakers and Writers in the North, 1830–1880.* New York: Oxford University Press.

Richardson, Marilyn, ed. 1987. *Maria W. Stewart: America's First Black Woman Political Writer.* Bloomington: Indiana University Press.

Simkins, Ann Marie. 1999. "The Professional Writing Practices and Dialogue Rhetoric of Two Black Women Publishers: Discourse as Social Action in the Nineteenth Century." Ph.D. diss., Purdue University.

Stewart, Maria W. 1987a. "Religion and the Pure Principles of Morality, The Sure Foundation on Which We Must Build." In *Maria W. Stewart, America's First Black Woman Political Writer*, ed. Marilyn Richardson, 28–42. Bloomington, Indiana University Press.

———. 1987b. "Mrs. Stewart's Farewell Address to Her Friends in the City of Boston." *Maria W. Stewart, America's First Black Woman Political Writer*, ed. Marilyn Richardson, 64–74. Bloomington: Indiana University Press.

Tannen, Deborah. 1994. *Gender and Discourse.* New York: Oxford University Press.

Thompson, Mildred I. 1990. *Ida B. Wells-Barnett: An Exploratory Study of an American Black Woman, 1893–1930.* In Hine, *Black Women in United States History*, vol 15. New York: Carlson Press.

Walker, Alice. 1976. *Meridian.* New York: Pocket Books/Simon and Schuster.

———. 1983. *In Search of Our Mothers' Gardens: Womanist Prose.* New York: Harcourt Brace Jovanovich.

———. 1988. *Living by the Word.* New York: Harcourt Brace Jovanovich.

———. 1997. *Anything We Love Can Be Saved.* New York: Random House.

Williams, Fannie Barrier. 1904. "An Extension of the Conference Spirit." *Voice of the Negro* (July): 300–303.

Williams, Patricia J. 1991. *The Alchemy of Race and Rights: Diary of a Law Professor.* Cambridge, Mass.: Harvard University Press.

———. 1995. *The Rooster's Egg: On the Persistence of Justice.* Cambridge, Mass.: Harvard University Press.

Literacy, Language, and Rhetoric

Berlin, James A. 1984. *Writing Instruction in Nineteenth-Century American Colleges.* Carbondale: Southern Illinois University Press.

Bruffee, Kenneth. 1984. "Collaborative Learning and the Conversation of Mankind." *College English* 46 (November): 635–52.

Burke, Kenneth. 1966. *Language as Symbolic Action: Life, Literature, and Method.* Berkeley: University of California Press.

———. 1969. *A Rhetoric of Motives.* Berkeley: University of California Press.

Campbell, Karlyn Kohrs. 1982. *The Rhetorical Act.* Belmont, Calif.: Wadsworth.

Chafe, Wallace L. 1982. "Integration and Involvement in Speaking, Writing, and Oral Literature." In *Spoken and Written Language: Exploring Orality and Literacy,* ed. Deborah Tannen, 35–53. Norwood, N.J.: Ablex.

———. 1994. *Discourse, Consciousness, and Time: The Flow and Displacement of Conscious Experience in Speaking and Writing.* Chicago: University of Chicago Press.

Clanchy, M. T. 1993. *From Memory to Written Record: England, 1066–1307.* 2nd ed. Oxford: Blackwell.

Coles, Robert. 1977. *Privileged Ones.* Boston: Little, Brown.

Cook, William. 1993. "Writing in the Spaces Left." *CCC* 44, no. 1: 9–23.

Cook-Gumperz, Jenny. 1986. *The Social Construction of Literacy.* New York: Cambridge University Press.

Corbett, Edward P. J. 1965. *Classical Rhetoric for the Modern Student.* 2nd ed. New York: Oxford University Press.

Cornelius, Janet Duitsman. 1991. *When I Can Read My Title Clear.* Columbia, S.C.: University of South Carolina Press.

Crowley, Sharon. 1994. *Ancient Rhetorics for Contemporary Students.* New York: Macmillan.

Dervin, Brenda, and Kathleen D. Clark. 1993. "Communication and Democracy: Mandate for Procedural Invention." In *Communication and Democracy,* ed. Slavko Splichal and Janet Wasko, 103–40. Norwood, N.J.: Ablex.

Fairclough, Norman, ed. 1992. *Critical Language Awareness.* London: Longman.

Farr, Marcia. 1994a. "Biliteracy in the Home: Practices Among Mexicano Families in Chicago." In *Biliteracy in the United States,* ed. D. Spencer. Washington, D.C.: Delta Systems and the Center for Applied Linguistics.

———. 1994b. "En los dos idiomas: Literacy Practices Among Chicano Mexicanos." *Literacy Across Communities,* ed. Beverly Moss, 9–47. Cresskill, N.J.: Hampton Press.

Foss, Karen A., and Sonja K. Foss. 1991. *Women Speak: The Eloquence of Women's Lives.* Prospect Heights, Ill.: Waveland.

Freire, Paulo. 1988. *Pedagogy of the Oppressed.* Trans. Myra Bergman Ramos. New York: Continuum.

Freire, Paulo, and Donaldo Macedo. 1987. *Literacy: Reading the Word and the World.* South Hadley, Mass.: Bergin and Garvey.

Gadamer, Hans-Georg. 1977. *Philosophical Hermeneutics.* Trans. and ed. David E. Linge. Berkeley: University of California Press.

Gardner, Howard. 1993. *Multiple Intelligences: The Theory in Practice.* New York: Basic.

Gatung, Johan. 1976. "Literacy, Education, and Schooling—For What?" In *A Turning Point for Literacy,* ed. Leon Bataille, 93–105. New York: Pergamon.

Geertz, Clifford. 1973. *The Interpretation of Cultures.* New York: Basic.

Goody, J., and I. Watt. 1963. "The Consequences of Literacy." *Comparative Studies in Society and History* 5, no. 3: 304–45.

Graff, Harvey J. 1988. "The Legacies of Literacy." In *Perspectives on Literacy,* ed. Eugene R. Kintgen et al. Carbondale: Southern Illinois University Press.

———. 1991. *The Legacies of Literacy.* Bloomington: Indiana University Press.

Greene, Jamie Candelaria. 1994. "Misperspectives on Literacy: A Critique of an Anglocentric Bias in Histories of American Literacy." *Written Communication* 2, no. 2: 251–69.

Havelock, Eric A. 1994. "The Coming of Literate Communication to Western Culture." In *Perspectives in Literacy,* ed. Eugene R. Kintgen, Barry M. Knoll, and Mike Rose, 127–34. Carbondale: Southern Illinois University Press.

Heath, Shirley Brice. 1983. *Ways with Words: Language, Life and Work in Communities and Classrooms.* Cambridge: Cambridge University Press.

Henderson, Mae Gwendolyn. 1992. "Speaking in Tongues: Dialogics, Dialectics, and the Black Women Writer's Literary Tradition." In *Feminists Theorize the Political,* ed. Judith Butler and Joan W. Scott. New York: Routledge.

Holquist, Michael, ed. and trans. 1981. *The Dialogic Imagination: Four Essays by M. M. Bakhtin.* Austin: University of Texas Press.

Holt, Thomas. 1990. "Knowledge Is Power: The Black Struggle for Literacy." *The Right to Literacy,* ed. Andrea A. Lunsford, Helene Moglen, and James Slevin, 91–102. New York: MLA.

Hymes, Dell. 1972a. "Models of the Interaction of Language and Social Life." *Directions in Sociolinguistics: The Ethnography of Communication.* New York: Holt, Rinehart and Winston.

———. 1972b. "On Communicative Competence." In *Sociolinguistics,* ed. J. B. Pride and J. Holmes, 262–93. London: Penguin.

Johnson, Nan. 1991. *Nineteenth-Century Rhetoric in North America.* Carbondale: Southern Illinois University Press.

Kaestle, Carl F. 1988. "The History of Literacy and the History of Readers." In *Perspectives on Literacy,* ed. Eugene R. Kintgen et al. Carbondale: Southern Illinois University Press.

Kay, Paul. 1977. "Language Evolution and Speech Style." *Sociocultural Dimensions of Language Change,* ed. B. Blount and M. Sanchez. New York: Academic Press.

Kintgen, Eugene R., Barry M. Knoll, and Mike Rose, eds. 1988. *Perspectives on Literacy.* Carbondale: Southern Illinois University Press.

Kirsch, Gesa, and Patricia Sullivan, eds. 1992. *Methods and Methodology in Composition Research.* Carbondale: Southern Illinois University Press.

Kitzhaber, Albert R. 1990. *Rhetoric in American Colleges, 1850–1900.* Dallas: Southern Methodist University Press.

Knoblauch, C. H., and Lil Brannon. 1984. *Rhetorical Traditions and the Teaching of Writing.* Upper Montclair, N.J.: Boynton/Cook.

Lunsford, Andrea A., Helene Moglen, and James Slevin, eds. 1990. *The Right to Literacy.* New York: MLA.

Mahiri, Jabari. 1994. "Reading Rites and Sports: Motivation for Adaptive Literacy of Young African-American Males." In *Literacy Across Communities,* ed. Beverly Moss, 121–46. Cresskill, N.J.: Hampton Press.

Mortensen, Peter, and Gesa E. Kirsch, eds. 1996. *Ethics and Representation in Qualitative Studies of Literacy.* Urbana, Ill.: NCTE.

Moss, Beverly, ed. 1994. *Literacy Across Communities.* Cresskill, N.J.: Hampton Press.

Murphy, James J., ed. 1990. *A Short History of Writing Instruction: From Ancient Greece to Twentieth Century America.* Davis, Calif.: Hermagoras.

Olson, D. 1977. "From Utterance to Text: The Bias of Language in Speech and Writing." *Harvard Educational Review* 47: 257–81.

Ong, Walter J. 1982. *Orality and Literacy: The Technologizing of the Word.* London: Methuen.

Portelli, Alessandro. 1999. "Friendly Fire and Collateral Damage: The Complex Memory of World War II Air Raids in Italy." Paper presented at the conference "Going Native: Recruitment, Conversion and Identification in Cultural Research," Ohio State University, Columbus, May 21.

Pyles, Thomas, and John Algeo. 1982. *The Origins and Development of the English Language.* 3rd ed. New York: Harcourt, Brace, Jovanovich.

Rose, Mike. 1988. "Narrowing the Mind and Page: Remedial Writers and Cognitive Reductionism." *CCC* 39, no. 3: 267–302.

Royster, Jacqueline Jones. 1988. "Reflections on the SAGE Women as Writer/Scholars Internship Program." *SAGE: A Scholarly Journal on Black Women* (Student Supplement): 4–6.

———. 1992. "Looking from the Margins: A Tale of Curricular Reform." In *Diversity and Writing: Dialogue Within a Modern University,* monograph 2, 1–11. Minneapolis: University of Minnesota Center for Interdisciplinary Studies of Writing.

———. 1996. "When the First Voice You Hear Is Not Your Own." *CCC* 47, no. 1 (February): 29–40.

Scott, Jerrie Cobb. 1990. "Maintaining the Cultural Integrity of Literacy Programs." In *Louisiana Literacy Forum 1990 Proceedings,* 107–17. Baton Rouge: Louisiana Endowment for the Humanities.

Scollon, R., and S. Scollon. 1981. *Narrative, Literacy and Face in Interethnic Communication.* Norwood, N.J.: Ablex.

Scribner, Sylvia and Michael Cole. 1988. "Unpackaging Literacy." In *Perspectives on Literacy,* ed. Eugene R. Kintgen, Barry M. Knoll, and Mike Rose, 57–70. Carbondale: Southern Illinois University Press.

Shuman, Amy. 1986. *Storytelling Rights: The Uses of Oral and Written Texts by Urban Adolescents.* New York: Cambridge University Press.

———. 1997. "The Rhetoric of Ethnography and the Possibility of Strategic Romanticism." Colloquium on Women in the History of Rhetoric, Ohio State University, Columbus, November 7.

Street, Brian V. 1995. *Social Literacies: Critical Approaches to Literacy in Development, Ethnography and Education.* New York: Longman.

Tannen, Deborah. 1982. "The Oral/Literate Continuum in Discourse." In *Spoken and Written Language: Exploring Orality and Literacy,* ed. Deborah Tannen, 1–16. Norwood, N.J.: Ablex.

———. 1994. *Gender and Discourse.* New York: Oxford University Press.

Vygotsky, Lev S. 1978. *Mind in Society.* Ed. Michael Cole et al. Cambridge, Mass.: Harvard University Press.

Weinstein-Shr, Gail. 1994. "From Mountaintops to City Streets: Literacy in Philadelphia's Hmong Community." In *Literacy Across Communities,* ed. Beverly Moss, 49–83. Cresskill, N.J.: Hampton Press.

Young, Stacey. 1997. *Changing the Wor(l)d: Discourse, Politics, and the Feminist Movement.* New York: Routledge.

The Public Sphere and the Periodical Press

Arendt, Hannah. 1958. *The Human Condition.* Chicago: University of Chicago Press.

Bullock, Penelope L. 1981. *The Afro-American Periodical Press, 1838–1909.* Baton Rouge: Louisiana State University Press.

Calhoun, Craig, ed. 1997. *Habermas and the Public Sphere.* Cambridge: MIT Press.

Dann, Martin E. 1971. *The Black Press, 1827–1890: A Quest for National Identity.* New York: G. P. Putnam's Sons.

Eley, Geoff. 1992. "Nations, Publics, and Political Cultures: Placing Habermas in the Nineteenth Century." In *Habermas and the Public Sphere,* ed. Craig Calhoun. Cambridge: MIT Press.

Fraser, Nancy. 1985. "What's Critical About Critical Theory? The Case of Habermas and Gender." *New German Critique* 35: 97–133.

———. 1989. *Unruly Practices: Power, Discourse and Gender in Contemporary Social Theory.* Minneapolis: University of Minnesota Press.

———. 1997. *Justice Interruptus: Critical Reflections on the "Postsocialist" Condition.* New York: Routledge.

Habermas, Jürgen. 1971. *Knowledge and Human Interests.* Trans. Jeremy Shapiro. Boston: Beacon Press.

————. 1974. "The Public Sphere: An Encyclopedia Article (1964)." *New German Critique* 1, no. 3: 49–55.

————. 1990. *Moral Consciousness and Communicative Action.* Trans. Christian Lenhardt and Shierry Weber Nicholsen. Cambridge: MIT Press.

Helly, Dorothy O., and Susan M. Reverby, eds. 1992. *Gendered Domains: Rethinking Public and Private in Women's History.* Ithaca, N.Y.: Cornell University Press.

Matthews, Glenna. 1992. *The Rise of Public Woman: Woman's Power and Woman's Place in the United States, 1630–1970.* New York: Oxford University Press.

Penn, I. Garland. [1891] 1988. *The Afro-American Press and Its Editors.* Salem, N.H.: Ayer.

Ryan, Mary P. 1990. *Women in Public: Between Banners and Ballots, 1825–1880.* Baltimore: Johns Hopkins University Press.

Swearingen, C. Jan, and Dave Pruett. 1999. *Rhetoric, The Polis, and the Global Village.* Mahwah, N.J.: Erlbaum.

Teigas, Demetrius. 1995. *Knowledge and Hermeneutic Understanding: A Study of the Habermas-Gadamer Debate.* Lewisburg, Pa.: Bucknell University Press.

Index

Page numbers for illustrations are in italic.